An
IRRESISTIBLE HISTORY *of*
southern
FOOD

An
IRRESISTIBLE HISTORY of
southern
FOOD

Four Centuries of Black–Eyed Peas,
Collard Greens & Whole Hog Barbecue

RICK MCDANIEL

Original photographs by Polly McDaniel, Robert Lahser and Royce W. Smith

Charleston · London

THE
History
PRESS

Published by The History Press
Charleston, SC 29403
www.historypress.net

Front cover (clockwise from top), archival images courtesy of: Lewis P. Watson Photographic Collection; Vanishing Georgia Collection, Georgia State Archives; Lewis P. Watson Photographic Collection; Georgia State Archives and North Carolina State Archives.

All food photography by Polly McDaniel unless otherwise credited.

Cover design by Natasha Momberger.

First published 2011

Manufactured in the United States

ISBN 978.1.60949.193.2

Library of Congress Cataloging-in-Publication Data
McDaniel, Rick.
An irresistible history of Southern food : four centuries of black eyed peas, collard greens, and whole hog barbecue / Rick McDaniel ; original photographs by Polly McDaniel, Robert Lahser, and Royce W. Smith.
p. cm.
Includes bibliographical references.
ISBN 978-1-60949-193-2
1. Cooking, American--Southern style. 2. Cooking--Southern States--History. 3. Cookbooks. I. Title.
TX715.2.S68M3325 2011
741.5975--dc22
2011008301

Notice: The information in this book is true and complete to the best of our knowledge. It is offered without guarantee on the part of the author or The History Press. The author and The History Press disclaim all liability in connection with the use of this book.

*To Georgia Pearl Long Styers, Margaret Styers Tate,
Bess Smith Chapman, Ruth Canipe Hill, Lorene Hovis Hill
and Josie Hill McDaniel—three generations of small women
who were giants in the kitchen.*

Contents

Acknowledgements

One of the biggest lies anyone can ever tell you is "I'm writing a book." Unless you are a true genius (and there are entirely too few of those running around these days), writing a book involves every friend and loved one you have, to one degree or another.

I'd like to thank my wife, Polly, and my son, Morgan, who put up with this obsession I had about putting my passion for Southern food onto the printed page. In addition to taking almost all the original photographs for the book, Polly provided advice, encouragement, editing and an uncanny knack for telling me when I was rambling on a tad too much about the virtues of lard. Morgan dutifully tramped over every plantation in the upper South, listening to me talk with fellow food historians, which he no doubt found far more interesting than video games. My sister, Cathy, and her husband, Darrell, gave me many of the nineteenth-century cookbooks in my reference collection, and the rest of my family provided opinions, constructive criticism, Scotch and cheerleading as needed.

The staff of the Charleston Library Society was immensely helpful during numerous trips down there to examine their rare cookbook collection.

Robert Lahser and Royce W. Smith provided more than thirty years of friendship and quite a few beautiful photos of the recipes.

The "China Dolls"—Carolyn Dorner, Rita Larkin, Nicole Orlovitz, Virginia Himmelheber and Carol Rifkin—loaned me most of the beautiful china and table linens you see in the original photographs, for which I am most grateful.

There are many historical photographs throughout this book, many seen in print for the first time. Many thanks are due to Steve Engerrand and Gail DeLoach at the Georgia State Archives, Karen Allen at the Olivia Raney Local History Library in Raleigh, Beth Bilderback at the Caroliniana Library at the University of South Carolina, Kim Cumber and Boyd

Cathey at the North Carolina State Archives and Keith Longiotti at the University of North Carolina Libraries.

For more than four decades now, John Masters has always been there to listen and give sage advice, even when I didn't ask for it or even know I needed it. He started my website and is the one who does all the grunt work while I sit back and get written up in the *New York Times*. Thanks, man. I owe you much.

John T. Edge, one of the best food writers of our generation and director of the Southern Foodways Alliance, has always given good advice and genuinely understands why a man needs his favorite barbecue joint on speed dial.

Damon Lee Fowler, author, food historian and one of the nicest people I have ever met, provided inspiration, knowledge, friendship and encouragement, for which I am very grateful.

Last, but certainly not least, a special thanks to everyone at The History Press, especially my editors, Jessica Berzon and Hilary McCullough. Jessica talked me out of several panic attacks during the craziness of turning a Word document into a book. Hilary, one of the best copy editors I have ever worked with, was amazing at finding glitches and gaffes my bleary eyes missed. Many thanks to you both, and to everyone else who had a hand at getting these words onto the printed page.

Introduction

More than twenty years have passed since the exchange I had with a waitress one winter morning in Clifton, New Jersey.

It was the first time in my life I had traveled North of the fabled Mason-Dixon line, and when asked what I wanted for breakfast, I naturally asked for country ham and grits with my eggs. "What's that?" came the reply, along with a genuinely perplexed look, and all of a sudden I realized that I was a long, long way from home.

"Southern hospitality" has always been synonymous with gracious entertaining and sumptuous feasts. This book looks at the foods Southerners have made their own during the four centuries since the first English settlers arrived in Virginia, where those foods came from and why those particular foods endured.

What we consider "Southern cooking" was not a revolution that occurred at any one time or place. It was an evolution of foods and cooking techniques from the many and varied ethnic groups who settled the region; some who came to start a new life, some who were stolen from the life they knew and forced into bondage and some whose lives changed forever when they saw the great white sails on the ships bringing strangers to their land.

Over the years, tens of thousands of books have been written about Southern cooking. The overwhelming majority of these books are reminiscences and recipes from someone who lived in a particular place in the South at a particular time. Very few books have been written about the food itself and where it came from; the aim of this book is to bridge the gap between history book and cookbook.

Food and history may seem like strange bedfellows at first, but the two are inescapably intertwined. From the moment of birth until death writes our final chapter, we take food for the nourishment of our bodies and the comfort of our souls. No matter who we are or what time period we may live in, the food we eat is largely determined by our social class and ethnic background, whether we realize it or not.

We grow up eating many of the same foods our parents ate, although each succeeding generation manages (for the most part) to eat better than the last. And no matter how long we might live or how far we may travel, the food of our youth always has an allure unmatched by any other.

For me, the food of my youth was the food of the American South in the early 1960s, a wonderfully simple time when the isolation of a small town of seven thousand souls kept the turmoil of a foreign war and inner-city strife confined to the flickering images on a black-and-white television set. It was a time of prosperity and plenty, as parents who had come through hard times and war made good on their promise to themselves that their kids would have a childhood far easier than theirs had been.

Churches still had dinner on the grounds on Homecoming Sunday, with wooden tables covered with more food than anyone not born in the South could imagine. There was always country ham and coconut cake at Christmas, and a Sunday dinner without fried chicken meant grandma wasn't feeling well at all, bless her heart.

Many of the foods I grew up eating were the same ones my great-great-great-grandfather ate two hundred years before. There was more of it, and we didn't have to work the land to raise our food, but the food itself was essentially the same—the vegetables that grew in that particular part of our state, pork and chicken. My ancestors, even back to colonial days, would have felt right at home at our Sunday dinner table. But our generation would witness major changes to Southern food, changes brought by a society becoming increasingly more concerned with convenience, speed and mobility.

History is what happens when ordinary people live through extraordinary times. You'll meet some of those folks in these pages; people who lived on the cutting edge of a New World, some who settled a new nation and some who lived through that nation trying to tear itself apart. They tell us through their receipt books, cookbooks, letters and diaries what life was like and what foods they loved in the South of their time. They tell us about the foods eaten by the extremely rich and the extremely poor but, more importantly, about the foods and recipes that sustained the average working family through the good times and bad times of four hundred years of daily living.

The recipes in this book were chosen after careful study of Southern cookbooks and recipe collections dating from 1756 to the present day. The recipes are modern adaptations of these historical dishes, along with recipes from my personal collection gathered over more than thirty years of studying the cuisine of my native South. All of the recipes are as relevant (and delicious) today at the turn of the twenty-first century as they were at the turn of the nineteenth century.

Oftentimes what makes a recipe Southern is as much a state of mind as it is a matter of geography; Southerners simply decide a particular food is Southern, and that is that. Black-eyed peas, for instance, are African, but they have been identified with the South for centuries and are now an integral part of our culinary heritage.

Geographically, the recipes span the length and breadth of the region, from Maryland crab cakes to Charleston she-crab soup to New Orleans jambalaya; chronologically, they span the four centuries from the founding of Jamestown in 1607 to the present day.

To Southerners, the memories of hearth and home give a comfort, a joy in knowing that Thomas Wolfe was wrong. You can go home again, even if only in your mind's eye; and mama will be there with a plate of hot biscuits, and grandma will have a cake made. Grandpa will greet you as he always did, with a cool glass of iced tea, and say, "It sure is good to have you home again. Let's go see what's for supper."

Courtesy of North Carolina State Archives.

CHAPTER 1

The Table of Our Ancestors

Southern Food, 1607–the Present

In the South, perhaps more than any other region, we go back to our home in dreams and memories,
hoping it remains what it was on a lazy, still summer's day twenty years ago.
—*Willie Morris,* North Toward Home

The South, more than any other region of the United States, has always been celebrated for its food. The cuisine that developed in the region is a truly unique blend of ingredients and cooking techniques drawn from a diverse group of cultures and nationalities, each drawn to the region's rich soil and bountiful waters.

Southern food has roots that run deep into European, Native American and African culinary traditions. Each group introduced the others to their native foods, along with ways of growing, preparing and preserving them. They also adapted cooking techniques one another; in many cases, the foods we consider "Southern" bear the mark of all three cultures.

To understand how Southern food developed, we need to take a look at the people who settled the region and the events that shaped the way they lived and ate.

After Columbus "discovered" the New World in 1492, Spanish-born Pope Alexander VI divided all the newly "discovered" land between Spain and Portugal, which promptly began exploring South and Central America, converting the native people to Catholicism at the point of a sword and relieving them of all that pesky gold they had been mining and wearing.

The Spanish also took note of a great many unusual foods in the Caribbean and Central and South America. When Columbus returned to Spain in 1493, he brought back examples of the native foods from each of the lands he had visited. This touched off two centuries of what historian Alfred Crosby called the Colombian exchange between the Old World and the New. This massive cross-pollination between Europe, Asia and the New World is why we have Chinese oranges in Florida, South American tomatoes in Italy, chocolate from Mexico in Switzerland and hot peppers from the Caribbean in Thailand. The Spanish were also responsible for bringing potatoes, vanilla, lima beans, sweet potatoes, peanuts and hot peppers from their native lands to the Southern table. Two other Southern staples introduced by way of Spanish Florida were oranges and peaches, both originally from China. The Spanish also introduced hogs and beef cattle to the New World.

The English Arrive

To counter the Spanish claim on the New World, the English made several failed attempts to colonize Virginia before finally getting a toehold at Jamestown in May 1607. They set out well prepared in terms of food, with good supplies of dried beef, salted fish and salt pork in addition to cows, pigs and thirty-seven chickens to serve as breeding stock. But a series of bad luck, ill planning, Indian attacks and the worst drought to hit Virginia in eight hundred years left them in such dire straits that the winter of 1609–10 was called the "Starving Time." Archaeological evidence and firsthand accounts tell of a diet of horses, dogs, cats, rats, poisonous snakes and even accounts of cannibalism as the settlers struggled to make it through the winter.

As attacks by the "salvages" (as they were referred to by several Jamestown residents, who weren't very good spellers) became less frequent and peaceful relationships with the native population ensued, the colonists moved away from Jamestown, which had always been plagued by a lack of dependable, safe drinking water, and into the surrounding countryside. There, they began to take stock of the bounty of their new land. John Smith, one of the Jamestown founders, wrote, "The rivers became so covered with swans, geese, ducks, and cranes that we daily feasted with good bread, Virginia peas, pumpions [pumpkins], and putchamins [persimmons], fish, fowl, and diverse sorts of wild beasts as fast as we could eat them."

The English brought their recipes and cooking techniques to the new land and soon roasted meats, fowl, fish, puddings (savory or sweet pies without crusts) and other familiar dishes from home were gracing the hearths of the first Virginia plantations. It wouldn't be long before the "savages" would start to change the English way of cooking.

Native American Influence

The first English settlers were ill prepared for life in the wilderness and owed their survival to the food they obtained and the skills they learned from the native peoples they would eventually usurp and annihilate.

The Native Americans of Virginia were skilled hunters and gatherers, but they were also equally skilled in agriculture. The Powhatans lived in villages with as many as one hundred

This 1585 illustration from Thomas Harriot's *A Briefe and True Report of the New Found Land of Virginia* of the Algonquin village of Secota in present-day North Carolina shows the garden plots surrounding each dwelling. *Courtesy of North Carolina Collection, University of North Carolina Libraries.*

homes, each with a large and carefully tended garden where they grew corn, beans, peas, squash, pumpkins and sunflowers. They also relied on fish and shellfish, nuts, fruits and berries to supplement what they grew in the garden.

The main subsistence crops of corn (maize), beans and squash were so vital to the Native Americans that they called them the "three sisters." These were the first Native American foods to be embraced by Southerners. Robert Beverley wrote about the Indians' love of corn in *The History and Present State of Virginia* (1705): "They delight much to feed on roasting ears; that is, the Indian corn, gathered green and milky, before it is grown to its full bigness, and roasted before the fire in the ear…And indeed this is a very sweet and pleasing food."

The introduction of maize (or "Indian corn," as the colonists called it) into the colonists' diet was a major event in the development of Southern food culture and was without a doubt the single most important event that ensured the survival of the European colonies. With farmland so hard to clear, a single crop that could yield fresh ears for roasting, be dried to last the winter and produce flour for bread was a godsend.

As the colonists learned how to grow, store and cook corn, English recipes were adapted to use the new crop. Soon Johnnycakes, corn pone and fry bread were a regular part of the colonists' diet.

An illustration by Roanoke Island colonist John White showing the clay stewpot used by Virginia Indians to make one-pot meals. *Courtesy of North Carolina Collection, University of North Carolina Libraries.*

One of the best records of Native American foodways in the early days of the South is found in *A New Voyage to Carolina* (1709), an account of the journey of John Lawson through the lands of almost every major Native American tribe in South Carolina.

Deer, wild hogs, raccoons, geese, turkeys and oysters from the Santee River were a few of the native foods Lawson found particularly to his liking. He also enjoyed peas, beans, nuts, corn and a type of bread made with peaches.

Hunting was one of the most valuable skills European settlers learned from their Indian mentors. In England especially, hunting was a matter of sport, not survival. The colonists soon learned methods of stalking, droving and even smoking out prey by setting fire to the forest (not the most ecologically correct thing to do, but it worked for them).

Native Americans also taught early Southerners how to smoke fish to preserve it for winter (a valuable skill when salt, which the English used for preserving food, was scarce) and the use of clay pots for cooking. These survival skills enabled the early settlers to move away from the abundant food supply of the coastline and into the primal forests that covered Virginia and the Carolinas.

Native Americans also introduced pumpkins, pecans, black walnuts, hickory nuts, persimmons, mulberries, blackberries, maple syrup and muscadines to Southern foodways.

Beyond Jamestown: Southern Foodways Prior to the American Revolution

The period between 1700 and the end of the American Revolution was marked by a huge contrast in the way Southerners ate. The foods and preparation techniques used by colonial Southerners varied greatly depending on their economic and social standing.

The sharp divisions of the English social class system began in His Majesty's colonies just as soon as the first "gentleman" got off the boat at Jamestown. Precious few people of this time period belonged to what would today be considered the middle class; you were either one of the small group of extremely wealthy aristocrats or you belonged to the other 95 percent of society and just barely scraped by.

At the top of the social ladder, the wealthy gentlemen planters dined on a dazzling variety of meats and breads and sweets at each meal, prepared in traditional English fashion by indentured servants or African slaves under the watchful eye of the lady of the manor.

Prior to the beginning of the Civil War, much of the South was still frontier, and the people who settled it led a radically different life from the gentry on the large plantations. For the majority of Southerners, elegant meals served on silver trays were as much a part of their daily lives as space travel.

The average Southern housewife woke up at 4:00 a.m. seven days a week. After stoking the fire in the kitchen, she milked cows and fed chickens before starting the day's cooking.

Simple soups, stews made from game and grain porridges (mostly cornmeal mush) cooked over the open hearth were what most Southerners ate. Hominy, made from cracked or ground corn and often flavored with salt-cured pork and vegetables, was also common fare for the frontier family. Charles Woodmason, an Anglican minister from England, traveled the Carolina backcountry for six years beginning in 1761. After the fine dining of London and the Charleston plantations, Woodmason found the daily fare of the Southern frontier somewhat lacking by his standards: "Nothing but Indian Corn Meal to be had, Bacon and Eggs in some Places—No Butter, Rice, or Milk—As for Tea and Coffee they know it not. These people are all from Ireland, and live wholly on…what in England is given to the Hogs and Dogs."

For rich and poor, dinner was the day's main meal, usually served around 2:00 p.m. Supper was usually leftovers from the afternoon meal, a practice that endures to this day in the Sunday evening meal served in many Southern households.

New Pots on the Fire: Scots-Irish, Germans and French

Beginning in the mid-1740s after the Battle of Culloden, Scots and the Scots-Irish (Scots who had colonized Northern Ireland) began pouring into the South via ports in Charleston and Philadelphia. They settled mostly in the Piedmont and mountains of North and South Carolina, bringing their own cooking techniques and foods to the South. Whiskey making was one tradition this group brought to the region.

A large number of the Scots and Scots-Irish moved west into the Appalachian Mountains after the American Revolution, settling on lands awarded to them in lieu of pay for their service in the Continental army. It was in the hills and hollows of the Appalachians and Blue Ridge that the marriage of Cherokee Indian and Scots-Irish foodways known as "mountain cooking" evolved.

The Cherokees were farmers who grew maize, squash, pumpkins, beans, potatoes, mulberries and serviceberries using a sophisticated system of sustainable agriculture. They gathered acorns and chestnuts and ground them into flour, mixing them with beans to make bread. The Scots befriended the Cherokees and adopted many aspects of their culinary traditions. The Cherokees taught the Scots-Irish how to smoke rainbow trout and how to make jerky out of deer meat. The Scots, who had no hang-ups about behaving like "proper English gentlemen," readily adapted to the diet of their native teachers. They introduced metal plows, Irish potatoes, turnips and the ubiquitous hog to the Cherokees, and a partnership began that lasted for years and resulted in a great number of intermarriages between the two groups.

Germans came to the South fleeing the religious persecution of Protestants that followed in the wake of the Thirty Years' War. In 1766, the Moravians, a Protestant sect from what is now the Czech Republic, built a settlement called Salem in the Piedmont area of North Carolina.

Salem was renowned to travelers of the day for its good food and commercial bakeries. One of these bakeries, Winkler's, is still in operation today, turning out traditional baked goods in huge, wood-fired ovens.

The influence of French cuisine was destined to take hold in many different parts of the South. Although the French settled throughout the region in the early eighteenth century (at one time, Charleston's population was 40 percent French), nowhere did they leave their cultural and culinary mark more than in south Louisiana. While the English primarily settled northern Louisiana, the southern part of the state became a Mecca for the French.

Beginning in 1715, French, French Canadians and settlers from the French colonies in the Caribbean started arriving in the Mississippi Delta, anxious to seek their fortunes. In 1764, the first four Acadian families (who would later be known as "Cajuns") arrived in Louisiana. The Acadians were the descendants of Frenchmen who had settled the Acadia region (today called the Maritime Provinces) of Nova Scotia in the late 1600s. These settlers brought the cooking techniques and recipes of France to the bayou and soon began intermingling them with Native American, Spanish (Louisiana was a Spanish colony for a while) and African influences to create the distinctive Cajun and Creole foods of Louisiana.

After the American Revolution, the French, who had assisted us in gaining independence, began to exert a much larger influence on Southern cuisine. Thomas Jefferson, who served the young republic as minister to France, developed a deep love for French cuisine and wines during his tenure in Paris. While he maintained his fondness for Southern staples such as sweet potatoes, Virginia ham and sweet corn, Jefferson was at the forefront of blending the cuisine of his native South with that of France.

Jefferson sent one of his slaves, nineteen-year-old James Hemings, to Paris for three years to train under a succession of French chefs and caterers. At the end of his apprenticeship, Hemings took over the kitchens at Jefferson's residence in Paris. When Jefferson returned to Monticello, Hemings brought his skill to the kitchen there. Daniel Webster noted that dinners at Monticello were "served in half Virginian, half French style, in good taste and abundance."

Jefferson's influential circle of friends soon took notice of the blending of "plantation food" with French cuisine, and French-trained chefs were in great demand among the Virginia aristocracy.

African and African American Influences

Although Europeans and Native Americans made significant contributions, no single group had a greater impact on Southern cooking than Africans and African Americans.

In 1619, an English privateer docked at Jamestown and traded a group of "Twentie and Odd" Africans he had taken as plunder from a slave ship for food. It is thought that these

"A slave auction at the south," from an original sketch by Theodore R. Davis, 1861. *Courtesy of Library of Congress.*

first Africans may have been viewed as indentured servants, meaning that after working for a specified time they were to be set free. At the time, there were no laws concerning slavery on the English books; by 1670, however, laws regulating a race-based system of slavery were on the books in Maryland and Virginia.

In 1650, there were fewer than one thousand slaves in America. By 1860, there were four million, the vast majority of them in the South.

In addition to their human cargo, slave traders brought some of the native foods of their captives: eggplant, okra (gumbo, as the Bantu called it), black-eyed peas sorghum, benne (sesame) seeds and watermelon. Peanuts were also brought to the South from Africa after first being brought there from Brazil. The Southern sweet potato was very similar to the yams of West Africa and was soon adapted.

In plantation houses from Maryland to Mississippi, the African cooks and their American descendants were introducing the foodways of their homeland to the South; soon collards, black-eyed peas and other foods that had once been African became Southern.

Slaves who came to America sometimes started their captivity in the West Indies. They were exposed to the spicy foods of the Caribbean and often learned to cook island dishes before ending up in Baton Rouge or Charleston, where the Caribbean influence melded with Creole or Lowcountry cuisine.

By the mid-1700s, a distinctly American cuisine was evolving in the South, as the foodways of Europeans, Africans and Native Americans converged and combined.

Plantation Fare for Master and Slave

By the end of the 1850s, Southern cooking had reached its antebellum zenith. Cookbooks like Mary Randolph's *The Virginia House-wife*, published in 1824, showed the world the gracious blend of English, French, Native American and African American cookery that was defining the cuisine of the antebellum South. *The Carolina Housewife*, published in 1847 by "A Lady of Charleston" (Sarah Rutledge), showed the rest of the country the dishes of what was to become known as the "Carolina Rice Kitchen."

For the wealthy planter class who owned the large cotton, rice and indigo plantations, meals were a social event that featured the finest native and imported foods. In *A Journey in the Seaboard Slave States* (1853), Frederick Law Olmsted wrote about breakfast at one of the smaller Virginia plantations: "There was fried fowl, and fried bacon and eggs, and cold ham; there were preserved peaches, and preserved quinces and grapes; there was hot wheaten biscuit, and hot short-cake, and hot corn-cake, and hot griddle cakes, soaked in butter; there was coffee, and there was milk, sour or sweet, whichever I preferred to drink."

Margaret Devereux's *Plantation Sketches* (1906) detailed the elegance and opulence of a typical meal:

> For a dinner of ten or twelve persons, including ourselves, there would be a ham at the head, a large roast turkey at the foot, a quarter of boiled mutton, a round of beef a la mode, and a boiled turkey stuffed with oysters. In the middle of the table would be celery in tall cut-glass stands, on the sides, cranberries in moulds and various kinds of pickles. With these would be served either four or six dishes of vegetables and scalloped oysters, handed hot from the plate-warmer. The dessert would be a plum pudding, clear stewed apples with cream, with a waiter in the centre filled with calf's-foot jelly, syllabub in glasses, and cocoanut or cheese-cake puddings at the corners. The first cloth was removed with the meats. For a larger entertainment, a roast pig would be added; ice-cream would take the place of stewed apples. The dessert cloth would be removed with the dessert, and the decanters and fruit set upon the bare mahogany, with the decanters in coasters; cigars would follow, after the ladies had left, of course.

In sharp contrast to the gastronomic luxury of the planters was the diet of the slaves who grew and prepared the master's daily feasts. The food provided to slaves varied greatly depending on time period, location, what food the plantation produced and the owner's economic situation.

Frederick Douglass, the escaped slave and abolitionist, wrote in 1845: "The men and women slaves received, as their monthly allowance of food, eight pounds of pork, or its equivalent in fish, and one bushel of corn meal."

In *The Life of Josiah Henson* (1849), Henson, who was born a slave in 1789 in Charles County, Maryland, wrote: "The principal food of those upon my master's plantation consisted of cornmeal and salt herrings; to which was added in summer a little buttermilk, and the few vegetables which each might raise for himself and his family, on the little piece of ground which was assigned to him for the purpose, called a truck-patch."

On coastal plantations, like those in the South Carolina Lowcountry, broken or dirty rice was plentiful and was a staple of the slave diet.

Archaeological evidence from excavations of slave cabins at Ashland Plantation in Louisiana shows that in some cases slaves added to their diet by fishing and trapping. The bones of opossums, raccoons, rabbits, wild birds and fish such as freshwater drum, gar, catfish, sunfish and mackerel have been found at the site. In *Flowerdew Hundred: The Archaeology of a Virginia Plantation, 1619–1864* (1993), James Deetz detailed food remnants from slave cabins. Deetz found that the foods most often eaten by slaves at Flowerdew Hundred were pork, catfish, various types of birds and fish, sturgeon, chicken, beef and opossum. Deetz also found evidence that slaves regularly supplemented their diets by keeping pigs and maintaining garden plots.

Patricia A. Gibbs, a former member of the research staff at Colonial Williamsburg, wrote:

> *Documentary and archaeological evidence shows that slaves grew a variety of plants in these gardens. Vegetables included lima beans, pole beans, cabbages, collards, corn, cymlings (patty pan squash), onions, peanuts, black-eyed or other field peas, potatoes (sometimes specified as red or sweet), and potato pumpkins. Fruits included apples, cherries, peaches, watermelons, and muskmelons…Most individual gardens produced only a limited number of vegetables and fruits. Potatoes, field peas, pole beans, cymlings, and collards were most commonly mentioned by travelers and planters.*

Although slave gardens were apparently fairly common in the eighteenth century, there is less evidence of them in the nineteenth century; they were rarely mentioned in travelers' accounts of Southern plantations of the time. Slaves of this period were more likely to be dependant on the food furnished by the plantation owner, with less supplemental vegetables available to them.

On rare occasions, house servants stole food from the plantation table to supplement their meager rations. In his autobiography, the Reverend Elijah P. Marrs wrote: "After I became seven or eight years old I was made a dining-room boy. I remember how Brother Henry and I used to steal the biscuits off the plates while carrying them into the dining-room, and how they would burn us while hot in our pockets." Plantation families prevented pilfering by keeping track of the food that left the kitchen.

Slaves became very adept at taking what they were given, what they could grow and what they could liberate and turning it into one-pot meals that needed little tending. In the eighteenth century, the cooking was often done in outdoor, communal fire pits in clay pots called "colonoware" by archaeologists. This pottery is similar to that used by Native Americans of the period, and some archaeologists suggest that it may have been made by Native Americans and sold to plantations for use by slaves.

By the 1850s, communal fire pit cooking gave way to a more efficient system. Olmsted wrote of the plantations he visited: "Except on the smallest plantations, where the cooking is done in the house of the proprietor, there is a cook-house, furnished with a large copper for boiling, and an oven. Every night the negroes take their 'mess' for the next day's breakfast and dinner, to the cook, to be prepared for the next day."

Food for the slaves was served in wooden bowls or trenchers and was often eaten with few, if any, utensils. Annie L. Burton wrote in *Memories of Childhood's Slavery Days* (1909): "Our dishes consisted of one wooden bowl, and oyster shells were our spoons. This bowl served for about fifteen children, and often the dogs and the ducks and the peafowl had a dip in it. Sometimes we had buttermilk and bread in our bowl, sometimes greens or bones."

No matter with what they were furnished or could procure for themselves, the diet of the slave was barely adequate in the best of times, especially considering the large amount of calories they expended. Malnutrition and the diseases it spawns were common among slaves, and the mortality rate was staggering, especially among the young.

Prosperity to Poverty: Southern Food, 1861–1865

When generations of simmering tensions between North and South finally boiled over into war in the spring of 1861, the impact on growing, preparing and storing food in the South was dramatic and immediate. Overnight, peaceful farms and towns exploded into hellish battlefields, and Southerners of all races and classes suffered through four agonizing years of hardship, danger and food shortages. The South had not been self-sufficient in any sense of the word while at peace, and war isolated the region even further from food sources in the North as well as at home.

One of the earliest casualties was the fertile Shenandoah Valley, which supplied food to people in all the region's major cities and to plantations where every inch of fertile ground was given over to cotton, tobacco or indigo production. Northern and Southern troops foraging for food descended on the lush valley like biblical plagues of locusts. Large portions of whatever crops didn't fall victim to fighting or foraging were diverted to Virginia to feed the Confederate armies in northern Virginia.

Three-quarters of a million Southern men marched off to war, many of them from farms and plantations. This led to a shortage of manpower for planting and harvesting. Slaves were taken away from tending crops and pressed into service digging trenches and breastworks for the army. The manpower shortage, coupled with the dwindling supply of food from the Shenandoah, soon led to food shortages.

Contemporary cookbooks such as *Confederate Receipt Book: A Compilation of Over One Hundred Receipts, Adapted to the Times*, published by "A Confederate Lady" in Richmond in 1863, offered recipes to help Southern women cope with the chronic shortages of everyday foods. It included tips for making coffee out of acorns, bread without yeast and piecrusts out of potatoes. Other recipes included apple pie without apples, artificial oysters made from green corn and, perhaps appropriately, a cure for dysentery.

After the fall of Vicksburg in July 1863 ended Confederate shipping on the Mississippi, getting by on less and less food became a way of life for soldiers and civilians alike. Federal troops advanced into the South's heartland, burning or trampling crops and emptying smokehouses of meat meant to last families through the winter. Horses, mules and oxen needed for planting and harvesting were run off, conscripted or simply shot to deny them to the Rebels. As Union troops captured and destroyed saltworks throughout the Confederacy, the lack of salt for curing led to widespread shortages of meat.

By 1864, inflation had rendered Confederate currency worthless, leading to desperation among Southerners living in cities, who depended on money to buy food. Judith McGuire of Virginia wrote about wartime food prices in her diary: "Coffee is $4 per pound, and good tea from $18 to $20; butter ranges from $1.50 to $2 per pound; lard 50 cents; corn $15 per barrel; and wheat $4.50 per bushel."

There were at least thirteen food riots in the Confederacy during the later years of the war. Jefferson Davis tried to stop a bread riot in Richmond by offering a mob of rampaging housewives money from his own pockets. His money was as worthless as theirs, and the angry mob only dispersed after Davis threatened that hastily assembled troops would open fire if they didn't go back home.

The more wealth a family had, the less impact the food shortages had on their daily lives. Mary Boykin Chesnut, a Charleston socialite whose husband, James, was an advisor to Jefferson Davis, recorded the menu of a "luncheon to ladies only" given by Mrs. Davis in late January 1864: "Gumbo, ducks and olives, chickens in jelly, oysters, lettuce salad, chocolate cream, jelly cake, claret, champagne, etc., were the good things set before us."

After capturing Atlanta in late 1864, Union general William Tecumseh Sherman marched his army through Georgia and the Carolinas, determined to deny food to Robert E. Lee's army in Virginia and to destroy the Southern people's will to fight.

Marching through Georgia and South Carolina without supplies, Sherman's sixty thousand men took the thirty tons of food they needed each day from the farms and homes of Southern civilians. To make sure this was carried out with maximum efficiency, Sherman had special maps drawn up from the 1860 census that showed the crop yields for each county in Georgia.

Dolly Burge, mistress of a cotton plantation in Zebulon, Georgia, recounted in her diary the feelings of helplessness as Sherman's "bummers" descended on her house:

> To my smoke-house, my dairy, pantry, kitchen, and cellar, like famished wolves they come, breaking locks and whatever is in their way. The thousand pounds of meat in my smokehouse is gone in a twinkling, my flour, my meat, my lard, butter, eggs, pickles…are all gone. My eighteen fat turkeys, my hens, chickens, and fowls, my young pigs are shot down in my yard and hunted as if they

were rebels themselves. Utterly powerless, I ran out and appealed to the guard. "I cannot help you, Madam; it is orders."

Emma LeConte was a seventeen-year-old girl living in Columbia, South Carolina, when Sherman's army came through her plantation after burning Columbia to the ground. Emma wrote about her family's shortage of food in her diary entry for January 23, 1865:

We live tolerably poorly. Two meals a day. Two plates of bread for breakfast, one of wheat flour as five bags of flour were recently made a present to us else we would only have corn bread. Corn itself is forty dollars a bushel. Dinner consists of a very small piece of meat, generally beef, a few potatoes and a dish of hominy and a pone of corn bread. We have no reason to complain, so many families are so much worse off.

Four weeks later, the LeConte family was living off meager rations supplied by the occupying Federal troops.

I hope relief will come before famine actually threatens. We have to cut our rations as short as possible to try to make the food hold out till succor comes. Father left us with some mouldy [sic]

After the Civil War, many newly freed slaves headed west and north to seek employment in food service or as caterers and cooks. *Courtesy of Library of Congress.*

spoiled flour that was turned over to him by the Bureau. We can only possible eat it made into battercakes and then it is horrid. We draw rations from the town every day—a tiny bit of rancid salt pork and a pint of meal. We have the battercakes for breakfast, the bit of meat and cornbread for dinner—no supper. We fare better than some because we have the cows. Mother had peas to feed them, and sometimes we take a few of those from them to vary our diet. Today as a great treat mother gave us boiled rice for dinner—some the Negroes had brought us in the pillage of the stores. We enjoyed it immensely—the first I have tasted in many days.

When peace finally came, the South was ravaged and many of its people scattered and destitute. In spite of relief efforts mounted by the federal government and an estimated $4 million in relief raised by private citizens in the North, the hunger Southerners suffered during the later years of the war still plagued them after the fighting stopped.

Frances Butler Leigh returned to her father's plantation on Butler's Island, Georgia, in 1866 after spending the war years in the North. She wrote about the trials facing Southerners during the years immediately following the war in *Ten Years on a Georgia Plantation Since the War* (1883):

I cook, and my maid does the housework, and as it has rained hard for three days and the kitchen roof is half off, I cook in the dining-room or parlour. Fortunately, my provisions are so limited that I have not much to cook; for five days my food has consisted of hard pilot biscuits, grits cooked in different ways, oysters, and twice, as a great treat, ham and eggs. I brought a box of preserves from the North with me, but half of them upset, and the rest were spoilt.

It would take another four years before food shortages became a thing of the past for most Southerners.

SOUTHERN COOKING FROM RECONSTRUCTION TO THE SECOND WORLD WAR

One of the most significant events relating to Southern food after the end of the Civil War was the return of the publication of *Mrs. Hill's New Cook Book* in 1867.

Annabella P. Hill of Atlanta published more than four hundred pages of recipes for traditional dishes and tips on everything from cooking vegetables to curing meat. Although it was published during Reconstruction, it is a celebration of antebellum recipes and foods. The book was widely circulated and had a significant impact on the way Southerners cooked in the latter years of the nineteenth century.

After the war ended, many African Americans who had been cooks on large farms or plantations headed west or north and found work in food service. Abbey Fisher, a former slave from Alabama, became a successful cook and caterer in San Francisco. In 1881, some of her patrons persuaded Mrs. Fisher, who couldn't read or write, to dictate the recipes she carried around in her head. The result was *What Mrs. Fisher Knows About Old Southern Cooking*. Although the book wasn't widely circulated, it was historically significant as the first cookbook published by an African American.

When Reconstruction ended in the mid-1870s, the South began to rise from the ashes and poverty brought on by the war. The new economic prosperity meant a return to entertaining, and cookbooks such as Marion Cabel Tyree's *House-Keeping in Old Virginia* (1877) and Mary Stuart Smith's *Virginia Cookery-Book* (1885) collected recipes from the old days and gave them to a new generation of Southern women.

In the period between the end of the war and the turn of the twentieth century, several new advances in technology would drastically change the way most Southerners ate. The wood cookstove had been invented in 1840 but was rare below the Mason-Dixon line prior to the end of the Civil War. By 1900, it was a fixture in Southern homes.

Piggly Wiggly stores revolutionized the way Southerners shopped for food. The abundance of canned goods meant fruits and vegetables were available year round. *Courtesy of North Carolina State Archives.*

Another attribute of the new stoves that revolutionized eating in the South was their ability to bake breads and cakes far better than any method used before. Cookbooks of the time abound with cake and pie recipes to satisfy the notorious Southern sweet tooth.

Advances in industrial production in the latter years of the nineteenth century led to the introduction of enamelware, also referred to as graniteware. These were pots, pans and other cookware made from thin sheet iron or sheet steel and covered with a nonporous coating of enamel. They were very inexpensive compared to cast iron and readily available at general stores and in the new mail-order catalogues from Sears, Roebuck and Company and Montgomery Ward. Their low cost enabled even families of modest means to own several different pots and pans. The one-pot meals that had made up the daily fare of most lower-class Southerners began to be replaced with meats and vegetables cooked separately in the new cookware.

The widespread availability of canned food was another major innovation that swept the South in the later part of the nineteenth century. By the beginning of the 1900s, general stores throughout the South were brimming with canned meats, fish, fruits and vegetables priced within the reach of working folks.

The early 1900s also brought the first widely available home refrigeration units, eliminating the need for icehouses and dripping blocks of ice. Recipes from the period reflect the changes, with "sweet milk biscuits," "icebox pie" and "refrigerator cookies" joining the list of Southern favorites.

In 1916, Clarence Saunders changed the way Southerners (and eventually the rest of the world) bought groceries when he opened Piggly Wiggly, the first self-service grocery store. The chain spread across the South, and the idea of shoppers filling their own carts (or buggies, as they're called in the South) became the industry standard.

Although the vast majority of Southerners were enjoying the fruits of these modern marvels, there was a group who lived in such abject poverty that the stereotype of their way of living and eating continues to stigmatize the South to the present day.

Sharecropping: The New Slavery

In the economic uncertainty immediately following the Civil War, some newly freed slaves remained on the plantations of their former owners, working the land as tenant farmers for a share of the crop. They were joined by a new underclass of desperately poor whites, some of who had been marginally poor farmers who were forced off their land for being unable to pay the four years' worth of back taxes demanded after the war by the federal government.

Sharecroppers, both black and white, often fell victim to the "crop lien" system, in which they received food, seeds and supplies on credit from the landowner or the local store. In 1938, the Works Progress Administration interviewed African American sharecroppers in Mississippi about their diet. They reported that the "furnishing men" supplied a peck of cornmeal, three pounds of salt meat, two pounds of sugar, one pound of coffee, one gallon of molasses and one plug of chewing tobacco, essentially the same rations their grandfathers had drawn as slaves. As these "furnishings" were advanced at inflated prices against their earnings from their share of the crop, most found themselves in debt to the landowner at the end of the season and beholden to work another year to pay off a debt that could never be paid.

Although these weekly "furnishings" were nearly identical to what they had lived on during slavery days, there was a major shift in their diet because of the crop lien system. The small patches of land used for the personal vegetable gardens that supplemented their diets during slavery were given up in order to grow more sale crops to help pay the debt. Soon the truly poor, black and white, were living almost exclusively on poor-quality cornmeal and molasses with no vegetables or meat other than fried hog fat. While they were taking in enough raw calories, their diet lacked enough protein and vitamins. This led to widespread malnutrition and disease until steps were taken to enrich cornmeal and flour with vitamins.

When World War I erupted in Europe in 1914, America remained neutral. By May 1916, the sinking of the British passenger liner *Lusitania* (with large loss of American lives) encouraged Americans to help with the war effort by supplying food to the Allies.

Food shortages in the winter of 1916–17 led Americans, including those in the South, to heed the calls by the U.S. Food Administration for voluntary food conservation. Food companies, eager to capitalize on the idea of food substitutes, started marketing campaigns touting the virtues of vegetable shortenings as a substitute for butter and lard, canned salmon as a meat substitute and the use of canned vegetables and other products. Soon patriotic Southerners

Sharecropper family, Hale County, Alabama. *Courtesy of Library of Congress.*

Sow the seeds of Victory!

plant &
raise
your own
vegetables

WRITE TO THE
NATIONAL
WAR GARDEN
COMMISSION ~
WASHINGTON, D.C.
for free books on
gardening, canning
& drying.

"Every Garden a Munition Plant"
Charles Lathrop Pack, President

In both world wars, Southerners faced food shortages and rationing but managed to make do by planting Victory Gardens like this 1918 poster encouraged them to do. *Courtesy of Library of Congress.*

flocked to their local Piggly Wigglys to snap up the new products. Thus salmon patties, canned soups and vegetables began to appear in the Southern pantry. At war's end, they became firmly ensconced in Southern foodways.

After the war ended in 1918, life returned to normal for the vast majority of Southerners. Many sharecroppers and tenant farmers, however, found themselves struggling to scratch out a living as cotton prices fell sharply during the early 1920s.

When the Great Depression hit in the winter of 1929, sharecroppers in the South were among those hardest hit. This led to the "Great Migration" of African Americans from the Mississippi Delta to the factories of the North. The emigrants left possessions, memories and sometimes families behind, but they took their food traditions with them. Hog meat, greens and cornbread were soon as much a part of supper in Joliet, Illinois, as they were in Jackson, Mississippi. In the rediscovery of African American history and traditions that marked the 1960s, this expatriated Southern cuisine would come to be called "soul food."

When America entered the Second World War in 1941, Southerners faced mandatory food rationing, beginning with sugar in April 1942. Coffee followed six months later, and by spring of 1943 a full-scale rationing system based on points and coupons was in place for the entire nation.

Rationing affected city dwellers more than people in more rural areas of the South, and recipes sprang up using creative substitutions for hard-to-find items such as sugar. Anyone who had even a small corner in their yard was encouraged to plant a "Victory Garden," and even city folks reaped the benefits of homegrown beans, okra and tomatoes.

THE ATOMIC AGE AND BEYOND:
SOUTHERN FOOD FROM 1945 TO THE PRESENT

The decades after the war brought sweeping changes to the way Southerners ate. Soldiers and sailors reared on hog and hominy had been exposed to a whole world of new foods from Europe and the Pacific.

The food shortages and rationing of the Depression and war years gave way to gleaming grocery stores brimming with new convenience foods. No longer did housewives have to bake loaf bread just for sandwiches—a quick trip to the supermarket, and a loaf of Wonder Bread was ready and waiting.

The new interstate highway system begun by President Eisenhower made long-distance transportation of food economical, and soon year-round produce from California and other western states replaced locally grown, seasonally available vegetables in Southern supermarkets.

The newly mobile Southerners started to eat on the run, and roadside diners, fish camps and barbecue lodges started with GI Bill money flourished. But the siren song of the ever-present television started to lure Southern children to hamburgers rather than ham biscuits and convinced time-conscious housewives that a mass-produced bucket of fried chicken was a special treat for the family.

By 1975, sales of microwave ovens had surpassed those of gas ranges. Just when it was beginning to look like traditional Southern cooking had been convenience fooded and microwaved out of existence, the regional cooking craze of the late 1970s and early 1980s got people interested in the foods of their heritage. An unlikely trio was on the forefront of the movement: a safety engineer from Louisiana turned Cajun cook (Justin Wilson); a peanut farmer who made it big (president Jimmy Carter); and a charming lady from the thriving megalopolis of Social Circle, Georgia (Nathalie Dupree).

With Carter's election in 1976, grits were served at the White House, while Wilson's and Dupree's cooking shows on public television came into homes across the South in the 1980s, extolling the virtues of red beans and rice and sweet potato pie. By the1980s, books by Dupree, Bill Neal, John T. Edge, Damon Lee Fowler, Ronni Lundy and John Egerton fanned the flames of a new generation of Southern cooks who wanted to learn how grandma had made things taste so good.

As Southern cooking enters its fourth century, it continues to change and evolve. Small family farms continue to hold out against agribusiness conglomerates, and a new breed of farmer— young, college educated, and Internet savvy—is riding the new wave of organic farming and sustainable, community-supported agriculture.

Instead of commercial feed, livestock on the new generation of Southern farms roam free and eat the same forage foods their ancestors ate for centuries. The result is a flavor not tasted in the South in the last fifty years. Fields are planted with sustainable crops, grown with natural methods that go against the conventional wisdom of big agribusiness but would be commonplace to a farmer of the 1800s.

A new generation of Southern chefs—Bill Lee, Frank Stitt, John and Robert Stehling, John Fleer and Hugh Acheson, to name just a few—are partnering with these farmers to bring heirloom fruits and vegetables bred for taste (not transportability) back to the Southern table. Sustainable agriculture groups are matching area farmers with nearby restaurants in "Buy Local" movements designed to encourage chefs to buy as much of their meats, dairy and produce as possible from farms within one hundred miles of their restaurants.

Photo by Frank R. Bealer, 1906. Courtesy of Georgia Archives, Vanishing Georgia Collection, tho372.

CHAPTER 2

The Southern Kitchen

My kitchen is a mystical place, a kind of temple for me. It is a place where the surfaces seem to have significance, where the sounds and odors carry meaning that transfers from the past and bridges to the future.
—Pearl Bailey

THE HEARTH

Before the revolution in cooking technology that occurred in the latter years of the nineteenth century, the Southern kitchen wasn't a particularly pleasant place to be. From the founding of Jamestown until the middle of the nineteenth century, cooking for plantation and backcountry cabin was done on the open hearth. Site-made brick was the material of choice for fireplaces, hearths and chimneys, but it was extremely labor intensive to make and expensive, so its use was mostly restricted to the wealthy. In most early Southern homes, fireplaces and chimneys were made from stones found on the property. If stones were scarce, the chimney above the roofline was often made of wattle and daub, which consisted of sticks held together with clay. While the stone hearths could withstand the high cooking temperatures, a layer of thick plaster usually protected brick hearths.

The goal of all homeowners was to have the kitchen separate from the main house to cut down on noise, odors, smoke and the ever-present danger of the main house burning down if a kitchen fire got out of hand. As soon as they could afford the time to do so, settlers built another room onto their cabins, separated by ten feet or more from the original structure. The old house became the kitchen, and the newer structure, with a smaller and less dangerous fireplace, became the living quarters.

Plantations, which had large numbers of mouths to feed, almost always had separate cookhouses, usually wood frame buildings with brick or stone floors. The interior walls were usually wood plank rather than plaster and were whitewashed regularly to keep them clean from the accumulation of soot from the large hearths.

The hearths in these cookhouses were huge, sometimes ten feet wide and four feet deep. Andirons set six feet apart held the large supply of oak and hickory logs needed to stoke the fire. The fires were kept going all day, and the coals were banked at night to make starting the next day's fire easier. The heat from these fireplaces was horrendous, especially in the stifling summers of the Carolinas and Georgia. An oven for baking was usually built into the side of the fireplace on larger farms and plantations. They would only be used once a week, as they made the already miserably hot kitchen an inferno.

This photo of the kitchen and fireplace at Cherry Grove plantation in Maryland shows pots hanging from the back bar. *Courtesy of Library of Congress.*

To prevent kitchen fires from destroying the main house, early Southern kitchens were often located away from the main house, like this one at the Harper House in Bentonville, North Carolina. *Courtesy of North Carolina State Archives.*

Plantation fireplaces were often state-of-the-art. The fireplaces were huge. The back bar, a long iron rod from which the pots and kettles hung, was sometimes as much as six feet above the fireplace floor. The back bar, or lodge pole as it was also called, was equipped with hooks of various lengths, designed so that the pots and kettles could hang at various distances from the fire to control cooking times. Trivets of different heights sat on the floor so that pots and skillets could be placed at exactly the desired distance from the hot coals.

Kitchens in larger plantations usually boasted several sizes of iron or brass pots, long-handled skillets (called spiders) equipped with legs and lids for placing coals under and over them and iron spits for roasting meats. In the homes of the extremely wealthy, such as the Colonial Governor's mansion in Williamsburg, Virginia, the spits were turned by elaborate wall-mounted clockwork mechanisms.

The equipment found in a typical plantation kitchen would include cast-iron pots with close-fitting lids, ranging from two to ten gallons in capacity, with rounded bottoms and three legs to keep them elevated from the hearth. Skillets with lids and legs, teakettles, a stew kettle, a biscuit baker and waffle irons rounded out the selection. Each piece had a lid, with an eye on top for lifting off with pothooks. Long, metal dripping pans were placed under meat as it roasted to catch drippings for gravy; root vegetables such as potatoes, carrots and parsnips were often put in these pans to simmer in the meat juices.

Other tools of the plantation cook's trade included long-handled shovels for banking coals and shoveling them under Dutch ovens and pots, pokers and bellows for tending the fire and long-handled tongs. Iron hooks of various lengths, called trammels, were used to suspend pots from the back bar at different heights above the fire to regulate cooking temperature.

The backcountry housewife, on the other hand, usually had to make do with one large stew pot and perhaps a single skillet. In the backcountry, food was generally served in wooden bowls, and wooden or pewter spoons were often the only utensils the family owned, in marked contrast to the fine china and silver usually found on the plantation table.

In addition to the pots and pans, standard kitchen furnishings included dressers with graduated shelves above them and double doors with drawers in the middle. The upper shelves held pewter and crockery, while the lower shelves and drawers held supplies and utensils. These dressers were supplemented by wall-mounted shelves used to store pots and pans. Cooking utensils of different sorts were often hung from wooden pegs mounted to the wall. Flour barrels covered with flat boards made handy worktables and served double duty as a place for the kitchen staff to take their meals.

The work of preparing the day's food was backbreaking and dangerous. Long cotton dresses, sleeves and aprons swept dangerously close to the open flames, and burns and scalding were common occurrences when pots slipped on the cranes. Some scholars estimate that 25 percent of all women killed in colonial times died as a result of cooking accidents. The invention of the fireplace crane in the early 1700s helped make open hearth cooking safer, but cooking was still risky business until cookstoves became common in Southern homes after the Civil War.

The Work Yard

Before electrical appliances became commonplace in the early years of the twentieth century, the Southern kitchen wasn't the self-contained room we think of today. Back then, the kitchen really started outside, where the cook would have her kitchen garden as close to the kitchen door as was practical. As Frances Phipps wrote in *Colonial Kitchens, Their Furnishings and Their Gardens*: "The orchard and the garden were set out, if at all possible, to the south and west of the shelter. The cornfield, the turnip lot, and the onion or cabbage patch usually began no more than fifty feet, if that, from the door."

The area immediately outside the kitchen door was called the work yard, and it was here that prep work such as peeling potatoes and shucking corn was carried out. A series of outbuildings was necessary to handle preserving, cooling and storage, especially on a family farm or plantation.

Milk, butter and other dairy products were stored in a dairy house or springhouse to keep them cool. A dairy house was a small shed or building with a dirt floor, usually dug down two or three feet below grade where the earth was cooler. There may have also been a pit dug a few feet deeper, lined with smooth stones or brick. This would serve to keep milk and buttermilk cool. The ideal was the springhouse, a small shed built of wood or, ideally, river rock. It would

The springhouse kept milk, butter, eggs and other perishables cool in the days before refrigeration. *Courtesy of Library of Congress.*

be built overhanging a shallow part of a creek or a natural spring where the milk could be put in stoneware crocks and placed directly in the cool water.

The smokehouse was a vital structure to the plantation; small farms usually had a small smokehouse or may have shared one with a neighboring farm. The smokehouse was used to cure and store meat of all kinds, although pork was the most common occupant (see chapter 6). Since the smokehouse needed to be able to hold in smoke efficiently, there were no windows and only one door. If the landowner was able to afford it, smokehouses were made of brick. If that wasn't practical, wood siding was employed to keep as much smoke in as possible.

Larger plantations also would have a well house and an icehouse, as well as root cellars for storage of sweet potatoes, carrots, "keeping" apples and Irish potatoes. These foods would be stored either beneath the floors of outbuildings or in separate storage sheds. The smokehouse, if not all of these buildings, would have been kept locked, and the mistress of the plantation was the keeper of the keys.

Cast-iron cookstoves began to replace the open hearth in Southern kitchens after the Civil War. *Courtesy of Library of Congress.*

THE MODERN SOUTHERN KITCHEN

In the period between 1866 and 1920, coal-fired cookstoves replaced the open hearth, making the kitchen a much safer and more pleasant place to be. Iceboxes replaced springhouses, and canned foods replaced the root cellar. Southern cooks enjoyed a life made markedly easier by these technological breakthroughs. When rural electrification made it possible for nearly everyone to have refrigerators, electric ranges and electric appliances, a new renaissance in cooking swept the South.

The remainder of this chapter looks at some of the basic equipment and ingredients necessary to prepare the recipes in this book. A lot of these are already in most modern kitchens, but there are a few ingredients you might have to obtain from your local organic grocer or specialty food store.

The Pantry: Staples for Southern Cooking

There are several ingredients called for in the recipes that may not be familiar to some readers. The following definitions and explanations will shed a little light on the subject.

BUTTER: Butter comes in salted and unsalted forms; in the days before refrigeration, salt had to be added to butter as a preservative. Salted butter is for spreading; unsalted is for cooking, as it allows for better control of the salt in the recipe.

CORNMEAL: Cornmeal is finely ground corn flour. White or yellow is a matter of personal preference; there is no discernible difference in taste. Self-rising cornmeal already has the baking powder mixed in and is more convenient. To use it in a recipe that calls for regular cornmeal, simply omit any baking powder or baking soda from the recipe.

EGGS: Unless otherwise stated, all eggs used in the recipes are USDA Large. If you buy a facsimile printing of one of the early cookbooks and want to try the recipes, use USDA Medium eggs.

FLOUR: All-purpose, self-rising and cake flour are essential ingredients for baking. All-purpose, as the name implies, is good for all types of recipes. Self-rising flour has a leavening agent mixed in with it, so it is almost exclusively used for baking. Cake flour is used in some cake recipes to give a lighter texture and finer "crumb" to the finished product.

In addition to baking, flour is used to thicken gravy and sauces and as a coating to prevent fried foods from sticking.

In the South, flours are "softer" than those found in the other regions of the United States—they contain less protein, giving a lighter texture to biscuits and other baked goods.

HAM HOCKS are the lower portions of the hog's hind leg, the small end of a ham. They are salt cured and may or may not be smoked.

HOT SAUCES: There are hundreds of bottled hot sauces used for additional heat and flavor in Southern cooking, especially in the cuisines of south Louisiana. Tabasco is probably the best known and widely distributed. Pepper vinegar, which is vinegar with tiny hot peppers in it, is much loved on greens by many Southerners.

MAYONNAISE: One of the five "mother sauces" of French cuisine; mayonnaise is widely used in the South for everything from potato salad to tomato sandwiches to shrimp remoulade. Southern mayonnaise tends to be sweeter than others; Duke's and JFG are the two most popular brands.

MILK PRODUCTS: There are three basic dairy products used in the preparation of traditional Southern recipes: whole milk (called "sweet milk" in old recipes), whipping cream (often just called cream) and buttermilk.

When a recipe calls for milk, it means whole milk. Whole milk is the closest thing to milk fresh from the cow.

Buttermilk was a staple in Southern recipes, especially in the days before refrigeration, when milk soured easily. Old recipes often called whole milk "sweet milk" to differentiate it from "sour" or buttermilk. The term buttermilk used to refer to clabber, the liquid left in the churn after butter was made. Modern buttermilk is made by adding cultures of bacteria to low-fat milk. This gives the resulting milk a thick texture and a slightly acidic taste. Some dairies add bits of butter to their buttermilk to give it that fresh from the churn taste.

Heavy cream, which is used to make really rich, thick whipped cream, is sometimes used in gravy and sauce recipes.

Some recipes call for half-and-half, which is half milk and half cream.

SALT PORK is the most commonly used of the flavoring meats in Southern cooking. Salt pork is similar to bacon but has much more fat and isn't smoked. Also known as side meat, it is cut from the sides and belly of the hog and is salt cured. If only the saltiness is desired, salt pork is fried to render all the fat and then added to the dish. Salt pork is used to flavor some vegetables and lends flavor and texture to pilaus.

Thick-sliced bacon may be substituted for salt pork in any of the recipes.

SPICES: Some recipes (especially those dating back to colonial times) will call for spices that may seem a little strange, such as nutmeg in a chicken dish. These spices were not only used for flavor but also to mask the taste of meats that were a little "off" in the days before refrigeration. Give them a try; you will be pleasantly surprised with the outcome.

SALT has been a highly sought-after commodity since biblical times. Early Southerners relied on salt not only as a seasoning but also as one of their most used materials for food preservation. A good, coarse-grained, non-iodized salt such as kosher or sea salt will make the recipes in the book more authentic.

BLACK PEPPER was widely used as a seasoning in the early South. Many of the recipes in this and many other cookbooks call for freshly ground black pepper, and the flavor difference from pre-ground black pepper is well worth the extra trouble.

There are several seasoning blends that are nice to have on hand to save time and effort in the kitchen. They are **CREOLE SEASONING**, **POULTRY SEASONING**, **"SOUL FOOD" SEASONING** and **SEAFOOD SEASONING**. Kitchen stores and large supermarkets will usually stock these, but if they are unobtainable in your area, they can be made up in advance and stored in empty spice bottles with screw-on tops, which are available at most kitchen stores.

Creole Seasoning Blend

Yield: about ⅔ cup

2½ tablespoons paprika
2 tablespoons salt
2 tablespoons garlic powder
1 tablespoon freshly ground black pepper
1 tablespoon onion powder
1 tablespoon cayenne
1 tablespoon dried oregano
1 tablespoon dried thyme

Combine all ingredients in a small bowl and spoon into small jars with tight-fitting lids. Store in a cool, dry area for up to 3 months.

Poultry Seasoning

Yield: ½ cup

¼ cup black pepper
2 tablespoons garlic powder
¼ cup onion powder
2 tablespoons celery salt

In a small stainless steel bowl, mix ingredients well and store in an airtight container.

Soul Food Seasoning

Yield: about ¾ cup

2 tablespoons ground black pepper
2 tablespoons garlic powder
2 tablespoons onion powder
1 tablespoon salt
1 tablespoon chili powder
1 tablespoon paprika
1 teaspoon parsley seasoning
1 teaspoon celery power
1 teaspoon thyme powder
1 pinch cayenne pepper

In a small mixing bowl, combine ingredients until well blended. Store in an airtight jar.

Seafood Seasoning

1 tablespoon celery seed
1 tablespoon whole black peppercorns
6 bay leaves
½ teaspoon whole cardamom
½ teaspoon mustard seed
4 whole cloves
1 teaspoon paprika
¼ teaspoon mace

Combine all ingredients in a spice grinder or small food processor. Grind well and store in a small glass jar.

Cookbooks and Receipt Books

In colonial times, cookbooks were few and far between. The lady of the house might have a copy of Hannah Glasse's *The Art of Cookery Made Plain and Easy* (1747) or Amelia Simmons's *American Cookery* (the first cookbook published in America in 1796), but for the most part she relied on her "receipt book."

Receipt books were handwritten kitchen journals, sometimes passed down from mother to daughter, in which the lady wrote her favorite receipts (or recipes, as we refer to them today). These books also contained instructions for the daily chores of running a household, from curing meats to curing colds.

Some of these old receipt books, such as the one begun by Harriott Pinckney Horry in 1770, have been reprinted and offer a fascinating glimpse of life as it was in the early days of Southern cooking.

In 1824, Mary Randolph published *The Virginia House-wife*, the first Southern cookbook. Over the next 180 years, an avalanche of books on Southern cooking hit the bookshelves of passionate cooks and continue to this day.

Many of these early Southern cookbooks have been reprinted in facsimile, and some are even available online as free downloads. Internet sites specializing in antique books such as Abebooks (www.abebooks.com) and Biblio (www.biblio.com) are good sources for those who wish to further explore historical cooking through collecting nineteenth-century cookery books.

Cooking from Historical Recipes

Cooks in the early days didn't have the standard measuring cups and spoons found in the modern Southern kitchen; they used the everyday utensils they had on hand. As they passed their receipts on to friends and family, they used measurements such as "one teacup," "a wineglass full" or "a lump of butter the size of a hen's egg."

The recipes in the following chapters have been adapted from original eighteenth-, nineteenth- and twentieth-century recipes and rewritten using standard measurements; but for those who wish to try recipes from the early texts such as *The Virginia House-wife* or *The Carolina Housewife*, these measurements will help in translating early recipes:

Liquid Measure
1 wineglass equals ¼ cup
1 gill equals ½ cup
1 teacup equals ¾ cup
1 coffee cup equals a little less than a cup
1 tumbler equals 1 cup

Dry Measure

1 peck equals 2 gallons, dry

A pinch or dash equals the amount that can be picked up between thumb and first two fingers

1 salt spoon equals $\frac{1}{4}$ teaspoon

1 kitchen spoon equals 1 teaspoon

1 dessert spoon equals 2 teaspoons or 1 soup spoon

1 spoonful equals 1 tablespoon

1 pound equals 4 cups flour; or $2\frac{1}{2}$ cups packed brown or confectioner's sugar; or 8 medium-size eggs

Butter the size of a hen's egg is about $\frac{1}{4}$ cup, or 2 ounces

Butter the size of a walnut is about 1 tablespoon

Oven Temperature

Slow oven: 300 degrees F

Moderate oven: 350 degrees F

Quick oven: 375 to 400 degrees F

Hot oven: 400 to 425 degrees F

CHAPTER 3

Appetizers, Knickknacks and Snacks

And the next morning, when he left, they would have him take along a bottle of "sperrits" for his stomach's sake, as well as a huge package of provisions, called in Southern parlance a "snack."
—*Daniel Robinson Hundley,* Social Relations in Our Southern States, *1860*

Curiously (especially for a region known around the world for lavish entertaining), appetizers were exceedingly scarce in the South until after the Second World War. Although some Southern cookbooks from the turn of the twentieth century had very small chapters devoted to appetizers, they were nearly all populated by recipes for canapés and other hors d'oeuvres not native to the region.

The reason for this lack of recipes is that everything that made up a Southern meal was traditionally brought to the table at the same time. Pickles, relishes, deviled eggs—all arrived together in a cornucopia that made mouths water and sideboards groan.

On occasion, toasted pecans, peanuts or cheese straws were put out in the parlor, but this was rare; no Southern hostess worth her salt wanted people to fill up on "knickknacks" and diminish their appreciation of the meal that had been hours in the making.

Snacking still managed to occur in spite of the best efforts of wives and mothers. Away from home, in the days before drive-throughs, Southerners snacked on pickled pig's feet, pickled eggs, bologna and crackers, sardines and the ubiquitous Vienna sausages, purchased from country stores, gas stations and dope wagons (push carts that sold drinks, sandwiches and snacks to millworkers; "dope" is an old Southern slang term for cola-flavored soft drinks).

At home, snacks were usually found on the back of the stove, where the leftovers from the last meal were kept warm by the residual heat from the massive black iron beast. There would usually be leftover biscuits and ham, bacon or sausage from breakfast. A raid on the pie safe for a little something sweet and a trip to the springhouse for a glass of cold buttermilk would calm a grumbling stomach until suppertime.

The modern Southern cook has a variety of appetizers and snacks in his or her repertoire, thanks in large part to the entertaining craze of the 1950s and '60s. An excellent source for early Southern appetizer recipes is *Charleston Receipts*, published by the Junior League of Charleston in 1950.

Deviled Eggs

Deviled eggs are so much a part of the food culture of the South that special containers for transporting them from place to place can be found in any housewares department worth its salt. China, cut glass and crystal deviled egg platters are cherished family heirlooms passed on from one generation to the next and the occasional cause of sisters not speaking to each other for a few years after mama passed away.

The term "deviled" to describe food prepared with hot spices first came into use in the eighteenth century, although recipes for stuffed eggs date back to medieval times. They made their way to the Southern table by way of the earliest English settlers.

Yield: two dozen eggs

12 eggs
4 quarts water
¼ cup mayonnaise
1 tablespoon Creole or Dijon mustard

1 tablespoon dill pickle cubes
salt and freshly ground black pepper to taste
paprika
fresh dill for garnish

Place eggs in a 4- to 6-quart saucepan and add water until the eggs are covered by about 1 inch of water. Bring to a vigorous boil and remove from heat. Let sit, covered, for 15 minutes, then remove and cool under running water. Peel eggs and allow to cool. Remove yolks and place in a mixing bowl. Set the whites aside, being careful not to break them. Break the yolks into small pieces using a fork or potato masher. Add the mayonnaise, mustard and pickles. Mix well. Season the mixture with salt and pepper. Spoon the mixture into the egg white halves. Chill completely and garnish with paprika and a sprig of dill.

Embellishments: Deviled eggs can be topped with almost anything from olive slices to shrimp to capers. Some favorites are rainbow trout caviar, fresh dill, minced chives, finely minced shallots, tiny slivers of country ham or bacon, crawfish tails and the little tiny peppers from empty pepper vinegar bottles.

Scotch Eggs

Scotch Eggs are a favorite Southern breakfast, enjoyed while hunting, fishing or tailgating. These portable and delicious morsels trace their ancestry back to nineteenth-century Scotland and England.

Yield: 8 eggs

2 pounds bulk pork sausage
2 tablespoons fresh parsley, chopped
2 tablespoons grated onion
½ teaspoon ground cinnamon

¼ teaspoon ground nutmeg
8 hard cooked eggs, shelled
1 cup fine, dry bread crumbs

Preheat oven to 350 degrees F.
In a medium bowl, combine all ingredients except for eggs and breadcrumbs; mix well. Divide mixture into 8 portions; shape into patties.
Place one egg on each patty, shaping the sausage mixture around the egg until the egg is completely covered. Roll in breadcrumbs.
Bake until golden brown, about 15 to 20 minutes.

Pickled Eggs

Pickled eggs date back to pre-colonial Europe, and recipes for them are found in the earliest Southern cookery books. There isn't a mom and pop store or "beer joint" anywhere in the South that doesn't have a gallon jar of pickled eggs on the counter, usually with a jar of Penrose pickled hot sausages and a jar of pickled pig's feet on either side.

Yield: two dozen eggs

24 large eggs
6 cups apple cider vinegar
2 tablespoon black peppercorns
1 tablespoon whole allspice
½ tablespoon mace

½ tablespoon coriander seeds
½ tablespoon cardamom seeds
½ tablespoon cloves
10 small hot red peppers
3 tablespoons granulated sugar

Place eggs in a 6- to 8-quart Dutch oven and cover with cool water to a depth of about two inches. Bring to a simmer and cook for about 15 minutes. Place eggs in cold water; remove shells and pack into sterilized quart jars. Place vinegar, spices and sugar into a 4-quart saucepan. Bring to boil, reduce heat and simmer for 5 minutes. Pour hot liquid over hardboiled eggs. Place lid on jar and store in refrigerator when cooled. Use within one month.

Pimento Cheese

Pimento cheese is a staple food across the South, beloved by rich and poor, young and old alike. Bill Neal, the great champion of Southern cuisine who presided over the kitchen at his legendary Crook's Corner in Chapel Hill, North Carolina, called it "the pate of the South." It dates back to at least the early years of the twentieth century: the earliest recipe I have found in print is from 1910.

Pimento cheese is eaten with crackers as an appetizer, as a sandwich on any number of breads and even as a topping for burgers, especially in South Carolina. It can be taken to a whole new level when the sandwich is graced with a little arugula and grilled lightly in butter, or for the ultimate Southern pimento cheese sandwich, add a thick slice of bologna, fried to perfection.

Yield: 3 cups

16 ounces aged white cheddar
one 2-ounce jar diced pimentos, drained
6 tablespoons mayonnaise
½ teaspoon chili powder

⅛ teaspoon freshly ground black pepper
⅛ teaspoon ground cumin
¼ teaspoon cayenne pepper, or to taste

Grate the cheddar by hand. Add the rest of the ingredients and stir lightly to mix. Refrigerate for 30 minutes. Serve with crackers.

Benne Wafers

Benne is the African word for sesame seeds. These thin, tasty crackers are a favorite snack in the South Carolina Lowcountry, and can be eaten alone or with dips or spreads such as pimento cheese.

Yield: about 3 dozen

½ cup sesame seeds
1 cup all-purpose flour
½ teaspoon baking powder
½ teaspoon salt

¼ cup butter
4 tablespoons milk
1 large egg, slightly beaten

Preheat oven to 350 degrees.

Sprinkle sesame seeds in a single layer onto an ungreased baking sheet and toast for 10 minutes. Let cool.

Sift together flour, baking powder and salt. Add butter, a small amount at a time, and cut into dry ingredients with a pastry blender until mixture resembles cornmeal. Add milk a little at a time, stirring until dough comes together. Stir in sesame seeds.

On a lightly floured surface, gently knead dough until no longer sticky. Roll out dough until it is no thicker than the sesame seeds themselves. Cut into 2-inch rounds and place on lightly greased baking sheet.

Using a pastry brush, brush each wafer with beaten egg.

Bake until golden brown, about 12 to 15 minutes. Allow to cool and store in an airtight container.

Cheese Straws

These are the quintessential Southern appetizers, showing up at nearly every party around the holidays.

This recipe is typical of many and is based on one published in the *Southern Cook Book of Favorite Southern Dishes*, published by the Gray & Dudley Hardware Company in Nashville about 1900.

Yield: about 6 dozen

8 tablespoons butter
½ pound sharp cheddar cheese
1¾ cups flour

½ teaspoon salt
¼ to ½ teaspoon cayenne pepper, or to taste
1 teaspoon Worcestershire sauce

Preheat oven to 300 degrees F.

In a food processor fitted with a metal blade, process butter and cheese until well blended. Add remaining ingredients; cover and blend thoroughly to form stiff dough.

Place the dough onto a lightly floured work surface and roll out to a thickness of ¼ inch. Using a dough scraper or sharp knife, cut dough into strips ½-inch wide by 2 inches long. Strips may be twisted together for a fancier look.

Arrange the pieces on 1 or 2 baking sheets.

Bake until they are crisp and lightly browned, about 20 to 25 minutes.

Boiled Peanuts

Boiled peanuts are distinctly Southern; you will find few non-Southerners who have even heard of them, let alone tasted them. They have been a part of Southern foodways since at least the nineteenth century and probably before then; they are so simple to make that most people never bothered to write down a recipe.

Travel any two-lane blacktop in South Carolina or Georgia between late May and early November, and you'll see people selling boiled peanuts from farm stands, shacks and even pickup trucks parked along the roadside.

Even among Southerners, boiled peanuts are an acquired taste; their flavor is closer to a bean (peanuts are legumes, after all) than the nutty flavor roasting imparts. This recipe is typical of many.

Yield: 3 pounds

3 pounds raw peanuts in the shell
1½ cups kosher salt

Fill sink with cool water. Place peanuts in sink and wash, changing water as needed until water is clear. Allow peanuts to soak for 30 minutes.
In a 10- to 12-quart stockpot, bring peanuts, salt and enough water to cover peanuts to a depth of 3 inches to a rolling boil. Reduce heat to medium and simmer for one hour. Using a slotted spoon, remove a peanut and crack it open. If peanut is soft, they are done. If still crunchy, allow peanuts to boil for ½ hour, then check again. It may take several hours before peanuts are soft, depending on the nuts. Serve hot with beer or RC Cola.

Spiced Pecans

"Toasted pecans" had probably been around for quite a while when Henrietta (Mrs. S.R.) Dull, the home economics editor of the *Atlanta Journal*, published her recipe in her *Southern Cooking* (1920). They are the perfect cocktail party snack—a little sweet, a little salty and a little spicy.

Yield: 1 pound, about 4 cups
¼ pound butter
¼ cup brown sugar, firmly packed
2 teaspoons salt

1½ teaspoons cayenne pepper
2 teaspoons Worcestershire sauce
1 pound pecan halves

In a 12-inch cast-iron skillet over medium heat, melt butter.
Add brown sugar, salt, cayenne and Worcestershire sauce; whisk until well blended and sugar melts.
Add pecan halves and toss until well coated and heated through.
Place in a large paper bag and shake to drain; allow to cool on a cookie sheet.

Sausage Cheese Balls

These spicy treats are a part of the post–World War II appetizer boom in Southern cuisine. They are a staple at Christmas parties but may be served any time of year.

Yield: about 5 dozen

1 pound hot sausage
4 cups (1 pound) grated sharp cheddar cheese
3 cups baking mix
vegetable oil (if needed)

Combine ingredients; depending on the fat content of the sausage, you may have to add a little vegetable oil (about a tablespoon) to get the sausage and cheese to blend.
Shape into walnut-sized balls and place about 2 inches apart on a non-greased baking sheet.
Bake on cookie sheet at 400 degrees F for 10 to 15 minutes. May be frozen before or after baking.
Serve hot.

Pickled Shrimp

Pickled shrimp were a favorite Charleston appetizer long before Harriott Pinckney Horry put a recipe for them in her handwritten receipt book in 1770. They are easy to make and very tasty. To sterilize the jar, place it, along with the lid, in a large pot, cover with water and bring to a rolling boil for 5 minutes. Remove with tongs and allow to cool without touching the inside of the jar or lid.

Yield: 6 to 8 pints

¼ cup crab boil seasoning
2 ½ pounds medium shrimp, peeled and
  deveined
¾ cup white wine vinegar
6 teaspoons celery seeds
1 teaspoon mustard seed

2 teaspoons salt
¼ teaspoon black pepper
1 cup extra virgin olive oil
1 large onion, thinly sliced
12 bay leaves

Place crab boil seasoning in cheesecloth and tie securely. Place in a large stockpot with six cups water. Bring to a vigorous boil; simmer for 5 minutes then add shrimp.
Boil shrimp for 3 minutes and drain.
In a small bowl, whisk together the vinegar, celery seeds, mustard seed, salt and pepper. Add oil, whisking continuously until well blended; set aside.
In a clean, sterilized one-quart canning jar, place a layer of about 15 shrimp and top with some of the onion and 4 bay leaves. Repeat layers of shrimp and layers of onions and bay leaves until all of the shrimp are used up. Top with the last of the onion and bay leaves.
Pour the dressing over the contents of the jar, pushing everything down so that the oil and vinegar mixture covers everything. Seal the jar and let marinate in the refrigerator for at least 24 hours.
When you remove shrimp, use a clean fork and make sure the remaining oil and vinegar mixture covers the remaining shrimp. Will keep, refrigerated, for about 2 weeks.
Serve shrimp skewered on toothpicks or with crackers or fried grits cakes (see page 60).

Pigs in Blankets

This recipe may come as a shock to anyone who has eaten those tiny cocktail wienies wrapped in biscuit dough.

In cookbooks from the turn of the twentieth century, the real recipe for pigs in blankets can be found, and it is a genuine treat. This recipe is based on one from *The Virginia Cookery Book: Traditional Recipes*, published as a fundraiser by the Virginia League of Women Voters sometime in the early 1920s.

Yield: 24 appetizers

24 large oysters, shelled, drained and picked over
12 slices bacon

Cut bacon in half crosswise. Wrap each oyster in a bacon slice and secure with a toothpick. Place on a very lightly greased cookie sheet and broil until bacon is cooked and oysters begin to curl at edges, about 10 to 15 minutes. Remove toothpick and serve with cocktail sauce.

Hoeing rice, South Carolina, circa 1904. *Courtesy of Library of Congress.*

Chapter 4

Rice and Grits

True grits, more grits, fish, grits, and collards.
Life is good where grits are swallered.
—*Roy Blount Jr., Southern humorist*

Grits

Rice and grits are two of the South's best-loved foods. Both take their place at breakfast and supper tables in every part of the region, singularly and as part of some of our most famous dishes. Since grits were here from the beginning, it's only fitting that they take their place in the spotlight first.

Grits has a special place in the hearts, minds and stomachs of Southerners. We are literally weaned on grits; go into the kitchen of almost any day-care in the South, and chances are there is grits in the cupboard.

There is a feeling Southerners get when we eat grits that no other comfort food can produce. It's warmth that transcends temperature; warmth that touches the part deep inside that makes you feel good and safe and comforted and loved.

Turner Catledge, a Southerner who for many years was an editor at the *New York Times*, called grits "the first truly American food." Catledge also addressed the unique grammar of grits when it comes to being singular or plural, saying it was up to the speaker to decide.

When the first English settlers arrived in the New World, they found the Powhatan Indians eating a hot porridge they called "rockahominy," which was made from dried maize, pounded and flavored with animal fat. Robert Beverley wrote about the use of hominy by the Powhatans in *The History and Present State of Virginia* (1705): "It is very common with them to boil fish as well as flesh with their homony [*sic*]; this is Indian corn soaked, broken in a mortar, husked, and then boiled in water over a gentle fire for ten or twelve hours."

Some linguists say the word grits may have come from the old English "grytt," which referred to any bran but in practice meant coarsely ground grain, while others say "grits" is a corruption of grist, the end product of grinding corn in a gristmill. Sarah Rutledge referred to grits as "grist" in her recipe from *The Carolina Housewife* (1824).

Prior to the Civil War, nearly every farmer in the South grew corn. Before gristmills became common in the frontier South, the dried corn was pounded in "hominy blocks," large wooden mortars and pestles that cracked the grains into a very coarse meal. By 1860, there was an average of forty gristmills per county in the Carolinas and Georgia, turning locally grown corn into hominy, grits and cornmeal to feed the region's growing population.

After the Civil War, grits was often one of the few foods available to ease the food shortages that plagued the South. In more modern times, the low cost and high nutritional value of grits helped many Southern families survive the Great Depression.

Traditionally, grits and hominy were made by soaking dried corn kernels in lye to remove the outer hull and germ. The resulting white, puffy kernels are called hominy and are sold in cans in most supermarkets. Older cookbooks sometimes refer to hominy as "big hominy" and grits as "little hominy." After drying, the hominy is ground into grits.

The mass-produced grits found in supermarkets are made by using steam instead of lye to loosen the outer husk. The corn kernels are split to remove the outer hull and cut it into uniform pieces about 1/16 of an inch across. The grits are separated from the cornmeal and corn flour and, depending on the degree of grinding and processing they undergo, classified as regular, quick cooking or instant. Regular grits require fifteen to twenty minutes' cooking time, while the quick variety is ready in five minutes. Instant grits are ready to eat as soon as boiling water is added, but at a cost of much texture and flavor compared to regular grits.

There are still a few mills across the South turning out old-fashioned stone-ground grits. Stone-ground grits take significantly longer to cook than their supermarket cousin, but have a flavor and "rightness" that many argue is well worth the extra time.

Creamy Grits

Yield: 6 to 8 servings

8 cups water
4 tablespoons butter
sea salt and freshly ground black pepper to taste
2 cups stone-ground grits (NOT instant or quick grits)
half and half or whole milk

In a 4-quart saucepan over high heat, bring water, butter, salt and pepper to a rolling boil. Slowly add grits, stirring constantly so that grits do not settle to the bottom and scorch; return to a boil. Reduce heat to a gentle simmer, so that only an occasional bubble breaks the surface. Cook, stirring occasionally and adding half and half or milk as needed, until liquid is absorbed and grits are done to your taste, about 30 to 45 minutes.

Cheese Grits

The first mention of cheese grits in print was by Marjorie Kinnan Rawlings in *Cross Creek Cookery* (1942), but there is little doubt that they existed long before that time.

To the recipe above, add ½ cup of shredded cheese of your choice (cheddar, American or gouda spring immediately to mind) after the bulk of the cooking liquid is absorbed, and adjust the consistency by adding water, milk or half and half.

Fried Grits Cakes

These delicacies can be served plain or topped with grated blue cheese, cheddar cheese, pickled shrimp (see page 54), chow chow or about any other tasty topping you can think of.

Yield: 4 to 6 servings

2 cups grits, cooked
½ teaspoon baking powder
2 eggs, beaten
½ cup butter
1 teaspoon flour

½ teaspoon salt
½ teaspoon pepper
3 eggs, beaten
¼ cup milk
vegetable oil for frying

Cook grits according to directions for Creamy Grits (page 59), with baking powder added to the water.
When grits are almost done, stir in 2 of the eggs, butter and flour, mixing well.
Cook until grits are tender, then pour grits into a shallow baking dish to a thickness of about ¾ inch. Cover with plastic wrap and refrigerate overnight.
Cut grits into squares and sprinkle with salt and pepper.
Beat 3 eggs well and add milk. Dip squares in egg mixture.
In a 10-inch cast-iron skillet, pour oil to a depth of ¼ inch. Fry grit cakes in hot oil until golden brown. Turn only once.
Drain on paper towels and serve immediately.

Rice

Drive down Highway 17 from Wilmington, North Carolina, to Savannah, Georgia, and you'll see an almost unbroken line of beachfront condominiums and luxury hotels.

Prior to the Civil War, that same coastal plain, known to its residents as the Lowcountry, was home to hundreds of thousands of acres of a type of rice sought after by every aristocrat in Europe—a crop that made the colonies rich and gave the fledgling United States its most successful exportable commodities.

The story of rice in the South began in 1685 when a Dutch ship sailing from Madagascar to New England was blown off course and forced to harbor at Charles Towne, as Charleston was then called. The ship's cargo was a type of golden, long-grain rice the colonists hadn't seen before. The captain gave a peck of the rice to a physician and amateur botanist named Henry Woodward, who planted it in the cypress swamps that border the Ashley and Cooper Rivers.

Workers carrying bundles of cut rice in South Carolina, circa 1890. *Courtesy of South Caroliniana Library, University of South Carolina.*

Europeans couldn't get enough of the unique flavor of the new rice, which was called Carolina Gold for the golden color of its outer husk. By 1726, the Port of Charleston was exporting about five thousand metric tons of Carolina Gold per year, and rice had become the top export of the American colonies. By 1770, exports had exploded to forty-five thousand metric tons.

Not all the rice was shipped to Europe, however. In addition to the citizens of the Lowcountry, who loved the new crop even more than the Europeans, American soldiers in the Revolutionary War regularly received rice as part of their food ration. By the later part of the 1700s, rice was being shipped overland to all parts of the Carolinas and surrounding colonies.

The agricultural schedule of the 1860 census of the United States tells the story of the importance of rice to the Lowcountry; of the 5 million bushels of rice grown in the United States that year, 3.5 million came from South Carolina.

Rice and Slavery

The wealth rice brought to the plantation owners came at a terrible cost in human suffering, however. As the demand for rice increased, the planters began to import more and more slaves from the Sierra Leone region of Africa, where the people had been growing rice since 1500 BC.

As profits increased, so did the demand for more production and more slaves. When Nathaniel Heyward, the most successful of the South Carolina rice planters, died in 1851, he owned seventeen rice plantations and 1,829 other human beings.

To convert the malarial swampland of South Carolina and Georgia into rice fields, the enslaved Africans cleared the swampland by hand, as oxen would sink up to their bellies in the mire. Cypress trees were felled with axes, and miles of containment walls and ditches were built with only shovels and mattocks.

The backbreaking work under the brutal Carolina sun took a huge toll; as many as one-third of Lowcountry slaves died within one year of their arrival. Of the eighty Africans who were brought to Somerset Place Plantation in North Carolina in June 1786 to prepare the land for rice cultivation, only fifteen were still alive by 1803.

Cultivation and Harvest

Slaves planted rice by covering the grains with clay to give them weight. As they walked the fields, they stubbed their toes into the soil, dropped in the weighted seed and then covered it with their heel, all in one smooth, repetitive motion.

During the growing season, the fields were flooded three times. The first, called the sprout flow, allowed the seed to germinate. The second, called the stretch flow, killed off grass and weeds and protected the plants from birds and insects. The third, called the harvest flow, supported the stalks as they grew and the rice ripened.

At harvest time, the rice would be cut with a small iron sickle and the stalks bundled and lay on the base of the cut plants to dry before being loaded onto a small boat and carried to the processing area of the plantation.

Female slaves used flails to remove the grain from the stalk. The grain would be separated from the chaff by throwing the rice up into the air in winnowing baskets or dropping it from a winnowing house. The rice would then be gathered and either sold as "rough rice," with the husks still on, or milled on-site or in Charleston or Savannah.

If the milling was done on-site, a rice mortar and pestle or a pounding mill would be used to remove the outer husk. The rice would again be thrown into the air from a sweetgrass basket to separate the husks. The rice would be "polished" in the mortar or pounding mill to remove the bran from the grains so the rice would not spoil during shipping or storage.

Carolina Gold rice was one of the earliest and most profitable export crops for the fledgling United States.

After the Civil War, planters didn't have the money to hire enough workers to replace the freed slaves. The swampy soil wouldn't support the weight of the new steam-powered equipment being used in Louisiana and Arkansas, and rice production in the Carolinas began a steady decline.

A series of hurricanes in 1880 and 1883 ruined crops and destroyed rice fields. When the hurricane of 1911 blew down the entire crop days before harvest, commercial rice production in the Carolinas came to an end.

Dr. Richard Schulze and his wife, Patricia, were responsible for the return of Carolina Gold to the Lowcountry. In the mid-1980s, they planted a small stand at Turnbridge Plantation in Bluffton, South Carolina, from seed obtained from a USDA seed bank. By 1986, they were producing enough rice to sell small amounts of Carolina Gold.

In 1987, small-scale commercial rice production returned to the Carolinas when Campbell Coxe of Darlington, South Carolina, planted Della rice on his hunting preserve, Plumfeld Plantation. A small group of dedicated farmers and enthusiasts is also attempting to bring commercial production of Carolina Gold back to the Carolinas from Arkansas, the only state producing it commercially at the time of this writing.

The Carolina Rice Kitchen

The abundance of rice in the South Carolina Lowcountry led to the birth of a cuisine known as the Carolina rice kitchen. This way of cooking reached its peak in the century between 1750 and 1850 and was a blending of ingredients and spices imported from Europe with native game and rice. The culinary influences of French Huguenots, English, Italians, Africans and Native Americans created a blend of flavors found nowhere else in the world.

Flour ground from rice was used for everything from bread to waffles to cookies. The pervasiveness of rice didn't mean blandness; the resources of the rice plantation kitchen would be the envy of any modern chef. Spices imported from the Orient, freshly picked vegetables and herbs, rice-fed beef, lamb and poultry and imported olive oils all found their way to the tables of Lowcountry plantations.

Steamed, buttered rice, with each grain fluffy and separate from the others, was called "Charleston ice cream" and to this day is the hallmark of Lowcountry cooking.

Basic Rice

This method for cooking rice has been followed in the Lowcountry for hundreds of years.

The basic formula for cooking rice is one part rice to two parts water; i.e., if you have one cup of rice, you need two cups of water. This recipe will give good results with any long-grain white or brown rice.

Yield: 6 to 8 servings

4 cups cold water
½ teaspoon salt
2 cups rice

In a mixing bowl, wash rice in several changes of water.
In a 2-quart saucepan with a tight-fitting lid, bring water and salt to a boil.
Sprinkle rice into water slowly (so that the water remains at a boil) and stir once with a fork to distribute the grains evenly. Cover and reduce heat to medium low; simmer (with bubbles just barely breaking the surface) for exactly 13 minutes. Do not lift lid.
Turn off heat and allow rice to steam for another 12 minutes, again without lifting the lid.
When ready to serve, gently fluff rice with a large fork and place in serving dish.

Jambalaya

Jambalaya was a favorite supper in south Louisiana long before Lafcadio Hearn published his recipe for Jambalaya of Fowls and Rice in *La Cuisine Creole*, published in New Orleans in 1885.

It's thought the name jambalaya is derived from the French *jambon*, meaning ham, an ingredient often found in the dish.

Yield: 8 servings

1 pound loin cut pork chops
1 pound chicken thighs
½ pound andouille, or other spicy smoked sausage
2 tablespoons bacon drippings
2 medium onions, chopped
2 bell peppers, chopped

2 ribs celery, chopped
2 cups uncooked long-grain white rice
1 tablespoon Cajun/Creole seasoning, or to taste (see page 43)
1 bunch scallions, chopped
2 tablespoons parsley, chopped

Place pork chops and chicken thighs in a 5- to 6-quart Dutch oven and add enough water to cover to a depth of 3 inches. Bring to a rolling boil, reduce heat and simmer until meat is tender enough to easily remove from bones, about 30 minutes. Reserve stock.

Remove meat from bones and cut into bite-size pieces. Return to Dutch oven over medium heat; add meat and andouille to bacon drippings and sauté until brown, about 5 minutes. Add vegetables and stir to coat with fat; sauté until tender, about another 5 to 10 minutes.

Pour the reserved stock into a measuring cup; note how much there is, pour into the pot and if necessary add enough water to make 6 cups of liquid. Add the rice and bring to a rolling boil. Reduce heat and simmer until rice is done, about 25 minutes. Adjust spice and garnish with chopped scallions and parsley.

Serve with hot sauce and French bread.

Pilau

This rice casserole of the Southern coastal regions has quite a few variations in spelling and pronunciation; there are as many as sixteen different spellings, including pilaf, perlo, plaw and perloo, each pronounced as it is spelled.

Noted food historian Karen Hess wrote in *The Carolina Rice Kitchen: The African Connection* (1992): "Pilau is the most characteristic dish of the Carolina rice kitchen, where its name is pronounced PUHR-*LOE* or *pi-LOE*."

In *Cross Creek Cookery* (1942), Marjorie Kinnan Rawlings wrote: "We pronounce the word 'pur-loo.' It is any dish of meat and rice cooked together. No Florida church supper, no large rural gathering, is without it. It is blessed among dishes for such a purpose, or for a large family, for meat goes farther in a pilau than prepared in any other way."

Both the word pilau and the dish it describes are Persian, and variations on word and dish are found in the Middle East, Africa, Spain, France, Turkey and India.

In its simplest form, a pilau consists of long-grain rice that has been washed, pre-soaked and added to some form of stock or broth. The rice is cooked until almost every drop of the liquid has been absorbed, leaving behind plump, juicy and flavorful grains, which are perfectly separate from one another and fall from spoon to plate in a glorious cascade. In many recipes, the washed and pre-soaked rice is sautéed in fat for even more flavor prior to simmering in the stock.

Pilaus may contain any vegetable, meat, fish or foul; the most popular ingredients (in historical as well as modern recipes) tend to be chicken, tomatoes, okra, ham and shrimp, either singularly or in combination.

Lowcountry Red Rice

Old recipes for this simple tomato pilau called it "mulatto rice" well into the 1930s. The name originated because the color of the dish was reminiscent of the ruddy skin color of mulattos, who were people of mixed African and Native American ancestry.

Red rice is served all along the coast of South Carolina and Georgia as an accompaniment to meat, game and seafood.

Yield: 4 to 6 servings

5 slices bacon or pork side meat
¾ cup chopped onion
1 cup uncooked rice, washed (see Basic Rice recipe, page 64)
2 cups fresh tomatoes, peeled, seeded and diced

½ teaspoon salt
½ teaspoon pepper
½ cup chicken stock
cayenne and hot sauce to taste

In a 12-inch cast-iron skillet, cook bacon or side meat until crisp; drain, crumble and set aside. Sauté onion in pork fat until tender.

Add the uncooked rice to the skillet and stir until the grains are coated with fat and heated through, about 3 to 4 minutes.

Add tomatoes, salt, pepper, stock and bacon. Bring to a boil, stirring often with a fork, and then reduce heat and simmer, covered, for 25 minutes. Remove from heat and allow to stand, still covered, for five minutes.

Using a large dinner fork, fluff the rice gently, add cayenne and hot sauce and serve.

Red Beans and Rice

Although this dish is most often associated with the Cajuns and Creoles of Louisiana, pilaus of rice and beans are from the African tradition and are found in all areas where enslaved Africans influenced the culinary culture.

Red beans and rice is traditionally served on Monday nights in New Orleans; legend has it that since everyone had spent all their money during the weekend, red beans and rice was easy on their depleted pocketbooks.

Yield: 8 servings

Rice and Grits

1 pound dry red beans	2 cups chopped onion
4 quarts water	½ cup chopped celery
2 ham hocks	1 bell pepper, chopped
8 cups chicken stock	1 bunch green onions, chopped
4 bay leaves	1 tablespoon minced garlic
1 teaspoon cayenne pepper	salt to taste
1 teaspoon black pepper	4 cups cooked hot rice
1 pound andouille sausage, divided	hot pepper sauce, to taste

Wash beans and soak overnight in the water. The next day, drain beans and wash well under cold running water.

In a 5- to 6-quart Dutch oven with lid, add beans, ham hocks and stock. Add more liquid if necessary until beans are covered to a depth of about two inches.

Bring to a boil and skim any film that collects on the surface. Reduce heat and add bay leaves, cayenne and black pepper. Simmer for 30 minutes.

Chop half of the andouille into ¼-inch pieces and place it in a 12-inch cast-iron frying pan. Cook for 5 minutes to render the fat and brown the meat.

Add onion and celery and cook until the vegetables are soft, about 10 minutes. Add bell pepper, green onions and garlic and cook an additional 5 minutes, then add to the pot of red beans.

Continue to cook beans until they are soft, about one hour. Allow the beans to cool; refrigerate, covered, overnight.

When ready to serve, bring beans to a simmer. Slice remaining andouille into ¼-inch slices and add to beans. Cook for about 10 minutes. Adjust seasonings.

To serve, place about ½ cup rice in center of each plate and spoon beans over rice. Serve with hot pepper sauce.

Hoppin' John

Hoppin' John is dearer to the hearts of South Carolinians than any other dish of the Lowcountry. Helen Woodward wrote in *200 Years of Charleston Cooking* (1930): "South Carolinians, like my husband, who have been away from home a long time, if they feel a culinary homesickness, always long for something called Hoppin' John, with the accent on John."

No one knows the exact origin of this traditional Southern dish or how it came by its unusual name. One theory is that it was concocted as an inexpensive food for slaves during the trip to

67

the New World. Alexander Falconbridge described the food served to slaves during the Middle Passage in a narrative written in 1788: "The diet of the Negroes, while on board, consists chiefly of horse-beans, boiled to the consistence of pulp; boiled yams and rice, and sometimes a small quantity of beef or pork."

Another speculation is that Hoppin' John originated in the slave cabins of the Lowcountry rice plantations, and some say that the dish arrived here by way of the sugarcane plantations of the Caribbean.

As to the name, *Webster's Ninth New Collegiate Dictionary* (1983) asserts that Hoppin' John is a corruption of the French *pois de pigeon* (pigeon peas). Since Huguenot French was widely spoken in Charleston, this version of the story can't be dismissed entirely. Karen Hess proposed that the name is a derivation of the Hindi *bahatta* (rice) and the Malay *kachang* (beans), which would imply that the Africans kept the names of the foods after they were introduced to them by Arab and Malay traders. After arriving in South Carolina, the name may have been transformed by filtering through the Gullah language, a mixture of several African dialects and English, until it reached its current form.

Hoppin' John is eaten on New Year's Day by Southerners black and white, rich and poor, young and old. The black-eyed peas are said to bring luck, and the collard greens served with it are said to bring wealth in the year to come. In many households, a dime is stirred into the pot just before serving; the person who finds it is supposed to have the most money in the coming year.

Yield: 6 servings

1½ cups dried black-eyed peas	1 recipe Basic Rice (see page 64)
1 tablespoon salt	salt and pepper to taste
6 strips salt pork or bacon, diced	dash of hot sauce
1 medium onion, chopped	½ cup minced green onions, including tops

Rinse peas and pick them over. Cover with cold water; add 1 tablespoon salt and let stand overnight.

Drain peas, discarding water, and place in a 6- to 8-quart stockpot. In a 10-inch cast-iron skillet, sauté salt pork or bacon until crisp; add it to the peas, reserving the drippings.

Add onion, a little salt and 2 cups water. Bring just to a boil, lower heat and simmer until peas are tender, about 20 minutes. A small amount of the cooking liquid should remain; if liquid is absorbed too quickly, add fresh water by ¼ cupfuls.

When peas are tender, add cooked rice to pot. Stir in 2 tablespoons of the reserved bacon drippings, salt, pepper and hot sauce to taste. Cover and simmer about 15 minutes longer so flavors combine and rice absorbed some of the remaining cooking liquid.

To serve, garnish with green onions.

Lowcountry Chicken Pilau

Chicken is the most common of the meats used in pilau recipes from the nineteenth and early twentieth centuries. This recipe is typical of recipes from that time period.

Yield: 4 servings

3 tablespoons vegetable oil, divided
1 chicken, cut up
2 onions, chopped
2 cups chicken broth
4 strips pork side meat or bacon, diced

½ cup celery, diced
2 cups long-grain white rice
salt and freshly ground black pepper to taste
1 cup tomatoes, peeled and chopped

In a Dutch oven over medium heat, brown the chicken in two tablespoons of the oil. Remove chicken and set aside. Add half of the onions to the drippings and sauté until tender.
Place the chicken back into the pot and simmer in one cup of the chicken broth until the chicken is tender, about 40 minutes.
Remove chicken, pour off and reserve the pan juices. Allow chicken to cool, skin and debone.
Heat the remaining 1 tablespoon of oil and the salt pork or bacon and sauté until brown. Add the remaining onion and celery and sauté until tender.
Add the rice and stir until it is coated with the fat and heated through. Add the salt and pepper, pour the reserved pan juices back into the pot and add the tomatoes. Cover and simmer until the rice is tender, adding more chicken broth if needed. Add the chicken pieces to the rice; heat 2 to 3 minutes. Adjust seasoning and serve.

Photo by Holland Studios, Albany, GA. Courtesy of Georgia Archives, Vanishing Georgia Collection, dgh083.

Chapter 5

The Southern Seas

Fish and Shellfish

And God created great whales, and every living creature that moveth, which the waters brought forth abundantly, after their kind, and every winged fowl after his kind: and God saw that it was good.
—*Genesis 1:21*

Fish from the Atlantic waters meant the difference between life and death for the Jamestown settlers. They lived on sturgeon and oysters the first year of the colony, along with whatever else they could pull from the waters.

Fish were so abundant off the Southern coasts that fishermen in the eighteenth century reported taking five thousand shad in one haul of a net.

Robert Beverley detailed the varieties of fish eaten by the early colonists in 1705, listing more than thirty-six species, including shad, trout, bass, crab and oyster. In the receipt book she began in 1749, Martha Washington gave recipes for sturgeon, eels, shrimp, pike, oysters, lamprey, mackerel, carp, trout and whiting, giving a good glimpse at what Virginia fishmongers had to offer in the mid-1700s.

Catfish

If there were an official Southern fish, the catfish would be it. Sarah Belk rather eloquently summed up the Southerner's love for catfish in *Around the Southern Table* (1991): "Catfish is one of those foods whose basic goodness transcends all economic and social levels. Catfish suppers—complete with hush puppies, fries, coleslaw and plenty of iced tea—create a 'get down' camaraderie that is as warm and genuine as Southern hospitality itself."

On the Southern frontier, catfish weighing up to one hundred pounds were sometimes encountered by the early pioneers.

Lettice Bryan gave recipes for stewed, boiled and grilled catfish, as well as catfish cutlets, catfish steaks and catfish "cavach," in 1839, although historically, more catfish take their final swim in hot grease than any other cooking method.

Fried Catfish Po' Boy

A po' boy is a sandwich made on French bread and filled with meat and gravy or fried seafood. It was invented in New Orleans in the 1920s to feed the "poor boys" who couldn't afford a full meal.

This recipe calls for either milk or beer as an ingredient for the batter; each gives its own unique flavor.

Yield: 2 sandwiches

oil for frying
2 catfish fillets, about ¼ pound each
1 egg, beaten
1 cup milk or beer
1 cup cornmeal
1 cup all-purpose flour

1 tablespoon Cajun spice
French bread, sliced length-wise
red or green leaf lettuce
sliced tomato
remoulade sauce (see page 191)

Place about one inch of oil into a 10-inch skillet and heat over medium-high heat until it shimmers but doesn't smoke, about 350 degrees F on an instant-read thermometer.
Inspect catfish fillets and remove any bones.
In a medium bowl, mix egg and milk or beer and set aside. In a large zipper-lock bag mix cornmeal, flour and Cajun spice.
Dip fish into liquid and gently shake to remove excess. Place into bag with coating mixture and gently shake to coat.

Place fish into hot oil and cook until one side is golden brown, about 2 to 3 minutes. Turn and cook other side until golden. Remove to paper towel to drain.
Serve on French bread with lettuce, tomato slices and remoulade sauce.

Courtesy North Carolina State Archives.

Salt and Pepper Catfish

This is the favorite way to prepare catfish in the Piedmont region of North Carolina. The coating is spicy, making it a nice contrast to the delicate flavor of the catfish.

Yield: 2–4 servings

1 cup buttermilk
4 whole catfish, cleaned
vegetable oil for frying
1 cup cornmeal

½ cup flour
1½ teaspoon kosher or freshly ground sea salt
2 tablespoons coarsely ground black pepper

Place buttermilk in a 2-quart baking dish; place fish in buttermilk and marinate for 15 minutes. Place oil in a 12-inch cast-iron skillet to a depth of about 2 inches. Heat until oil registers 365 degrees F on an instant-read thermometer.
In a large, zipper-lock food storage bag, mix remaining ingredients by zipping them inside bag and shaking until well blended. Remove fish from buttermilk; allow excess liquid to drain. Place fillets in bag and shake gently until completely coated.
Gently shake off excess coating mixture and carefully place into hot oil. Fry until golden brown, about 5 minutes on each side. Drain on paper towels and serve hot.

Catfish Evangeline

This dish combines several flavors beloved to south Louisiana: catfish, crawfish and a rich, buttery Creole sauce. The dish is named for Evangeline, a legendary Academe heroine who was also the subject of the Longfellow poem by the same name.

Yield: 4 servings

4 catfish fillets
4 tablespoons butter, melted
2 teaspoons fresh lemon juice
salt and pepper to taste

For the Sauce:
4 tablespoons butter
1 medium onion, chopped
½ cup celery, chopped
½ cup bell pepper, chopped

1 clove garlic, minced
1 teaspoon salt
¼ teaspoon black pepper
¼ teaspoon cayenne pepper
1 tablespoon tomato paste
2 teaspoons cornstarch dissolved in ¾ cup
  water
1 to 2 cups boiled crawfish tails or shrimp
1 green onion, chopped
cooked rice (see page 64)

Preheat oven to 400 degrees F.

Wash catfish and pat dry. In a small bowl, mix butter and lemon juice. Dip each fillet into mixture and place on a wire rack over a baking sheet. Sprinkle with salt and pepper.

Bake until fish flakes when touched with a fork, about 10 to 15 minutes.

To Prepare the Sauce:

In a 10-inch skillet over medium heat, melt butter and sauté onion, celery, bell pepper and garlic until soft. Stir in salt, black pepper, cayenne and tomato paste. Simmer for 20 minutes, stirring occasionally. Add cornstarch and water mixture and simmer until sauce thickens. Add crawfish or shrimp and green onion. Serve over white rice and top with sauce.

Baked Fish Creole

Yield: 8 servings

	For the Dressing:	For the Sauce:
1 large red fish or red snapper	2 tablespoons oil	3 tablespoons vegetable oil
salt and pepper to taste	1 pound medium shrimp, peeled	1 small onion, minced
3 cloves garlic, sliced	3 ribs celery	1 bunch green onions, minced
butter (to coat dish)	4 green onions	3 (15-ounce) cans tomato sauce
juice of 2 lemons	1 tablespoon flour	1 bay leaf
	1 cup breadcrumbs	½ teaspoon thyme
	1 egg, beaten	chopped parsley
		salt and pepper to taste

Clean fish thoroughly; wash, pat dry and season inside and out with salt and pepper. Using a sharp paring knife, make several small slits on the top of fish and insert garlic slices.

Make the dressing by sautéing shrimp, celery and green onions in oil until vegetables wilt and shrimp turn pink. Add about one tablespoon flour and stir, simmering for about two minutes. Add breadcrumbs and egg and mix well. Allow mixture to cool.

Stuff fish and close opening with toothpicks. Place in a buttered baking dish and squeeze lemons over the fish. Set aside in refrigerator.

Preheat oven to 350 degrees F.

Make the sauce by sautéing onion and green onions until tender. Add remaining ingredients and simmer for 15 to 20 minutes. Pour over stuffed fish.

Bake until fish flakes when touched with a fork, about 30 to 45 minutes.

Trout

Of all the fish native to the Southern United States, few are as beautiful and sought after as the rainbow trout.

Trout were an important part of the foodways of the mountain South long before Lettice Bryan published recipes for fried and boiled trout in *The Kentucky Housewife* in 1839.

Pecan Crusted Trout

Yield: 4 servings

1 egg
1 teaspoon heavy cream
¼ cup flour
¼ teaspoon salt
¼ teaspoon black pepper
4 trout fillets, skin on
1 cup ground pecans
2 tablespoons vegetable oil
lemon wedges for serving

Preheat oven 375 degrees F.
In a shallow baking dish, beat egg and cream together.
In another shallow dish, mix flour, salt and pepper. Dredge fillets in flour mixture, shaking gently to remove excess. Dip flour-coated fillets in egg mixture, then coat well on all sides with pecans. In a 12-inch skillet over medium heat, heat oil until it shimmers but doesn't smoke. Gently place fillets in oil skin side down and sauté for 2 minutes on each side. Transfer the fillets to a baking sheet and bake until fish flakes when prodded with a fork, about 10 minutes. Serve with lemon wedges.

SHRIMP

Shrimp are eaten everywhere in the South, although nowhere are they more beloved than the Lowcountry of South Carolina.

Shrimp recipes in Southern cooking date back to colonial times; Eliza Smith's *Complete Housewife*, published in London in 1735 and the most widely used cookbook in the American colonies, featured several shrimp recipes.

Lowcountry Shrimp Boil

Yield: variable

salt
Old Bay seasoning
garlic
black pepper
cayenne pepper
lemon juice
3 new potatoes per person
1 carrot per person
¼ pound kielbasa per person
1 ear of corn per person
½ pound raw shrimp per person, shells on
Tabasco sauce

optional:
2 small onions per person
1–2 blue crabs per person

Fill a large stockpot with water; season with salt, Old Bay, garlic, black pepper, cayenne and lemon juice. Bring to a rolling boil. Add potatoes, allow to return to a full boil and cook for 10 minutes.
Add carrots, sausage and onions. Return to a boil. When potatoes and carrots are almost tender, add corn and crabs. Return to a rolling boil, then add shrimp.
Cook until shrimp are just done, about 3 minutes. (If you are cooking more than 2 pounds of shrimp, you might have to slightly increase cooking time, but be careful not to overcook.) Drain and pour onto platters. Serve with melted butter, cocktail sauce, hot sauce and plenty of iced tea or cold beer.

Shrimp and Grits

There are as many ways to cook this classic dish of the Lowcountry as there are people in Charleston; there is no right or wrong way to make shrimp and grits, only delicious and more delicious ways.

The base grits can be regular breakfast grits, creamy grits, cheese grits or creamy cheese grits. The shrimp can be medium, large or jumbo; personal preference is for large, as they are more tender than jumbo and there are fewer to peel than medium.

The sauce can be as simple as a little freshly squeezed lemon juice and butter, as in the "Breakfast Shrimps" preferred by some Charlestonians, or the spicy brown gravy with onions and celery favored by others.

Charleston "Breakfast Shrimps"

This is the classic Charleston breakfast in its purest (and some would say best) form.

Yield: 6 servings

½ cup unsalted butter
1½ pounds medium shrimp, peeled
sea salt and freshly ground black pepper to taste
pinch of garlic powder (optional)
one recipe Creamy Grits (see page 59)

In a 10-inch skillet over medium-high heat, melt butter. Season shrimp with salt and pepper and garlic powder (if desired).
Sauté shrimp in butter until they just turn pink, shaking pan or stirring gently as they cook.
Spoon grits into bowls and top with shrimp and butter mixture.

Spicy Shrimp and Grits

This version of the dish is heartier and has a nice, spicy flavor.

Yield: 6 servings

2 pounds large shrimp, peeled and deveined
2 tablespoons bacon grease
3 ribs celery
1 medium Vidalia onion
8–10 turns freshly ground sea salt
8–10 turns freshly ground black pepper

2 tablespoons flour
1 cup shrimp stock (see page 80)
Louisiana hot sauce to taste
1 recipe creamy or cheese grits (see page 59)
green onions for garnish

In a 12-inch cast-iron skillet over medium-high heat, sauté shrimp in bacon grease until just pink; remove and place in a bowl. Add the celery, onions, salt and pepper and sauté until tender; add the flour to the vegetables and stir until it is brown but not burned. Slowly add enough of the shrimp stock, stirring continuously, to make a brown gravy. Season to taste with hot sauce; the dish should have a nice burn but not be fiery.
Ladle grits into bowls, top with the shrimp sauce and garnish with green onions.

Shrimp á la Creole

This may well be the best known of all Creole dishes. It combines shrimp with a rich, buttery tomato sauce. Note: Save the shrimp shells and the end pieces from the vegetables. They will be needed later.

Yield: 8 servings

2 pounds medium shrimp, shells on
1½ quarts water
4 bay leaves
2 tablespoons tomato paste
1 tablespoon garlic, minced
3 ounces vegetable oil
1½ cup onion, diced
1 cup celery, diced
1 cup bell pepper, diced

1½ sticks butter, divided
3 tablespoons all-purpose flour
two 15-ounce cans chopped tomatoes
1 bunch flat leaf parsley, finely chopped
salt and pepper to taste
cayenne pepper to taste
hot buttered rice (see page 64)
diced green onion for garnish

Peel and devein shrimp, reserving shells.

In a 2-quart saucepan, make a shrimp stock by combining shrimp shells, water, bay leaves, tomato paste and vegetable trimmings.

Bring stock slowly to a boil; reduce heat and simmer for 30 minutes.

While stock is simmering, in a 4-quart pot over medium heat, sauté garlic in the oil; add onion, celery and bell pepper. When vegetables are softened, add ½ stick of the butter and allow to melt completely. Stir in the flour and cook, stirring constantly, until the roux is a light brown, about the color of peanut butter.

Strain the shrimp stock and discard the shells and vegetable trimmings; add the stock to the roux, stirring constantly.

Add tomatoes and bring to a boil; reduce heat and simmer for 45 minutes, adding water if necessary. Add shrimp and parsley and continue to cook until shrimp is pink, 5 to 10 minutes.

Season to taste with salt, black pepper and cayenne; add the remaining stick of butter while stirring constantly to thicken the sauce.

Serve in shallow bowls with a mound of hot buttered rice in the middle; garnish with diced green onions.

Crabs

Crabs are found in the coastal waters from Maryland to the Gulf Coast. Southerners have eaten crabs in all manner of dishes from Jamestown to the present day; Mary Randolph said that eggplant tasted like crab but gave no recipes for crabs. One early recipe for crab is the one for boiled crabs that Harriot Pinckney Horry put in the handwritten receipt book she started in 1770.

Crab Imperial

Yield: 6 to 8 servings

2 pounds lump crabmeat
½ pound butter
1 cup flour
2 cups milk
½ cup celery, diced
½ cup mushrooms, diced
½ cup parsley, diced

½ cup green onions, diced
½ cup pimento, diced
½ teaspoon Worcestershire sauce
½ teaspoon Tabasco sauce
salt and pepper, to taste
breadcrumbs

Preheat oven to 350 degrees F.

Gently pick over crabmeat to remove any bits of shell, being careful not to break up lumps.

Melt butter in 12-inch skillet over low heat. Add flour and whisk together to make a roux. Cook roux, whisking constantly over low heat until golden brown.

Add milk, whisking constantly, until well blended. Add celery, mushrooms, parsley, green onions and pimentos; cook until vegetables are tender, then fold in crabmeat, being careful not to break up lumps. Add Worcestershire sauce, hot sauce, salt and pepper to taste.

Pour mixture into individual baking dishes and top with breadcrumbs. Bake until breadcrumbs are golden brown and mixture is heated through.

Crab Cakes

Crab cakes are found along the entire length of the Southern coastline. Although some variations call for onions, green pepper, celery and who knows what else, this recipe is for true Maryland-style crab cakes: just crab meat, a little seasoning and some stuff to hold it all together.

Yield: 4 to 6 servings

1 pound lump crabmeat
¼ cup mayonnaise
2 eggs, beaten
2 teaspoons Old Bay Seasoning
2 slices bread, toasted and finely crumbled
1 tablespoon bacon drippings

Gently pick over crabmeat to remove any bits of shell, being careful not to break up lumps.

In a mixing bowl, whisk together mayonnaise, eggs and Old Bay seasoning. Add breadcrumbs and crabmeat. Gently fold mixture together with a rubber spatula, again being careful not to break up the crabmeat.

Form the crab mixture into cakes ½ inch thick. Put the bacon drippings into a 12-inch cast-iron skillet and heat over medium-high heat until the bacon grease is almost to the smoking point, then gently transfer the cakes to the hot fat with a spatula, being careful not to crowd them.

Fry cakes, turning once, until golden brown on each side.

Oysters

Although they have yet to win a beauty contest, oysters have been prized throughout history for their taste.

Indians in the South used oysters for food, tools, jewelry and currency thousands of years before the first Europeans arrived. Early European settlers found oysters near Jamestown up to a foot long and, after eating them, used the shells for tools and as construction material for buildings and roads.

Oysters Bienville

"Count" Arnaud Cazenave, founder of Arnaud's restaurant, invented this New Orleans specialty in 1920. This is my version of this classic dish.

Yield: 8 servings

2 dozen oysters on the half shell, drained
⅔ cup mushrooms, diced
1 tablespoon olive oil
4 tablespoons butter
1½ teaspoon garlic, minced
½ cup bell pepper, diced
1 tablespoon shallots, minced
rock salt
½ pound boiled shrimp, finely diced
1 tablespoon flour

½ cup brandy
½ cup heavy cream
6 tablespoons freshly grated Parmesano-
  Reggiano cheese
4 tablespoons dry breadcrumbs
¼ cup parsley, minced
1 teaspoon salt
1 teaspoon ground white pepper
½ teaspoon cayenne

Shuck oysters and reserve meat; save shells. Thoroughly wash oyster shells and pat dry.
In a 4-quart saucepan, sauté mushrooms in oil. Remove from pan and set aside. Melt the butter and sauté garlic, bell pepper and shallots until tender. Add the shrimp, then sprinkle in the flour, stirring constantly. Add the mushrooms. Continue stirring and add brandy to deglaze pan. Stir in the cream and cook until smooth.
Add the cheese, breadcrumbs, parsley, salt, pepper and cayenne. If the mixture is too thick, add 1 or 2 tablespoons of milk and whisk to blend. Remove from heat, allow to cool and then refrigerate for about 1½ hours.

In a 4-quart saucepan, simmer oysters in water just until edges curl. Remove from heat. Spread rock salt in a layer about ¼ to ½ inch deep over the bottom of 4 glass or metal pie pans. Put oysters on shells and place six in each pan of rock salt. Spoon one heaping tablespoon of sauce over each oyster. Broil until golden brown and bubbly, about 5 to 7 minutes.

Courtesy of the Lewis P. Watson Photographic Collection, Olivia Raney Local History Library, Raleigh, NC.

CHAPTER 6

The Incredible, Edible Pig

There was nothing on the table, when I was invited to it, except some cold salt pork and pickled beets;
but as long as I remained, at intervals of two or three minutes, additions would be made, till at last
there had accumulated five different preparations of swine's flesh, and two or three of corn, most of
them just cooked; the only vegetable, pickled beets.
—*Frederick Law Olmsted,* A Journey in the Seaboard Slave States

THE PIG IN SOUTHERN HISTORY AND CUISINE

As soon as they hit the beach at Jamestown, Southerners began their love affair with what John Egerton called "the noble pig, sustainer of the South through four centuries of grief and glory."

While fried chicken is most often associated with the South, it was a very rare delicacy prior to the twentieth century. Pork in one form or another was daily fare for most Southerners, and our love for all things porcine was not immune to literary sniping, even from our own backyard. Dr. John S. Wilson, a resident of Columbus, Georgia, in the 1850s wrote: "The United States might properly be called the Great Hog Eating Confederacy or The Republic of Porkdom."

In the eighteenth and nineteenth centuries, eating pork was not only a way of life; it was a matter of life and death. Salt-cured pork was usually the only meat a family would have to last them through the winter when game was, at best, scarce and, at worst, completely unobtainable.

Prior to the 1840s, the hogs found on Southern farms were a far cry from the pampered pink piggies found at today's county fair. The typical Southern hog was lean and mean, usually a cross between the European domestic pig and feral hogs descended from domestic stock brought to Florida by Hernando de Soto in 1539 that roamed the pine forests and occasionally came courting domesticated sows.

Beginning in the early years of the 1840s, Southern hog producers began importing higher quality breeding stock from England and the Northern United States and began practicing improved husbandry methods that led to increased meat yields. By 1850, there were more than two million hogs in Georgia alone, and the pig had become by far the most important source of meat in the South.

Pigs were the perfect animals for farmers; a sow reached sexual maturity at six to eight months of age and could have two litters a year with an average of six to eight piglets per litter. Piglets born in spring were ready for slaughter by early winter. This was a major economic advantage, because only breeding stock had to be fed over the winter with precious stored grain.

Pigs were generally self-sufficient during spring, summer and fall, feeding on acorns, grubs, fallen orchard fruit, sweet potato vines and anything else they could root up. Whatever food they found was put to good use; hogs are by far the most efficient of all livestock at turning forage into meat; 24 percent of the energy eaten by hogs is made available for human consumption, as compared to only $3^{1}/_{2}$ percent for beef and mutton.

HOG-KILLING TIME

After the hogs had fattened themselves up during the spring, summer and fall, they were slaughtered during a weather-dependent period that ran from late autumn to early January, depending on the geographic area. The outside temperature had to be cold enough so that the meat wouldn't spoil before it was used or cured but not cold enough to make the people doing the work miserable.

Hog-killing time was a social event as well as a time for work. Children stayed home from school, and neighbors came to help with the work and enjoy the fresh meat. While the men and older boys worked, children played together and the women caught up with news of new babies, brides and local goings-on as they prepared the midday dinner for the workers.

Work began at first light to maximize the available daylight. The hogs were killed, usually by a cut to the throat, and then dipped into huge kettles or barrels of boiling water to loosen the bristles, which were scraped off with a knife, sometimes on a door borrowed from the house.

After scraping, the hogs were hung by the feet from a tree limb or a timber frame and gutted. Hams, sausage, side meat and bacon were smoked, cured or both and were destined for consumption weeks or months later. The liver, neck bones, backbones, tenderloin, tongue, ears and tail were eaten in the first few days after killing day. The jowls were cured and saved for New Year's Day to be eaten with the traditional field peas and collard greens. The head was used to make souse, a carryover from Elizabethan England. Almost every part of the pig was

Courtesy of the Lewis P. Watson Photographic Collection, Olivia Raney Local History Library, Raleigh, NC.

used, even down to the feet, which were pickled. Even the hog's bladder was washed, scalded and blown up for use as a ball in the days before store-bought toys.

Excess fat, especially the leaf fat that surrounded the kidneys, was cooked down and rendered into lard, which was used for frying and baking.

In the days before home refrigeration, any type of meat not consumed within hours after the animal was killed had to be preserved by one of four methods: smoking, salting, drying or curing, which was a combination of the first three.

Two methods were used for curing pork—wet and dry. In the wet method, meat was soaked in a brine (sometimes referred to in early texts as a "pickling") solution of salt, sugar or molasses and saltpeter dissolved in water. In both wet and dry curing, salt did the majority of the preservation work, with the sugar or molasses added for flavor. Saltpeter (potassium nitrate, for the chemically curious) assisted with some antimicrobial duties and improved the color of the meat, adding a more natural-looking reddish hue.

After the hams and shoulders had been removed and set aside for dry curing, the trunk of the hog was cut into pieces and immersed in a barrel filled with brine. The ribs were sometimes removed and reserved for smoking and curing to make bacon and then brined for preserving.

The salt solution penetrated deep into the cells of the meat and did an effective job of preserving it from bacteria and insects. The resulting brine-cured meat was referred to as salt pork, side meat or middling meat and is composed of the fat from the hog's belly and sides, usually containing one or more streaks of lean. Salt pork is often confused with fatback, which is also belly fat but is not salt cured.

The side meat was stored in the family's pork barrel and removed as needed as the nine months to a year between hog-killing times passed. The family with a full pork barrel was happy and secure; this gave rise to two American slang terms still in use today. When politicians allocate government funds for projects in their home districts that will make their constituents happy, the money is referred to as "pork barrel" funds. And if someone has run out of money or times are hard, they are said to be "scraping the bottom of the barrel." This expression stems from the fact that (especially in colonial and antebellum days) salt was scarce and expensive, and none was wasted. When a pork barrel had reached the end of its days or when times were hard, the salt was scraped from the bottom and sides and reused. It wasn't as desirable as fresh salt, thus the negative connotation of "scraping the bottom of the barrel."

Country Ham

Of all the meats consumed in the Southland, none has the mystique of country ham. Although modern commercial production methods and marketing have muddied the waters somewhat, traditionally country ham refers to the upper portion of the hind leg of a hog, which is dry cured, aged and very often smoked.

Curing hams was a very important activity in the rural South in the days before refrigeration. Dry-cured hams, if properly prepared, would keep for more than a year, ensuring a supply of meat through the winter. These hams were also used to barter for goods and services at trading posts on the Southern frontier.

Hams were cured nearly everywhere in the South, but Virginia has always been noted for quality hams. In 1760, Reverend Andrew Burnaby pronounced Virginia hams superior to any found in Europe. In 1806, the *Charleston Courier* published a recipe for "The Virginia Mode of Curing Ham." Although the recipe used the same ingredients as recipes published in early cookbooks, the mystique of Virginia hams spread throughout the South.

The first step in dry curing country hams was to completely cover the ham in salt. The hams and shoulders would be placed in a "meat box" or curing trough and buried in salt for four to six weeks to draw out moisture. Salt boxes ranged in size from a few feet long for a small farm to the massive, twenty-foot-long cypress salt trough used by the Stone family at Hope Plantation in eastern North Carolina. The plantation processed several tons of pork each year to feed the Stone family and their slaves; when David Stone died in 1819, his estate inventory listed more than 4,700 pounds of stored pork, plus more than 330 pigs awaiting their turn in the trough.

The salting process removed a significant amount of moisture from the meat; a twenty-five-pound ham would weigh about fifteen pounds when it came out of the meat box.

After their time in the salt, the hams were washed and scrubbed to remove the excess salt and then coated with a mixture of salt, saltpeter and red pepper, which was used to discourage insects from laying eggs on the ham. Sometimes molasses or brown sugar was added to the "cure," with each family or cure master having their own special and secret blend of ingredients for their hams.

If the hams were to be smoked, they were taken to a smokehouse, a structure specially designed to retain smoke from a low, smoldering fire. The fire could be made from most any hardwood, but hickory and oak seemed to be the preferred woods. Dried corncobs and sawdust were also used, as they produced a great deal of smoke without much heat.

After smoking, hams were sometimes coated with wood ash to further discourage insects. The hams were placed in cloth bags and hung from the rafters of the smokehouse, barn or, on small homesteads, the main house itself.

"Boiled" Country Ham

This is a traditional way to cook a whole country ham. The name must not be taken literally, however. The idea is to gently simmer the ham and *never* allow it to boil. This will produce a moist, flavorful ham that does justice to the cure master.

Yield: 25 to 30 servings

one 12- to 14-pound country ham
water
2 cups apple cider or apple juice

Place ham in sink and cover with cold water. Soak ham 8 to 12 hours or overnight, changing water twice. Drain sink and refill it with fresh, warm water. Using a stiff brush, scrub ham to remove any mold and rinse well.
Dry ham with paper towels and place in a covered roasting pan or large stockpot. Add cider or juice and then add enough water to cover the ham to a depth of two inches.
Heat roasting pan or stockpot on stovetop or in a 300-degree F oven until water reaches a very gentle simmer (bubbles just barely reach the surface). Simmer, covered, for about 25 minutes per pound or until the internal temperature reaches 160 degrees F on an instant-read thermometer. Remove from heat and allow ham to cool. Remove from water and pat try with paper towels. Using a sharp knife, remove skin. Carve ham into thin pieces and serve warm or cold.

Fried Country Ham for Biscuits

Most early Southern cookbooks only contain recipes for cooking whole hams because they were written by the wives of plantation owners who usually had a houseful of family and guests to feed. For the small farmers (especially in the frontier South) with only a few mouths to feed, ham was usually prepared by cutting off thin slices for frying, then rubbing the exposed meat with salt, red pepper and wood ash to keep insects away from the newly exposed meat.

In the modern South, far more country ham is cooked by frying than any other cooking method.

Yield: 4 servings

1 pound center-cut country ham slices
1 tablespoon bacon drippings or lard

If present, trim rind (skin) from outside of ham slices.
Add bacon drippings to a 10-inch cast-iron frying pan over medium heat. When it dissolves, add ham slices and cook slowly until just brown. Turn and brown other side. Serve with hot biscuits, grits, scrambled eggs and gravy.

Maryland Stuffed Ham

In southern Maryland, hams are cured by the same process used for corned beef, giving them a very distinctive flavor. They are then stuffed with cooked vegetables for one of the most unique dishes of the South.

Yield: 20 servings

one 12-pound corned ham (or country cured)
3 pounds kale, chopped
2 pounds green cabbage, chopped
1 bunch celery, chopped
1 large onion, chopped
1 hot red pepper, chopped

5 tablespoons salt
5 tablespoons black pepper
2 tablespoons celery seed
2 tablespoons mustard seed
2 tablespoons red pepper flakes
2 teaspoons Tabasco sauce

Place the ham in a large, deep roasting pan and add enough water to cover it to a depth of at least two inches. Place the roasting pan on top of the stove over two burners. Bring water to a rolling boil, reduce heat and simmer for twenty minutes. Allow to cool enough to handle and remove skin and excess fat with a sharp knife.

Boil greens, celery, onion and pepper in boiling water until thoroughly cooked; drain well. Add seasonings and mix.

Starting at the butt end of the ham, cut three lengthwise slits, 2 inches long, completely through the ham. Continue this pattern, making several rows of slits, being careful that they do not overlap or split into each other.

Using your fingers, push the seasoned greens into the slits, first from the top and then from underneath the ham, until all the slits have been filled with the seasoned greens. Place any remaining greens over the top of the ham. Place ham, skin side up, on a large piece of cheesecloth. Fold the ends over tightly and pin with a clean safety pin.

Return to roasting pan and simmer 15 minutes to the pound.

Eat hot or cold as a sandwich on plain white bread.

BARBECUE: NATURE'S MOST PERFECT FOOD

Barbecue is one of the South's most beloved foods and has long played an important role in the foodways of the region. As much as we Southerners love our country ham, tenderloin biscuits and smothered pork chops, we will run over them all to get to a plate of barbecue. It is a subject that is guaranteed to get two people from different parts of the South into a spirited discussion ending in either a lifelong friendship or a fistfight.

Almost everywhere in the region, but especially in North Carolina, barbecue is spoken of in the reverential tone usually reserved for '65 Mustang convertibles, large bass that slipped the line and the cheerleader everyone was in love with in high school.

The word barbecue more than likely entered the English language via the Spanish, who observed native people in the West Indies using a method of slowly cooking meat over coals they called *barbacoa*. Native Americans were cooking meat over coals using essentially the same method as the West Indian peoples, and the English settlers who set up shop in the South were soon happily cooking pigs over hot coals.

The typical method for barbecuing a hog was to dig a pit or trench and build a hardwood fire in it. After the fire had burned down to coals, the hog was placed on poles or a sheet of corrugated iron laid across the trench. Barbecue made by this method came to be known as "pit

Community barbecue, LaGrange, Georgia, late 1920s. *Courtesy of Georgia Archives, Vanishing Georgia Collection, trp259.*

cooked," and the term is still in use today. Even in modern barbecue restaurants where the hole in the ground has been replaced with concrete block cookers, they are still called pits, and the person who is the head cook is called the pit master or pit boss.

In the modern South, the word barbecue is most often used as a noun, as in a plate of barbecue. It is rarely used as a verb, as in "we barbecued a pig." Most people who do so simply say they cooked a pig, with the cooking method implied. In a final note on usage, nothing will mark someone as a barbecue novice and possible Yankee spy quicker than referring to a grill as a barbecue or using the term in any connotation when referring to cooking hamburgers or hot dogs.

The Hog, the Whole Hog and Nothing but the Hog

While folks in other places use the same cooking method on beef brisket, chicken, and God only knows what else, to the overwhelming majority of Southerners, barbecue means exclusively pork. In *The Art of Cookery Made Plain & Simple*, published in England in 1747, Hannah Glasse gives two recipes for barbecue, both using pork. Since the English are famous for their love of beef, this speaks volumes for the pig's rightful place as the one true source of barbecue.

During the colonial period, plantation owners held social events called barbecues where whole hogs and an occasional beef found their way onto the coals. By the antebellum period, barbecue was a fixture at plantation social events.

Roasting a pig was a community event that brought family, friends and neighbors together. It's often said that politics and religion make strange bedfellows; obviously the person who thought this up has never been to a church barbecue. Many churches in the South hold barbecues as part of their yearly "homecoming" celebrations, when people who have moved away return for fellowship and pig in their former church. Other churches hold barbecues as fundraising events, like the Mallard Creek Presbyterian Church in Charlotte, North Carolina. The church held a barbecue in 1929 to pay for the new Sunday school room. The event has been held every year since, and the four pigs they cooked the first year has grown to 14,000 pounds of pork barbecue, 2,500 gallons of Brunswick stew and two tons of coleslaw for the twenty thousand people who attend each year. Politicians running for any local, state or national office from that part of the state wouldn't dream of missing the event. They know, just as their antebellum forefathers did, that barbecue draws crowds of people from all classes and beliefs, each one of them a potential voter.

Just as barbecue transcends politics and religion, it bridged racial barriers as well. African American slaves made up the overwhelming majority of cooks tending barbecue pits in antebellum days. After freedom came at the end of the Civil War, some of them sold barbecue from open fire pits. As they made enough money, a tin-roofed, wooden building known as a barbecue shack sprung up.

Since these early "shacks" were carryout only, white Southerners made their way up to the counter in a strange reversal of Jim Crow. Unfortunately, this barbecue-induced racial harmony didn't last. The end of the Second World War brought a new birth of drive-in barbecue restaurants to the highways and byways of the South. With inside dining being the new trend, these new pig palaces were segregated. Like white-owned lunch counters, the barbecue joints became battlegrounds in the war against racial discrimination. Rulings against Ollie's Barbecue in Birmingham, Alabama, and Maurice's Piggie Park in Columbia, South Carolina, ensured that Southerners of all races could enjoy barbecue wherever they pleased.

Although it's easy to get Southerners to agree that barbecue should be pork cooked slowly over coals made from hardwood, from that point on, the consensus rapidly falls apart. Barbecue, perhaps more than any other food in the South, varies greatly by state and even regions within the states. John Sheldon Reed, an astute observer of Southern culture, wrote, "Southern barbeque is the closest thing we have in the U.S. to Europe's wine and cheeses; drive a hundred miles and the barbeque changes."

In the Piedmont of North Carolina, for example, shoulders are cooked, and the meat is sliced, chopped or pulled from the bone and served with a thin, tomato and vinegar sauce referred to as "dip." East of Raleigh, the only common ground is the chopped or pulled part. People "down east" cook the hog, the whole hog and nothing but the hog. They use a "mop sauce" made of vinegar and peppers to baste the meat as it cooks, and it comes to the table covered with the same sauce. Each camp believes their side to practice the One True Way and considers the other side to be ignorant, godless heathens and possibly communists.

In Georgia and South Carolina, shoulders are the preferred cut, either chopped or sliced, and the sauce is a tangy, yellow mustard and pepper affair.

Shoulders also rule the roost in the eastern part of Tennessee, but they prefer a slightly thick, slightly sweet ketchup-based sauce sometimes referred to as "Tennessee Red." In Memphis, pulled pork from shoulders reigns supreme, with a thicker, sweeter tomato sauce made with vinegar and molasses or brown sugar with an occasional dash of Tennessee whiskey added for flavor.

In Alabama and Mississippi, pulled and chopped pork is the meat of choice, and spicier red sauces are preferred. One exception is Alabama White, a mayonnaise-based table sauce.

No matter where in the South it is prepared, barbecue is always cooked "low and slow," meaning at low temperatures and slowly. The medium for the sacred flame is wood, not gas nor even charcoal, and especially not charcoal pre-soaked in lighter fluid. If you don't have access to good, dried hardwood such as hickory, you can use charcoal briquettes, but if you can find lump charcoal, so much the better. Let the fire burn down to low coals, add wood chips soaked overnight in water and keep the temperature of the grill or smoker between 250 and 275 degrees Fahrenheit for the required cooking time, adding more coals from a supply started in another grill or fire pit if needed to maintain the temperature.

Barbecued Suckling Pig

Since a whole hog can dress out at more than two hundred pounds, barbecuing a suckling pig is one way to get the taste of whole hog barbecue without having to roast an entire hog. Early recipes abound for roasting suckling pigs and young hogs known as shoats. Suckling pigs dress out at around fifteen to twenty pounds, depending on their age when slaughtered. The hardest part is finding a shoat or suckling pig; your local butcher might be able to order one. If not, you may be able to get one from a local farmer.

Once you have obtained the pig, salt and pepper it well inside and out, or use the dry rub on page 97. Use a stick to pry the mouth open and wedge a small apple in there.

After preparation, put the pig on the grill or smoker. If you are roasting directly over the coals, pile the coals at the hams and shoulders. If you are using a smoker, put the butt end closest to the coals.

For best results, cook slowly until an instant-read thermometer inserted deep into one of the hams reads 155 degrees F. If the snout, tail and ears begin to brown before the rest of the pig is done, cover them with aluminum foil.

BARBECUE VOODOO: RUBS AND MOP SAUCES

Rubs and mop sauces are two of the pit master's secret weapons for imparting his or her own unique flavor to the finished barbecue. These concoctions are made up of various and sundry combinations of herbs, spices, liquor, beer, sugar and heaven knows what else. For the most part, the recipes for these rubs and sauces are carefully guarded secrets, but some have become common knowledge.

Mop Sauce

James Battle Avirett may have been the first person to record the classic eastern North Carolina pepper and vinegar mop sauce in *The Old Plantation* (1901): "My sakes! How busy was old Uncle Shadrac in barbecuing five or six whole hogs…taking care to baste them well with a long handled mop that had been dipped into a pan of vinegar, salt and home grown red pepper so that there should be no lack of highly flavored seasoning."

Mop sauces are applied to the pork as it slowly cooks. Although "Uncle Shadrac" used a real mop for his whole hog barbecue, modern versions in miniature sizes called barbecue mops are available for smaller cuts of meat.

Mop sauces are applied to barbecue while it's cooking, like this unidentified North Carolinian is doing, sometime in the 1940s. *Courtesy of North Carolina State Archives.*

Yield: about 3¼ cups

3 cups cider vinegar
3 tablespoons red pepper flakes
1½ teaspoons kosher salt
1½ teaspoons black pepper

In a 1-quart mixing bowl, whisk all ingredients together until well blended. Apply to all surfaces of pork with a barbecue mop during the last 3 hours of cooking.

Wet Rub

As the name implies, wet rubs are made with some form of liquid as an ingredient and are rubbed onto the pork prior to cooking.

Yield: about ⅔ cup

¼ cup olive oil
2 tablespoons salt
1 tablespoon garlic powder
1 tablespoon onion powder

1 teaspoon sage
1 teaspoon fresh ground black pepper
1 teaspoon cayenne

In a small mixing bowl, combine all ingredients. Using your hands or a sauce mop, rub over all surfaces of pork before cooking.

Lexington-Style Dry Rub

Lexington, North Carolina, is the spiritual, if not actual, home of the Western North Carolina style of barbecue.

Yield: ¼ cup

3 tablespoons paprika
4 teaspoons brown sugar
1½ teaspoons black pepper

1½ teaspoons dry mustard
1 teaspoon garlic powder

In a small mixing bowl, stir all ingredients until well blended. Apply using your hands to all surfaces of pork prior to cooking.

FINISHING AND TABLE SAUCES

Many different types of sauces are used on barbecue after it has been cooked. If the sauce is added to the meat before it is served, the sauce is called a finishing sauce. If the sauce is served alongside the barbecue, it's called a table sauce.

Eastern North Carolina–Style Finishing Sauce

Yield: 2¼ cups

2 cups apple cider vinegar
2 teaspoons granulated sugar
1 tablespoon plus 2 teaspoons red pepper
flakes

1½ teaspoons Tabasco sauce
1 tablespoon freshly ground black pepper
2 teaspoons kosher salt

In a 1-quart mixing bowl, whisk together ingredients until well blended. Serve over cooked, pulled pork barbecue.

Western North Carolina–Style Sauce ("Dip")

This sauce can be used as a finishing sauce or as a table sauce. When it's used as a table sauce, folks in the western part of North Carolina call it "dip."

Yield: 1½ cups
1 cup ketchup
1 cup brown sugar, firmly packed
½ cup lemon juice

3 tablespoons butter, melted
¼ cup onion, minced
1 teaspoon hot sauce
1 teaspoon Worcestershire sauce

In a 1-quart saucepan over medium heat, combine all ingredients and bring to a boil. Reduce heat and simmer 30 minutes, or until slightly thickened.

Tennessee-Style Table Sauce

Yield: 3½ cups
1 cup ketchup
½ cup lemon juice
3 tablespoons butter, melted
¼ cup onion, minced

1 teaspoon hot sauce
1 teaspoon Worcestershire sauce
½ cup bourbon
1 teaspoon dry mustard
3 tablespoons sorghum molasses

In a 1-quart mixing bowl, whisk together all ingredients until well blended.

South Carolina/Georgia Golden-Style Mustard Sauce

In South Carolina and some parts of Georgia, sauces based on yellow mustard are the norm. They can be used as finishing or table sauces. This type of sauce dates at least to antebellum days.

Yield: 2 cups

¾ cup yellow mustard
¾ cup apple cider vinegar
¼ cup granulated sugar
2 tablespoons butter, melted

1½ teaspoons Worcestershire sauce
1½ teaspoons black pepper
½ teaspoon salt
½ teaspoon red pepper sauce

In a 1-quart mixing bowl, whisk together all ingredients. Brush on pork the last 15 minutes of cooking time and serve at the table.

Western North Carolina Pulled Pork Barbecue Sandwich

Yield: 6 to 8 large sandwiches
1 Boston butt pork roast, 4 to 6 pounds
¼ cup apple cider vinegar
¼ cup hot sauce
¼ cup kosher salt
¼ cup black pepper

Wash roast and pat dry with paper towels. In a small bowl, combine vinegar and hot sauce. Using your hands, rub roast with vinegar and hot sauce mixture, then rub on salt and pepper.
In a kettle-style grill (or ideally, a side-box smoker), make a fire out of charcoal, using paper to start the fire, not lighter fluid. Allow the fire to burn down to hot coals. Add some hickory wood chips that have been soaking overnight in water to the fire, place the Boston butt on the grill and close the lid. Use a spray bottle filled with one ounce of vinegar and seven ounces of water to douse any flames that spring up.
Build another fire in an outdoor fire pit or another grill. Use these coals to replenish the main coals as needed.
Cook 3 to 4 hours, turning every 30 minutes to ensure even cooking.
After the meat has cooked, allow it to rest for 30 minutes, then pull it apart with two large forks. Serve on hamburger buns with a tablespoon of Western North Carolina–Style Sauce (see page 98) on each sandwich. Top with Red Barbecue Slaw (see page 155).

Southern-Style Pork Ribs

Yield: 4 to 6 servings

4 pounds pork ribs
1 recipe Wet or Dry Rub (see page 97)
1 recipe Mop Sauce (see page 96)
1 recipe Barbecue Sauce (your choice, see pages 97–99)

Rub ribs on all sides with wet or dry rub. Cover with plastic wrap and refrigerate 2 hours or overnight.

Preheat grill to medium or preheat oven to 450 degrees F. Place ribs on rack on grill or in broiler pan. Brush ribs with mop sauce. Cook 20 minutes on each side or until instant-read thermometer inserted into thickest part of meat registers 160 degrees F, brushing occasionally with mop sauce. Serve with barbecue sauce of choice.

CHOPS AND OTHER PRIME CUTS

Beginning in the late 1870s, advances in refrigeration and sanitation led to greater availability of fresh pork such as tenderloin, ribs and chops throughout the year, shipped down from the new meatpacking plants in the Midwest.

Many rural Southerners, however, still produced their own meat until after the Second World War, when the small farm started down the road to near extinction. For them, fresh cuts of pork were a rare treat and cause for celebration.

Smothered Pork Chops

In Southern cooking, the term "smothered" is used to refer to meat that has been fried and then served in a pan sauce or gravy that usually contains onions.

Yield: 6 servings

2 tablespoons cornstarch
2 cups chicken stock or chicken broth
¼ teaspoon black pepper
1 tablespoon lard or vegetable shortening

6 pork chops, ½ inch thick
¼ teaspoon salt
2 onions, sliced

Mix cornstarch, stock and pepper until smooth and set aside. In a 10-inch cast-iron skillet over medium heat, melt shortening until it shimmers but doesn't smoke.

Season chops with salt and pepper and cook in two batches until brown, about 5 to 10 minutes on each side. Remove chops and set aside.

Remove the skillet from the heat and add a little more shortening if necessary. Add the onion and cook over medium heat until tender. Stir cornstarch mixture and add to skillet. Cook until gravy boils and thickens, stirring constantly. Return chops to pan, cover and cook over low heat for 10 to 12 minutes or until the chops are done.

Everything but the Oink

Pigs were the most versatile animals ever to trod Southern soil. Every part from snout to tail found its way to the table, and nothing was wasted. Brains were scrambled with eggs for breakfast, ears were fried, tails were stewed and feet were barbecued. Anything left over would find its way to the sausage grinder.

Sausage

Every European country that contributed settlers to the South had long histories of making pork sausage. Sausage was usually made from the meat alongside the backbone (this cut is called the "chine"), along with any trimmings left from other parts of the hog. The meat was put through a hand-cranked grinder, and then mixed with red pepper, salt and herbs. Harriott Pinckney Horry's recipe (1770) called for mace, cloves, nutmeg, allspice, dried sage, thyme and parsley, dampened with water and a little Madeira wine. The sausage went into casings made by boiling the intestines and then was taken to the smokehouse to cure. After smoking, sausage was placed in earthenware crocks and covered with lard. This kept air away from the meat and prevented it from spoiling; sausage preserved in this method would keep between six months and two years.

Liver Mush

One of North Carolina's best-loved breakfast foods is "poor boy's pâté," better known as liver mush. This delicacy, fried crisp and served with grits and eggs, is the classic breakfast of the Piedmont region of both Carolinas. Liver pudding uses meat other than the liver and usually has a smoother consistency.

Yield: 1 loaf pan of liver mush, 8–10 servings

1 fresh hog liver
1½ pounds fresh pork fat
salted water to cover

2 cups cornmeal
salt, red and black pepper and sage to taste

In a 4-quart saucepan over medium heat, cook liver and pork fat in enough salted water to cover until tender. Remove the liver from broth, reserving the broth, and grind liver through the fine screen of a meat grinder into a large mixing bowl.

Return the ground liver to the saucepan and add cornmeal and spices to taste. Add just enough of the broth to soften mixture. Return saucepan to heat and cook until cornmeal has cooked, stirring constantly.

Place liver mush into a loaf pan lined with waxed paper. Fold paper over top and place a brick, covered in aluminum foil, on top of the loaf pan to weight it. Refrigerate overnight to allow liver mush to set. Slice and serve cold or pan fry.

Pork Neck Bones and Rice

When the backbone was cut away from the ribs, there were still some good scraps of meat remaining close to the bone. When the entire backbone was cooked, it was called "chine" in early recipes. Neck bones and rice is a soul food classic.

Yield: 4 to 6 servings

4 pounds pork neck bones
1½ teaspoon onion powder
1 teaspoon garlic powder
1 teaspoon black pepper
½ cup bacon drippings
1 large onion, chopped

3 cloves garlic, minced
2 ribs celery, diced
1 cup uncooked long-grain white rice
½ cup all-purpose flour
1 cup water

Wash neck bones in warm water, drain and pat dry with paper towels.

Sprinkle neck bones with onion powder, garlic powder and pepper; refrigerate for 15 minutes.

In a 6-quart Dutch oven over medium-high heat, brown neck bones in the bacon drippings and remove to warm platter.

Sauté onion, garlic and celery in pan drippings until tender; return neck bones to the pot. Add enough water to cover, plus another 2½ cups.

Bring to a boil over high heat; reduce heat to medium-low and simmer, covered, until tender, about 1½ to 2 hours.

Remove 2½ cups of liquid from the pot and bring to a boil in a separate 1½-quart saucepan; add rice and return to a boil. Reduce heat and simmer, covered, until rice is done, about 25 minutes.

In a small bowl, rapidly whisk flour into water; slowly add to broth, a little at a time, stirring well after each addition until broth is desired consistency.

Uncover pot, bring to a gentle simmer over low heat and allow to cook down for 30 minutes.

Serve with additional cooked rice if desired.

Chitterlings (Chitlins)

The megalopolis of Salley, South Carolina, is the chitlin' capital of the world. One day each fall, the population of Salley swells from four hundred people to more than fifty thousand, making it (on that day) the fifth largest city in the state.

People come from all over the United States for the annual Chitlin' Strut, where the humble hog intestine is raised to an art form.

Definitely an acquired taste, chitlins are first washed, then boiled and lastly fried to a crispy golden brown.

Courtesy of Georgia Archives, Vanishing Georgia Collection, gwn099.

CHAPTER 7

The Gospel Bird

Chicken

*Nothing rekindles my spirits, gives comfort to my heart and mind, more than a visit to Mississippi…
and to be regaled as I often have been, with a platter of fried chicken, field peas, collard greens, fresh
corn on the cob, sliced tomatoes with French dressing…and to top it all off with a wedge of freshly
baked pecan pie.*
—*Craig Claiborne,* Craig Claiborne's Southern Cooking

CHICKEN IN SOUTHERN HISTORY

Any Southerner will tell you that the miracle of the loaves and fishes was the only church supper in history that didn't include fried chicken.

For those of us who grew up in the post–World War II South, chicken was a pretty regular part of our diet. But prior to the end of the war, chicken was a rare treat for most Southerners. The reason for this was economic: unlike hogs, which had to be killed to use them for food, chickens produced eggs, a renewable food source.

Like hogs, chickens were essentially self-supporting and free range. They were able to feed themselves on bugs, grubs and animal droppings. Chickens are good mothers, and unless a predator got in the henhouse, chicks usually reached adulthood.

Eggs were not only food but could also be bartered for goods or sold for cold, hard cash. This meant that chickens were generally left alone until after they had stopped producing eggs, at which time they were ushered to the chopping block.

These mature hens needed to be cooked for long periods of time in moist heat to make them tender. Dishes such as chicken and dumplings, stewed chicken and chicken country captain evolved to make use of these older birds.

The dry heat and short cooking times used for frying requires a young, tender chicken, one capable of egg production. For Southerners of modest means, sacrificing one or more laying hens so their guests could have fried chicken was the ultimate expression of hospitality, one reserved for Sunday dinner with company or when the preacher came calling.

After the Second World War, commercial poultry production finally made the Republican campaign slogan of 1932 a reality: a chicken in every pot.

Fried Chicken

The first mention of "Southern fried chicken" in print was in 1925. An earlier mention of "Fried Chicken—Southern Style" is found in Kate Brew Vaughn's *Culinary Echoes from Dixie*, published in 1917. The dish itself goes back to at least the early 1800s. The earliest published recipe for what Southerners would consider fried chicken was in the third edition of Mary Randolph's *The Virginia House-wife*, published in 1828.

Although it may come as a shock to some below the Mason-Dixon line, Southerners didn't invent fried chicken. Nearly every culture on earth has some dish involving a chicken and a skillet or pot of hot fat, from *pollo fritto* in Italy to *ga xao* in Vietnam. As to how fried chicken came to the South, the most popular theory credits African slaves. The Scots also fried several different foods, including chicken, so the jury is still out.

There are almost as many ways to prepare a chicken for a date with a pan full of hot grease as there are people who want to snatch a drumstick when it's done. Sarah Rutledge had one of the simplest formulas for fried chicken in *The Carolina Housewife* (1847): "Having cut up a pair of young chickens, lay them in a pan of cold water to extract the blood. Wipe them dry, season them with pepper and salt, dredge them in flour and fry them in lard." She goes on to give directions for making gravy, which is good information to have if the preacher is on his way for dinner.

Other variations on the theme involve replacing the water bath with buttermilk, sweet milk or no bath at all; dipping the pieces in an egg and milk mixture before or during breading; and replacing the flour with cornmeal, cracker crumbs or some combination thereof.

Traditionally, rice was the most common side dish served with fried chicken, along with cream gravy made from the drippings from the frying pan and hot biscuits. Some Southerners, particularly in Maryland, serve the gravy poured over the chicken, but the gravy is most commonly served on the rice instead.

Basic Fried Chicken

Yield: 4 servings

2 cups cold water
2 teaspoons kosher salt
1 chicken, cut into serving pieces
fat for frying (vegetable oil, lard, shortening)

1½ cups all-purpose flour
1 teaspoon salt
1 teaspoon black pepper

In a shallow baking dish, combine water and salt. Place chicken pieces in dish and refrigerate for at least 30 minutes.

In a 12-inch cast-iron skillet over medium-high heat, place enough fat (vegetable oil, shortening or lard) to come to a depth of about two inches. Heat the fat until it shimmers but does not smoke, about 350 degrees F on an instant-read thermometer.

Whisk remaining ingredients together in a shallow baking dish. Remove chicken pieces one at a time from water, drain them and dip into the flour mixture, then carefully place them into the hot fat. Cook for five minutes, then gently lift with tongs to see if chicken is cooking evenly; rearrange pieces if necessary. Continue cooking until chicken is evenly browned, about five more minutes. Turn chicken with tongs and continue cooking until brown all over, about 10 to 12 minutes longer.

OTHER CHICKEN RECIPES

Stewed Chicken

Stewing was one method for cooking an older hen that had stopped producing eggs. Recipes for this dish almost always call for the chicken to be covered in gravy, like Hannah Glass's recipe in *The Art of Cookery Made Plain & Easy* (1747). This recipe is based on several from the early nineteenth century.

Yield: 6 to 8 servings

one 3- to 4-pound whole chicken
2 tablespoons poultry seasoning
2 tablespoons plus 2 teaspoons cornstarch
1 cup milk

2 cups chicken stock or chicken broth
salt and pepper to taste
2 tablespoons melted butter
hot sauce to taste

Place chicken in a 6- to 8-quart Dutch oven and cover with water to a depth of 2 inches. Add poultry seasoning and bring to a rolling boil, then reduce heat and simmer, covered, until tender, about 2 hours.

Remove chicken from pot and allow to cool enough to handle. Pull meat from bones and discard skin. Using a fine-mesh strainer, strain the cooking liquid and return to pot. Return liquid to a rolling boil.

In a 1-quart mixing bowl, whisk cornstarch into milk. Add chicken stock, salt, pepper, melted butter and hot sauce. Whisk mixture into cooking liquid, reduce heat to simmer and add chicken. Simmer until mixture thickens and chicken is heated through, about 5 minutes.

Chicken and Dumplings

Dumplings are small dough balls or strips that are cooked in liquid. They are found in several different cultures, especially English, central European, Chinese and Italian.

Dumplings most likely came to the Southern table courtesy of our German friends. This recipe is based on several from the turn of the twentieth century, including one from Kate Brew Vaughn's *Culinary Echoes from Dixie* (1917).

Yield: 6 to 8 servings

1 chicken, cut into quarters
1 tablespoon chicken seasoning
2 cups flour
3 tablespoons baking powder

1 cup whole milk
2 teaspoons lard or vegetable shortening
1 egg, beaten
1 teaspoon salt

Place chicken in a large Dutch oven. Add chicken seasoning and enough water to cover chicken with at least 2 inches of water. Bring to a rolling boil, then reduce heat and simmer, covered, until meat can easily be removed from bones. Remove chicken, leaving liquid in pot.

Remove meat from chicken and place meat back into pot. Bring back to a boil.

Mix remaining ingredients to form a dough and spoon into boiling chicken pot liquid.

Cover pot and simmer until dumplings are cooked, about 10 to 15 minutes.

Chicken Fricassee

Fricassee was always a source of curiosity for us baby boomers raised on Saturday morning cartoons. All we knew of this Southern favorite was that Wile E. Coyote was always looking at a recipe for Roadrunner Fricassee in his cookbook but never managed to catch the main ingredient.

Fricassee is a cooking method in which meat (usually chicken) is sautéed in butter and then slowly simmered. The end result is tender meat in a rich gravy.

The French have used this technique since the Middle Ages, and fricassees first appeared in English cookery books in the 1500s. The dish was popular from colonial days through the Great Depression as a way to turn a tough old chicken into a dish fit for company.

Harriott Pinckney Horry recorded recipes for two types of fricassees in her receipt book (1770). This recipe is based on several from the mid-1800s.

Yield: 6 to 8 servings

1 roaster or stewing chicken, cut into serving
  pieces
1 cup milk
½ cup water
1½ teaspoons salt
1 tablespoon poultry seasoning (page 43)
½ teaspoon salt
½ teaspoon freshly ground black pepper

¼ teaspoon ground allspice
4 tablespoons butter
1 tablespoon flour
2 egg yolks
1 cup heavy cream
⅓ cup white wine
½ cup chopped parsley
1 recipe Basic Rice (page 64)

Lay chicken pieces in a shallow baking dish. In a small mixing bowl, whisk together milk, water and salt. Pour over chicken. Cover with plastic wrap and refrigerate for 1½ to 2 hours.

Remove chicken from milk mixture and pat pieces dry. In a small bowl combine poultry seasoning, salt, pepper and allspice. Rub mixture on both sides of all the chicken pieces.

In a 12-inch cast-iron skillet over medium-high heat, melt butter and place chicken pieces in pan. Lightly brown chicken on all sides and remove from pan. Whisk flour into pan drippings and stir until light brown.

Return chicken pieces to skillet and add enough water or chicken stock to cover the pieces (about 3½ to 4 cups). Cover the pan, reduce heat and simmer slowly until chicken pieces are tender, about 45 minutes to 1½ hours, depending on size of chicken. Remove pieces to serving platter.

In a small bowl, whisk egg yolks into cream; add wine. Remove skillet from heat and pour mixture into liquid remaining in skillet; gently increase flame and stir gently just until bubbles begin to break the surface. Remove from heat and stir in chopped parsley. Pour sauce over chicken pieces and serve over rice.

Chicken Country Captain

This Georgia favorite is thought to have been brought to Savannah by a British sea captain (or British army officer, depending on the version of the story) by way of India. The recipe dates back to at least the middle of the nineteenth century; Eliza Leslie published a recipe for it in her *New Cookery Book* in 1857.

In the 1940s, President Franklin Delano Roosevelt was served this dish in Warm Springs, Georgia, and he helped rekindle interest in this Southern classic. There is some variation in recipes, but they all contain curry powder, raisins or currants, onion and tomatoes.

Yield: 6 to 8 servings

⅔ cup flour
1 teaspoon salt
¼ teaspoon black pepper
¼ cup butter
one 3- to 4-pound chicken cut into serving
  pieces
½ cup onions, finely chopped
½ cup green pepper, finely chopped

2 cloves garlic, minced
2 teaspoons curry powder
½ teaspoon salt
½ teaspoon dried thyme
2 cups fresh tomatoes, chopped
¼ cup golden raisins
½ cup toasted slivered almonds
1 recipe Basic Rice (page 64)

In a 1-gallon zipper-lock food storage bag, combine flour, salt and pepper. Add chicken pieces and toss to coat.

In a 12-inch cast-iron skillet over medium-low heat, melt butter; add chicken, increase heat to medium and cook until chicken is browned on all sides.

Remove chicken from skillet and set aside; add onion, green pepper, garlic, curry, salt and thyme to skillet and sauté until tender. Add tomatoes, breaking them up into bite-sized pieces with a large kitchen spoon. Simmer, uncovered, for 10 minutes. Return chicken to skillet and simmer, covered, until chicken is fork tender, about 45 minutes. Add raisins and cook 5 minutes longer. Remove from heat and transfer chicken to a deep platter. Spoon vegetables and sauce around the chicken and sprinkle with almonds. Serve with hot cooked rice.

Georgia Chicken Mull (Chicken Jallop)

Mull is one of the more interesting contributions our neighbors in Georgia have made to Southern cuisine.

Mull is a thick stew made of chicken or other meats (sometimes in combination) and thickened with soda cracker crumbs. The dish is a fixture at church suppers and political fundraisers in northeast Georgia, where it is called mull. Folks in south Georgia call the same dish jallop and often make it with seafood rather than chicken.

Yield: 6 to 8 servings

1 broiler chicken, cut into serving pieces
1 tablespoon poultry seasoning (page 43)
1 cup fresh lima beans
1 cup corn

½ cup carrots, diced
salt and pepper to taste
2 cups milk
one 1-pound box saltine crackers

Wash chicken and place in a 6- to 8-quart Dutch oven. Cover with water, add poultry seasoning and bring to a rolling boil over high heat. Reduce heat and simmer, covered, until chicken is tender, about 45 minutes to 1 hour. Reserve cooking liquid.
Remove chicken pieces and de-bone, discarding skin. Cut into bite-size pieces and set aside. Add vegetables, salt and pepper to cooking liquid and return to a boil. Reduce heat and simmer, covered, until vegetables are tender, about 10 to 15 minutes.
Return chicken to pot and heat through. Add milk and heat until it just begins to boil. Reduce heat and coarsely crumble crackers into liquid as it boils, stirring and adding more crackers until desired consistency is reached.

Chicken Bog

Bog is a casserole or thick stew served in the Lowcountry. If you want to attract a politician in North Carolina, all you have to do is start cooking a pig and at least three people running for office will magically appear and start shaking hands and kissing babies. The same is true for bog in South Carolina.

There are many variations on the theme; some add more vegetables, such as lima beans or corn. Bog is also frequently made with shrimp instead of chicken. This recipe is based on several from the early twentieth century.

Yield: 6 servings

1 chicken, about 3 pounds
6 cups water
1 tablespoon salt
1 medium onion, finely chopped
1 cup long-grain rice

½ pound spicy bulk sausage
2 tablespoons poultry seasoning (page 43)
2 hard-boiled eggs, finely chopped (optional)
green onion, chopped (optional)

Place chicken in a 6- to 8-quart Dutch oven and add enough water to cover to a depth of one inch. Add salt and onion and boil until chicken is tender, about 45 minutes. Remove chicken, let cool and de-bone, reserving the cooling liquid.

Cut chicken into bite-sized pieces. Skim fat from the cooking liquid and pour 3½ cups of this broth back into the Dutch oven. Add rice, chicken pieces, sausage and poultry seasoning.

Bring pot to a boil, reduce heat and simmer until rice is tender, about 30 minutes. Garnish with egg and green onion if desired. Serve with coleslaw and corn bread.

Chicken Pie

Recipes for poultry or beef baked in a pastry crust can be traced back to medieval times in the British Isles.

The term "potpie" originally referred to the cooking method (cooked in a pot) rather than to the dish itself and first appeared in American cookbooks in the late 1700s.

Yield: 6 servings

1 chicken, cut into serving pieces
water
2 tablespoons poultry seasoning (page 43)
3 carrots, diced
2 cups green peas
1 medium onion, diced
2 hard-boiled eggs, sliced (optional)
4 tablespoons butter
⅓ cup flour
2 cups reserved chicken broth
2 cups milk

For the Crust:
1 cup self-rising flour
1 stick margarine, melted
1 cup milk

Put chicken pieces in a 6- to 8-quart Dutch oven and add enough water to cover chicken pieces to a depth of about three inches. Add poultry seasoning and bring to a rolling boil. Reduce heat and simmer, covered, until chicken is cooked, about 45 minutes. Remove from the pot and allow to cool, reserving the cooking liquid.

Preheat oven to 375 degrees F.

Remove meat from cooled chicken and cut into bite-sized pieces, discarding skin. Place chicken, vegetables and eggs in a buttered 9- by 13-inch glass baking dish, making two layers.

In a 10-inch cast-iron skillet over medium heat, melt butter and add flour, whisking constantly until flour is a golden brown color. Whisk in reserved chicken broth and cook until thick, about two or three minutes. Stir in milk and remove from heat. Allow to cool slightly and pour over chicken and vegetables, stirring to mix if necessary.

In a medium mixing bowl, mix together ingredients for crust and spoon or pour on top. Bake for 30 to 45 minutes or until crust is golden brown.

Courtesy of Georgia Archives, Vanishing Georgia Collection, gly075.

CHAPTER 8

Wild Game

Wild hogs and cattle, rice birds, possum, coon or fox, anything that moved was considered game, but it was turkey hunting that came under the heading of art.
—*William P. Baldwin*

WILD GAME ON THE SOUTHERN FRONTIER

From the early 1600s to the late 1800s, food from the forest played a major role in the diet of many Southerners, especially those living in rural areas or on the frontier.

Long before the landing at Jamestown, hunting in England and many parts of Europe had become a sport for the wealthy, as the vast majority of Europeans didn't own land.

For the Scots and Germans especially, the abundance of game on the Southern frontier must have seemed like heaven after the food shortages both groups had faced back home. Buffalo (which was never plentiful but did exist east of the Mississippi) was an especially sought-after treat. By 1797, buffalo had been driven east of the Kentucky frontier by hunters, with elk close behind. Black bear was another favorite in the mountain South and is hunted in the Blue Ridge and Appalachian Mountains today.

For the most part, smaller, less threatening game such as deer, rabbits, squirrels, raccoon, possum, ground hogs (also called "whistle pigs") and many other types found their way to the table. Settlers in the backcountry of the South also dined on pheasant, passenger pigeons (which were hunted to extinction), bobcat, crane, alligator, quail, robins and waterfowl. Panther, beaver tails and even woodpeckers also found their way into the pot.

While the Kentucky rifle is most often thought of as the weapon of choice on the frontier, a majority of Southerners preferred the more versatile shotgun. It took less skill to use than the rifle and could be loaded with large single balls for large animals such as bear or multiple small shot for birds or squirrels. Trapping was also used to put meat on the table, especially by slaves, who weren't allowed to possess weapons.

VENISON

Deer meat, or venison, played an important part in early Southern foodways and is still enjoyed by large numbers of Southerners when deer season begins each November.

When European settlers saw the large number of deer in the colonial South, they were dumbfounded. In Europe, and especially England, deer had been hunted to the point that they existed only on the country estates of noblemen, and their meat was highly prized.

Deer were an ideal food source for several reasons. They were much safer to hunt than buffalo, elk or bear, and since a large buck could yield one hundred pounds of dressed meat, it only took one shot of precious gunpowder to feed several families for several days. As an added bonus, deer hide was highly prized for clothing. The leather made from doeskin was silky soft and tough; the Southern colonists sold the hides to the English, who turned them into doeskin pants, the fashion craze of the 1700s. The money from the sale of deer hide was used to buy coffee, tea, nails, pewter dishes, whiskey, sugar and other foods that made life on the Southern frontier more bearable. The trade was very lucrative; between 1690 and 1714, the Carolina colony exported an average of fifty-four thousand buckskins per year.

Venison Stew

This stew is similar to recipes found in cookbooks dating from the mid-nineteenth to mid-twentieth centuries.

Yield: 8 servings

3 pounds venison, cut in cubes
enough flour to coat venison cubes
½ cup cooked, crumbled bacon
2 tablespoons oil to brown meat
1 cup onion, chopped
1 cup carrots, chopped
1 cup celery, chopped

1½ cups dry red wine
1½ cups beef stock
salt and pepper to taste
1 clove garlic, crushed
1 tablespoon Worcestershire sauce
1½ teaspoon paprika

Brown floured meat cubes in oil. Place meat in casserole dish. Add remaining ingredients. Bake, covered, at 350 degrees F for 1½ hours or until tender.

Roast Venison

Yield: 6 to 8 servings

2 cups red wine
2 cloves garlic, minced
½ teaspoon tarragon
½ teaspoon rosemary
freshly ground black pepper
1 venison saddle roast

1 cup water
dash of ginger
1 teaspoon lemon juice
⅓ cup sour cream
1 teaspoon brandy

In a medium mixing bowl, whisk together wine, garlic, tarragon, rosemary and pepper. Pour into a shallow baking dish and place the roast in the mixture. Allow to marinate overnight, turning frequently.

Remove the roast and discard the marinade. Place the roast on a rack in a covered roasting pan and add a small amount of water to the roaster.

Roast, covered, in a 350-degree oven until the meat reaches an internal temperature of at least 165 degrees F, basting frequently with the pan juices.

Remove the roast and allow to rest for 20 minutes before carving.

To the remaining pan juices, add water, ginger, lemon juice, sour cream and brandy; bring to a boil. Thicken slightly if necessary with a slurry of 1 teaspoon cornstarch in ¼ cup of water.

ALLIGATOR

Alligator can be found from the Florida Everglades up to the Lowcountry of South Carolina, with an occasional stray causing a commotion in North Carolina. Once on the verge of extinction and federally protected, the alligator has made great strides in repopulating itself.

Marjorie Kinnan Rawlings, writing in *Cross Creek Cookery* (1942), commented that alligator was like liver and veal in that it has to be cooked either quickly or for a long time, with anything in between producing a tough, chewy result.

Alligator Sauce Piquant

This is a Cajun recipe that makes a thick stew traditionally served over rice.

Yield: 8 to 10 servings

3 pounds alligator meat
½ cup vegetable shortening
1¼ cups all-purpose flour
3 large onions, chopped
1 large green bell pepper, chopped
8 ribs celery, chopped

1 (8-ounce) can tomato sauce
1 (6-ounce) can tomato paste
salt and cayenne pepper to taste
1 cup water
1 recipe Basic Rice (page 64)

Cut alligator meat into bite-sized pieces.

In a 6- to 8-quart Dutch oven, heat three tablespoons of the shortening and add alligator meat. Cook until meat is browned. Remove meat and set aside.

Make a roux by adding the remaining shortening and flour to the pot and cook slowly, stirring constantly until the roux is the color of peanut butter. Add onion, green pepper and celery. Sauté slowly until vegetables are tender. Add tomato sauce and tomato paste and mix well. Add cayenne pepper and water. Cover and simmer over medium heat for 30 minutes.

Stir in reserved alligator meat. Cook for 1 hour or until meat is tender. Serve over cooked rice.

Rabbit

Many a Southern boy has spent the fall afternoons of his youth hunting the wily cottontail, a fast-moving target that has challenged the skill of hunters for hundreds of years.

As forests were cleared in the early South and the rabbits' natural predators pushed farther back into the remaining wilderness, the cottontail population thrived, making them the most widely hunted game animal even after the Civil War.

Fried Rabbit with Soppin' Gravy

Lettice Bryan published a recipe for fried rabbit with gravy in *The Kentucky Housewife* (1839). The buttermilk marinade helps tenderize the meat.

Yield: 4 to 6 servings

1 rabbit, cut into serving pieces
2 cups buttermilk
1 cup all-purpose flour
1 teaspoon salt
¾ teaspoon pepper
1 cup vegetable shortening

For the Gravy:
3 tablespoons pan drippings
¼ cup flour
1½ cup milk

Place rabbit pieces in a large, zipper-lock freezer bag. Cover with buttermilk and soak for at least 2 hours, preferably overnight.

Dredge rabbit in flour seasoned with salt and pepper. In a 12-inch cast-iron skillet over medium heat, melt shortening and heat until it shimmers but does not smoke, about 360 degrees F on an instant-read thermometer.

Carefully place rabbit in skillet and brown on all sides. Lower heat and cook until done, turning once. Transfer to serving dish and place in a 200-degree F oven to keep warm.

To make the gravy, drain all but 3 tablespoons shortening from skillet. Add flour, stirring to loosen brown bits. When brown and smooth, stir in milk and cook over low heat until thickened.

Rabbit Stew

Lettice Bryan also appears to have been one of the earliest Southern cookbook authors to give a recipe for rabbit stew. Since this recipe calls for cooking the rabbit slowly in addition to the buttermilk marinade, the meat is exceptionally tender.

Yield: 4 servings

1 rabbit, cut into serving pieces
2 cups buttermilk
flour
salt and pepper
3 tablespoons butter

1 cup corn
2 large potatoes, cubed
¼ teaspoon cayenne
1 large onion, diced
2 cups fresh tomatoes

Cut rabbit into serving pieces. Marinate in buttermilk for 2 hours; drain and pat dry with paper towels.

In a large bowl, mix flour, salt and pepper. Dredge rabbit pieces in flour.

In a large Dutch oven, melt the butter over medium-high heat. Add the rabbit pieces and brown on each side. Add the corn, potatoes, cayenne and onions; fill with salted water until Dutch oven is ¾ full.

Cover and bring to a rolling boil, then reduce heat and simmer for 1½ to 2 hours. Add the tomatoes and continue to simmer another hour, or until rabbit is tender.

Squirrel

Squirrel Dumplings

This dish is a favorite of the southern Appalachians. Squirrels have always been abundant in the South and to this day are a challenging target for a young boy with a .22 rifle.

Yield: 4 servings

2 squirrels
1 quart buttermilk
2 cups water
1 teaspoon salt
dash of black pepper
butter

For the Dumplings:
2 cups all-purpose flour
½ teaspoon baking soda
½ teaspoon salt
3 tablespoons shortening
1 cup buttermilk

Skin and gut squirrels, removing any shot. Wash thoroughly in cold water and cut into serving pieces.

Place squirrels in a glass baking dish and cover with buttermilk; cover dish, place in the refrigerator and allow squirrels to marinate for 6 to 8 hours.

Remove squirrel pieces, wash in cold water and pat dry. Place into Dutch oven, add water and salt. Bring to a rolling boil, then reduce heat. Simmer, covered, until squirrel is tender, about 2 to 3 hours. The meat should be almost falling from the bones.

Add pepper and butter to pot and bring to a rolling boil. Combine the flour, baking soda and salt. Cut the shortening into the flour with fingertips until mixture resembles coarse crumbs. Add the buttermilk, stirring just until moistened. Turn dough out onto a floured surface and knead 4 or 5 times.

Roll the dough to a thickness of ¼ inch, then cut into 2-inch strips.

Lay the dumplings on top of the water in the pot, cover tightly and cook for 12 to 15 minutes.

Turkey

Turkeys were such an important source of food in colonial America that Benjamin Franklin proposed the wild turkey for our national bird. John Lawson described the abundance of turkeys on the South Carolina coast in the early 1700s: "Near the Sea-Board, the Indians kill 15 Turkeys a Day; there coming out of the Swamp (about Sun-Rising), Flocks of these Fowl, containing several hundred in a Gang, who feed upon the Acorns."

Smoked Turkey

Smoking turkeys gives an incredibly moist and flavorful result.

Yield: 8 to 10 servings

one 12-pound turkey
½ cup olive oil
2 tablespoons fresh rosemary
2 tablespoons fresh thyme

4 cloves garlic, minced
2 large Vidalia onions, quartered
1 pound thick sliced smoked bacon

If using a frozen turkey, allow to thaw in refrigerator for about three days prior to starting the recipe.

Wash turkey inside and out, remove giblets and pat dry inside and out with paper towels. Sprinkle salt and pepper inside bird.

In a medium mixing bowl, combine olive oil, rosemary, thyme and garlic. Mix well and apply to outside of bird using a pastry brush.

Separate onions into single layers and cover entire turkey with onion, securing them by sticking a toothpick into each onion slice. Cover turkey with bacon by spearing the bacon with the toothpicks.

Place turkey in smoker, using charcoal and hickory wood chips for the fire. Smoke according to smoker manufacturer's directions, at least 6 to 8 hours.

Courtesy of Georgia Archives, Vanishing Georgia Collection, cow179.

CHAPTER 9

The Old Iron Pot

Gumbos, Soups and Stews

Gumbo is not, as many people suppose, a vegetable, but is a very thick soup made from a combination of young boiled chicken and okra, flavored with a soupcon of garlic, and well seasoned with salt, pepper, and rich, fresh butter an unforgettable delicacy.
—*Elizabeth (Mrs. T.P.) O'Connor,* My Beloved South

Marjorie Kinnan Rawlings summed up the place of soup in Southern cuisine pretty well in her 1943 work, *Cross Creek Cookery*: "I associate soup with either poverty or formal elegance."

While some may consider this an oversimplification, Southerners do tend to rely on soups as one of the courses for an elegant dinner, while our stews claim their heritage from the coast or frontier and are mostly descended from the hearty one-pot meals that were once the daily fare of the common man.

Stews and gumbos have always been a welcome way to feed a lot of people with a little meat or to ensure a meal that did not require a whole lot of tending. In the backcountry of the colonial South, the kettle generally never left the fire. It contained whatever stew was left over from the last meal, and periodically a fresh squirrel or two, possum or groundhog would be added, along with a few potatoes and maybe some corn to simmer until it was time to eat again. This practice had been copied from the Powhatans and Cherokees, who also kept cooking vessels filled with stews constantly bubbling on their campfires.

On the plantation, soups served as first courses or, more rarely, as light suppers. Mary Randolph, in *The Virginia House-Wife* (1824), listed recipes for sixteen different soups, including barley, dried peas, green peas, ochra (okra), rabbit, "any kind of old fowl," catfish, onion, turtle and mock turtle.

Some Southern soups have all but died out, especially calf's head soup, which, as the name implies, was a means of using almost every part of the cow. At the "other end" of the spectrum, oxtail soup is still considered a soul food delicacy to this day.

Along the coast, soups and stews made use of the abundant fish and shellfish the Atlantic and Gulf had to offer; fish, oysters, shrimp and crabs filled the pots of our ancestors and gave us some of the region's most popular fare.

GUMBO

Gumbo is, without a doubt, the best known of all Southern soups. If you ask anyone in any part of the world to name a dish from New Orleans, odds are the answer will be gumbo.

Gumbo is a thick soup or stew that evolved out of the unique fusion of French, African, Spanish and Native American cuisines native to south Louisiana.

Gumbo probably began life as bouillabaisse, a fish and shellfish soup native to Provence and brought to "New France." Native Americans contributed their knowledge of local shellfish and seafood, along with dried sassafras leaves as a thickener. The Spanish influence came in the form of fiery cayenne peppers that still grow on Avery Island west of New Orleans to this day. Africans brought okra (called *gombo* in the Bantu language) to the mix; while gumbos may or may not contain okra, it gave the dish its name.

Gumbo most likely evolved during the latter years of the eighteenth century; by 1824, it had made its way to Virginia, where Mary Randolph published a recipe for it in *The Virginia House-Wife*, identifying it as a "West India Dish." Another early recipe is found in Lettice Bryan's *The Kentucky Housewife*.

Both Mrs. Randolph and Mrs. Bryan also offered recipes for ochra (okra) soup; the difference between the two seems to have been the inclusion of a soup bone with the two soups, while the gumbos relied on the broth made by cooking down the vegetables.

Lafcadio Hearn used the traditional spelling *gombo* and offered nine recipes in *La Cuisine Creole* (1885), and *The Picayune's Creole Cook Book* (1900) addressed gumbo in reverential tones before giving variations containing everything from squirrels to cabbage.

Gumbo seems to be more of a state of mind than a dish with set ingredients; about the only conclusion anyone who studies gumbo recipes past and present is likely to reach is that gumbo consists of vegetables (or no vegetables), several kinds of meat (or one kind, or no meat) and seafood (or not) and is always thickened with a flour and fat mixture called a roux, unless something else entirely is used.

Except for *gombo z'herbs* (gumbo with herbs), gumbo recipes from about the mid-twentieth century onward generally contain one or more meats such as chicken, duck, sausage or ham. Seafood gumbos can contain fish, shellfish or a mixture of the two. Other gumbos combine everything that runs, swims or crawls. Hearn said in *La Cuisine Creole*, "Oysters, crabs, and shrimp may be added when in season, as all improve the gombo."

As for vegetables, early recipes almost always contain okra and tomatoes; after the middle of the twentieth century, recipes began using what came to be called the "Holy Trinity" of Cajun and Creole cookery: bell pepper, onions and celery.

A great majority of gumbo recipes call for making a roux (pronounced roo), which provides flavor and color for the stew. Roux is made by cooking flour in some type of fat over low heat until it turns nut-brown or darker. The first published recipe for gumbo using a roux dates to 1852.

Duck and Sausage Gumbo

There is something magical about the combination of duck and andouille sausage. This recipe is similar to several found in New Orleans cookbooks from the 1950s to the present day, although the recipe doubtless goes back much further.

Yield: 6 servings

1 duck, about 5 to 6 pounds, cut into pieces
1 tablespoon vegetable oil
1 pounds andouille or other smoked sausage, thinly sliced
6 cups chicken stock or chicken broth
3 cups water
3 tablespoons all-purpose flour
1 onion, chopped
2 celery ribs, chopped
1 red bell pepper, chopped
1 green bell pepper, chopped
¼ teaspoon cayenne, or to taste
1 recipe Basic Rice (see page 64)
⅔ cup green onions, thinly sliced

Using a sharp knife, prick the skin of the duck in several places on each piece.

In a 12-inch cast-iron skillet over medium-high heat, heat oil until it shimmers but doesn't smoke. Add duck pieces and brown on all sides; remove duck from skillet and drain on paper towel. Add andouille to pan and brown; drain on paper towel. Leave fat from duck and sausage in skillet and set aside.

Place andouille, duck, water and stock into a 6- to 8-quart Dutch oven and bring to a rolling boil. Pour off all but ¼ cup duck fat from skillet. Over low heat, whisk in flour to make a roux. Cook over low heat, stirring constantly, until roux is medium-brown in color, about 30 minutes. Add onions, celery and bell peppers and cook, stirring occasionally, until vegetables are tender. Add vegetable mixture to Dutch oven and stir until roux is well blended.

Bring gumbo back to a boil, then reduce heat and simmer uncovered for 1½ to 2 hours. Let cool. Remove duck, discard skin and de-bone, tearing or cutting meat into bite-sized pieces. Place duck meat back into Dutch oven.

Refrigerate gumbo overnight. Skim fat from surface and discard. Reheat gumbo over medium-high heat until it starts to simmer. Season to taste with salt and cayenne. Serve over rice and garnish with green onions.

Filé Gumbo

Filé (fee-lay) is a light brown powder made from ground sassafras leaves used as a thickener in soups and stews and was introduced to the early settlers of Louisiana by the Native Americans. It is similar to root beer in taste and is best used to thicken gumbo in the serving bowls, as it can become a stringy mess if used improperly. To use it to thicken a pot of gumbo, add it after the gumbo is off the heat, just moments before serving.

Yield: 10 to 12 servings

½ pound butter
1 rib celery, chopped
1 onion, finely chopped
½ green pepper, finely chopped
2 teaspoons garlic, minced
½ cup flour
1 gallon shrimp stock or water
3 bay leaves

½ pound smoked ham, diced
6 crabs (cleaned and quartered)
½ pound hot smoked sausage, cut into ¼-inch slices)
½ pound shrimp, peeled and deveined
salt, black pepper and cayenne pepper to taste
2 tablespoons filé powder
1 recipe Basic Rice (see page 64)

In a 6- to 8-quart Dutch oven over medium heat, melt butter. Add celery, onion, green pepper and garlic; sauté until vegetables are tender, about 5 minutes. Reduce heat to low.

Make a roux by adding flour and stirring constantly until mixture is the color of dark peanut butter, about 15 minutes. Add stock or water and bay leaves. Heat over medium flame for 20 minutes. Stir in ham, crabs and sausage; cook for 30 minutes.

Return pot to boil, stirring to avoid sticking. Add shrimp, salt, pepper and cayenne. Allow to return to the boiling point again. Remove from heat and stir in filé powder; serve immediately over rice.

Southern Soups and Stews

She-Crab Soup

She-crab soup is a creamy bisque made from, as the name implies, female crabs. More specifically, the roe (eggs) found inside female crabs during laying season are what gives this soup its unique flavor and pale pink color.

Scottish settlers to the Carolinas brought with them recipes for a soup called partan-bree made with crab and rice, two things found in abundance in the Lowcountry of South Carolina.

According to Charleston tradition, William Deas, an African American butler employed by Goodwyn Rhett, mayor of Charleston in the early 1900s, was the inventor of she-crab soup. President William Howard Taft, who is known to history for his girth more than anything he ever did as president, visited Rhett on several occasions. Deas, taxed with "dressing up" the traditional crab soup, added cream, roe and sherry to create what has become Charleston's signature dish.

Over the one hundred or so years since its creation, legions of Charleston chefs have added things to the recipe, making (in some cases) a soup that has too much cream in it and is entirely too thick. Peppers, onions, carrots and God knows what else have also been added as each chef pits his or her spin on the dish.

Luckily for purists, Blanch Rhett, the mayor's wife, gathered the recipes for the classic book *200 Years of Charleston Cooking* (1930) and recorded what the book says is Deas's original recipe. This recipe follows, along with a modern version that is thickened with more flour than the original but is still true to its roots.

William Deas's Original She-Crab Soup

Yield: 6 servings

1 dozen she-crabs
1 tablespoon butter
1 small onion
black pepper and salt to taste
2 cups milk

½ cup cream
½ teaspoon Worcestershire sauce
1 teaspoon flour
1 tablespoon sherry

Cook the crabs until tender—about twenty minutes in boiling, salted water. Pick the meat from the shells and put the crabmeat with the crab eggs in a double boiler. Add the butter, onion and a little black pepper. Let simmer for five minutes. Heat the milk and add to the mixture. Stir together and add the cream and the Worcestershire sauce. Thicken with the flour, add the sherry and salt to taste. Cook over a low flame for one half hour.

"Modernized" She-Crab Soup

This "modern" version of she-crab soup is thicker and richer than Deas's original and is closer to what you would get in a Charleston restaurant today.

Yield: 4 servings

2 tablespoons butter
1 onion, minced
1 bay leaf
2 tablespoons all-purpose flour
2 cups shrimp stock or chicken broth
2 cups milk
1 cup cream

2 teaspoons paprika
1 pound cooked blue crabmeat, divided
½ cup crab roe, divided (may substitute yolks
    of hard-boiled eggs, finely crumbled)
salt and pepper to taste
4 tablespoons dry sherry
2 tablespoons fresh chives, chopped

In a 5- to 6-quart Dutch oven, melt butter over medium heat. Add onion and bay leaf and sauté until onion is translucent, about 2 minutes. Whisk in flour until it dissolves, then add the stock, stirring constantly until smooth. Gradually add milk, cream and paprika; continue to whisk until well blended. Add half the crabmeat and roe to the mixture and season with salt and pepper. Cook until thick and heated through, about 15 minutes.

To serve, place 1 tablespoon of sherry in each of 4 bowls. Ladle the soup into the bowls, spooning a portion of the remaining crabmeat and roe in the center of each bowl. Garnish with chopped chives.

Okra Soup

Mary Randolph published a recipe for "ochra" soup in *The Virginia House-Wife* (1824), and the hearty soup had probably been a staple on Virginia plantations for at least a generation by that time. Modern recipes nearly always call for a beef soup bone, although Sarah Rutledge wrote in *The Carolina Housewife* (1847) that "a ham-bone boiled with the other ingredients is thought an improvement by some people."

This recipe is typical of many from the nineteenth century.

Yield: 6 servings

1½ quarts water
1 beef shank bone
1½ pounds stew beef
one 24-ounce can tomatoes
1 cup fresh butter beans

3 cups sliced okra
1 large onion, chopped
salt and pepper to taste
cooked rice

Place water, beef shank bone and beef in a 5- to 6-quart covered Dutch oven. Bring to a rolling boil, reduce heat and simmer for 2 hours.
Add remaining ingredients and return to a boil. Reduce heat and simmer until vegetables are tender, about 1 to 1½ hours. Serve in soup bowls with ¼ cup rice placed in the middle.

Virginia Ground Nut Soup

"Ground nut" is an early term for peanuts; this soup is a delicacy in some parts of the South, particularly in Virginia. Modern recipes nearly always call for peanut butter, which makes a much thicker soup than the original recipes (if you use peanut butter, replace the 3 cups peanuts with 2 cups of unsweetened peanut butter).

This recipe is faithful to the originals in use before peanut butter became a staple. It is based on a recipe by Rufus Estes, who wrote one of the first cookbooks published by an African American, *Good Things to Eat, As Suggested by Rufus*, published about 1911. Estes was born a slave and, after emancipation, became executive chef for the Pullman Railroad Car Company in Chicago.

Yield: 6 servings

3 cups unsalted peanuts

2 quarts water

2 bay leaves

1 stalk celery, finely diced

¼ cup sweet onion, finely diced

½ teaspoon ground mace

1 cup heavy cream

Soak peanuts in water for at least eight hours.

After the nuts have soaked, add bay leaves, celery, onion and mace to water. Bring to a boil, reduce heat and simmer slowly for 4½ hours, stirring frequently to keep from burning.

Strain soup and rub softened peanuts through sieve or puree in food processor and return to soup mixture. Return soup to burner and simmer to heat through. Whisk in cream to thicken, adjust seasonings and serve hot with croutons.

Black-Eyed Pea Soup

Black-eyed pea soup was probably a fixture in antebellum slave cabin cookery, but it doesn't show up in Southern cookbooks written by whites until the late nineteenth century. This recipe is based on one found in the "Recipes popular when the club was founded" section of *Famous Recipes from Old Virginia*, published by the Ginter Park Woman's Club of Richmond in 1941.

Yield: 6 servings

1 cup dried black-eyed peas

2 tablespoons bacon drippings

1 small yellow onion

1 teaspoon salt

cayenne pepper to taste

1 tablespoon flour

Wash and pick over peas. Place peas in a 4-quart mixing bowl, cover with water and soak overnight.

Discard remaining liquid. In a 6- to 8-quart Dutch oven over medium heat, sauté onion in bacon drippings until tender. Add peas, salt and cayenne; cover with 2 quarts water and bring to a rolling boil. Reduce heat and simmer until peas are tender, about 45 minutes. Check cooking liquid; if it hasn't reduced by one half, increase heat and cook until approximately one quart of liquid remains. Add flour and stir to thicken. Serve with hot corn bread.

Brunswick Stew

While Brunswick County, Virginia, Brunswick County, North Carolina, and Brunswick, Georgia, all claim it, the most popular story for the origin of this popular Southern stew is that it was stirred up sometime around 1828 by "Uncle" Jimmy Matthews, an African American cook to Dr. Creed Haskins, a member of the Virginia legislature. Matthews is said to have made the dish when Haskins asked for something new to feed his hunting party.

Traditional recipes for Brunswick stew always call for some type of game, usually squirrel, and always include corn. The early cookbooks avoid the issue; neither Lettice Bryant (*The Kentucky Housewife*, 1839) nor Annabella Hill (*Mrs. Hill's New Cook Book*, 1867) offers recipes for Brunswick stew.

A recipe for "Virginia Stew" appeared in the September 2, 1862 issue of the *Southern Recorder* (Milledgeville, Georgia); this is one of the earliest recipes for what we would today consider Brunswick stew. The identification with Virginia would seem to bolster Uncle Jimmy's claim. Marion Cabell Tyree published the earliest recipe for Brunswick stew by that name in *Housekeeping in Old Virginia* (1877).

Regardless of where it came from, Brunswick stew has become a Southern staple, particularly at barbecue restaurants throughout the Carolinas and Georgia, where pork and/or chicken replaces the wild game.

Yield: 15 to 20 servings

2 pounds pork shoulder meat
2 large onions, sliced
2 pounds diced tomatoes
2 pounds fresh lima beans
3 medium potatoes, diced
4 cups fresh corn, removed from cob
3 teaspoons salt
1 teaspoon pepper
1 tablespoon sugar

Cook pork in 2 quarts water, until meat can easily be removed from bones. Reserve cooking liquid; remove pork, allow to cool, de-bone and shred meat. Place in covered bowl and refrigerate. Add vegetables to broth and simmer uncovered, stirring occasionally, until potatoes are tender. Add shredded pork and the seasonings and heat until pork is warm.

Burgoo

Kentuckians have always had a soft spot for lamb, and it has been enjoyed there ever since Colonel Richard Callow brought the first sheep to Boonesboro in 1775. Lamb is most often the meat of choice for burgoo, a rich, thick stew that is probably the state's best-known dish.

The origin of the dish and its name are the subject of much debate. Some attribute the dish to French sailors who reportedly brought the dish to these shores from Europe. Others claim a man named Colonel Gus Jaubert brought the dish to Kentucky around 1810.

Burgoo is the main event at Kentucky political rallies and community events, and recipes abound that make the dish in biblical proportions, hundreds of gallons at a time. Although recipes vary in terms of ingredients, lamb and lima beans are nearly universal.

This recipe is typical of several burgoo recipes from the late nineteenth and early twentieth centuries.

Yield: 10 to 12 servings

1 stewing chicken (about 4 pounds)
2 pounds lamb, cut into bite-sized pieces
2 quarts water
2 teaspoons coarsely ground pepper
½ teaspoon cayenne pepper
one 14-ounce can tomato puree
12 Irish potatoes, cubed
2 large onions, chopped
1 head cabbage, finely chopped

8 medium tomatoes, peeled and chopped, OR
   one 24-ounce can chopped tomatoes
4 cups fresh carrots, sliced
8 ears of corn, cut off the cob
2 tablespoons salt
1 teaspoon pepper
½ cup Worcestershire sauce
2 cups fresh or frozen butterbeans

Place chicken, lamb, water and black and cayenne pepper in a 6- to 8-quart Dutch oven, adding more water if necessary to completely cover chicken. Bring to a rolling boil; reduce heat and simmer, covered, until lamb is tender and chicken falls off the bone, about 45 minutes to 1 hour. Remove chicken from pot, leaving the lamb in the cooking liquid. Discard skin and remove meat from bones. Shred meat and return to the cooking liquid. Add tomato puree, potatoes, onions, cabbage, tomatoes, carrots and corn. Season with salt, pepper and Worcestershire sauce. Cook slowly, stirring from the bottom to prevent scorching until burgoo is the consistency of a thick stew, about 3 to 4 hours. Add water, if necessary, to keep from sticking, then add butterbeans and cook until tender, about 15 minutes more.

Oyster Stew

Oysters have been an important source of food for Southerners in coastal areas since the days of the Jamestown colony. One of the earliest printed recipes for oyster stew is in a manuscript receipt book that belonged to Ann Chase of Maryland. Her recipe was called "Oyster Soup Mr. Paca's way" and referred to William Paca, a signer of the Declaration of Independence. Since Mr. Paca died in 1799, it's safe to assume the recipe predates his demise. The original recipe, which was reprinted in the book *Maryland's Way*, published by the Hammond-Harwood House Association in 1964, is a rich stew thickened with a teacup of butter and a pint of heavy cream and spiced with nutmeg. Over the years, the recipe has remained basically the same, with milk or half and half sometimes taking the place of the heavy cream.

My father made this dish more Saturday nights than I can remember. This was his recipe.

Yield: 4 servings

2 pints oysters, juice reserved
4 tablespoons butter
½ gallon whole milk
salt and pepper to taste

In a 3- or 4-quart saucepan over medium heat, bring oysters and reserved oyster liquid to a boil. Add butter, stirring until melted. Stir in milk and add salt and pepper to taste. Return to a rolling boil and cook for about five minutes.
Serve hot with saltine crackers.

Carolina Seafood Muddle

This rich, thick fish stew dates back to colonial times and is eaten from Tidewater Virginia to the South Carolina Lowcountry. The term "muddle" comes from Old English and means "a mess of fish."

Yield: 4 to 6 servings

2 tablespoons vegetable oil
2 large onions, thinly sliced
2 medium carrots, peeled and finely chopped
1 rib celery, thinly sliced
1 clove garlic, minced

2 ripe tomatoes, seeded and chopped
2 medium potatoes, cut into small pieces
6 cups fish stock or bottled clam juice
salt and freshly ground black pepper to taste
12 small clams, scrubbed
1 pound fish (cod, flounder or snapper), cut into 2-inch pieces
½ pound medium shrimp, peeled and deveined
12 small mussels, rinsed and beards removed
¼ cup finely chopped fresh parsley

Heat oil in an 8-quart Dutch oven over medium-high heat. Add onions, carrots and celery. Cook, stirring often, until vegetables are softened, about 3 to 5 minutes.

Add garlic to vegetables and cook 1 minute longer. Stir in tomatoes and potatoes.

Reduce heat to medium-low, cover and cook until potatoes are slightly softened, about 10 minutes. Pour in fish stock and increase heat to high. Bring to a boil, reduce heat to medium and season with salt and pepper. Simmer until potatoes are completely cooked, 10 to 15 minutes. Add clams and cook until they start to open, about 5 minutes. Add fish, shrimp and mussels. Cook about 10 minutes longer, until fish is opaque, shrimp are pink and clams and mussels are fully opened (discard any clams or mussels that remain unopened). Season with salt and pepper, sprinkle with parsley and serve hot.

Pine Bark Stew

Pine bark stew is a variation on muddle and also hails from the North Carolina coast. The stew gets its name, the story goes, because it was cooked in big iron pots over fires made from chunks of pine bark.

Yield: 6 servings

½ cup bacon, chopped
1 cup onion, chopped
2 cups tomatoes, seeded and chopped
1 cup tomato catsup
2 tablespoons Worcestershire sauce

2 cups potatoes, cut into 1-inch cubes
2 pounds red snapper or other firm white fish, cut into 1-inch cubes
2 teaspoons sea salt
½ teaspoon pepper, or to taste

In a 6- to 8-quart Dutch oven over medium heat, cook bacon until crisp. Remove with a slotted spoon and set aside, reserving drippings. Add onion to bacon drippings and sauté over medium heat until tender. Add tomatoes, catsup, Worcestershire sauce and potatoes and bring to a boil.

Reduce heat to low and simmer for 30 minutes. Add fish, salt and pepper. Simmer until potatoes are tender, about 15 to 20 minutes. Add crumbled bacon, adjust seasoning and serve.

Courtesy Lewis P. Watson Photographic Collection, Olivia Raney Local History Library, Raleigh, NC.

CHAPTER 10

The Southern Garden

Vegetables and Fruit

> *Thank God, who made the garden grow,*
> *Who took upon himself to know*
> *That we loved vegetables so.*
> *I served his plan with rake and hoe,*
> *And mother, boiling, baking, slow*
> *To her favorite tune of Old Black Joe,*
> *Predestined many an age ago.*
> *Pearly corn still on the cob,*
> *My teeth are aching for that job.*
> *Tomatoes, one would fill a dish,*
> *Potatoes, mealy as one could wish.*
> *Cornfield beans and cucumbers,*
> *And yellow yams for sweeteners.*
> *Pickles between for stepping-stones,*
> *And plenty of cornmeal bread in pones.*
> —*John Crowe Ransom,* Poems About God *(1919)*

Since the South was chiefly an agrarian society for the first three hundred years of its existence, it shouldn't come as a surprise that Southerners have always celebrated the vegetables that come from the region's rich soil.

Robert Beverley tried to give a comprehensive list of the crops being grown in Virginia at the close of the seventeenth century in his *The History and Present State of Virginia* (1705). The list included cherries, mulberries, plums, persimmons, hickory nuts, hazelnuts, walnuts and maple syrup produced from native trees. Native shrubs yielded cranberries, currants, huckleberries and raspberries, and the colonists had transplanted wild strawberries and grapes into their gardens. Pumpkins, watermelons, yellow squash, red and white potatoes, several varieties of peas, kidney beans and lima beans were also being cultivated by the close of the seventeenth century.

At a time when the success or failure of a family's garden could mean the difference between life and death, great attention was given to finding crops that would grow successfully in the new land. Two decades after Beverley's list, Governor William Byrd II of Virginia, trying to encourage people to move into his state's backcountry, made another listing of the agricultural bounty awaiting new settlers. He listed artichokes, asparagus, beans, beets, broccoli, four kinds of cabbage, carrots, cauliflower, cress, cucumbers, several varieties of lettuce, mustard, onions, parsnips, potatoes, rhubarb, spinach, truffles and turnips as being regularly cultivated by the first half of the eighteenth century.

From the earliest days, Southern tables have groaned under the cornucopia of vegetables at harvest time. In *The Virginia House-Wife* (1824), Mary Randolph gave recipes for preparing fifty vegetable dishes, ranging from green salads to mashed potatoes to French beans. At Monticello, Thomas Jefferson grew 250 varieties of more than seventy different vegetables in his extensive gardens. Jefferson's table included salads made from endive grown in the garden and dressed with oil from the sesame seeds he planted as an alternative to the olive trees that didn't survive the Virginia winters. Other vegetables from the Monticello gardens included eggplant, tomatoes, peppers from Mexico, broccoli, cauliflower, scarlet runner bleans, okra, asparagus and figs.

THE THREE SISTERS: CORN, BEANS AND SQUASH

Corn

No other plant has been more responsible for the sustenance, succor and survival of the Southern people than corn. Corn started its journey to the Southern table in Mexico and Peru, where the native peoples raised several varieties, each suitable for different uses. Corn is divided into popcorn, dent corn, flint corn, soft corn and sweet corn. Of these, dent and sweet corn had the greatest impact on Southern foodways.

Dent corn gets its name from a slight crease in the kernel. It grows well in the South (flint is its Northern counterpart). Also known as field corn, feed corn or grinding corn, dent corn has low sugar content and comes to the table as grits, hominy or cornmeal.

Sweet corn, which as the name implies has a high sugar content, is served as a vegetable, either on the cob or off. Although sweet corn was cultivated in Virginia by the late 1770s, it really didn't catch on as a vegetable until the early years of the twentieth century. Prior to that time, most of the corn served as a vegetable on Southern tables was "green corn," the immature ears of the dent varieties.

Sweet corn owes its naturally sweet taste to a recessive gene that significantly reduces its ability to change sugar to starch inside the kernels as they age after picking. Today, sweet corn hybrids such as Silver Queen, Platinum Lady, Calico Belle and Bodacious are enjoyed on the cob or in a number of favorite Southern dishes.

Creamed Corn

Yield: 6 servings

6 ears fresh corn
¼ cup unsalted butter
¼ cup water
1 teaspoon sugar
1 tablespoon flour
½ teaspoon salt
½ teaspoon coarsely ground black pepper
¾ cup milk

Using a sharp knife, carefully cut corn from cobs. Scrape cobs with the back of the knife to remove milk.
In 4-quart saucepan over medium heat, melt butter. Stir in corn and corn milk, water and sugar. Cook corn until tender, about 10 minutes. Stir in flour, salt and pepper. Gradually add milk, stirring constantly. Simmer until mixture reaches desired thickness. Do not boil.

Corn Pudding

Corn pudding has been around since colonial days and was one of the earliest cooked corn dishes. This recipe is adapted from *Mrs. Charles H. Gibson's Maryland and Virginia Cook Book* by Marietta P. Gibson, published in 1894.

Yield: 4 to 6 servings

8 ears fresh, sweet corn
4 eggs, separated
1 teaspoon sugar

1 teaspoon flour
1 tablespoon butter, melted

Preheat oven to 350 degrees F. Using a sharp knife, carefully cut corn from cob and place it in a small bowl, using the back of the knife to scrape the bare cob to remove any juice. Add this to the corn kernels.

Beat egg yolks, sugar and flour together and add to corn mixture. Beat egg whites until stiff peaks form, then fold into corn and egg yolk mixture.

Place into a buttered 2-quart casserole dish and bake until set, about 30 to 45 minutes.

Beans

Beans, peas and various other legumes have been a source of nourishment for Southerners since the earliest days of the Virginia colony.

"Green beans" is the generic term for a dazzling assortment of different types and varieties of the immature seed pods of any member of the largest family of legume called *Phaseolus vulgaris*, literally translated as "common bean."

American bean species were originally native to South America and made their way to North America centuries before Columbus. Native Americans planted beans in the same holes as their corn as part of a relationship that benefited both plants: the beans gave the corn much-needed nitrogen, and the corn provided a natural trellis for the beans to climb. Another benefit of the corn and bean combination unknown at the time was that beans contain an enzyme (lacking in corn) that helps humans digest and absorb protein.

Thomas Harriot was one of the first Europeans to comment on the beans raised by Native Americans. In *A Briefe and True Report of the New Found Land of Virginia*, an account of his trip to Roanoke Island in 1586, he wrote, "Called by us beans, because in greatness and partly in shape they are like to the beans in England, saving they are flatter, of more divers colours."

Europeans took to the American bean species quickly, as they were very similar to European bean varieties. The common green bean, also called the string bean or snap bean, and lima beans were very popular in the colonial South. European beans were imported and planted early in Virginia, although some of them didn't take very well to the scorching Virginia summers. One particularly popular European bean, according to Wesley Greene, garden historian at Colonial Williamsburg, was a variety of English broad bean (fava bean) called the magazan. Mary Randolph (*The Virginia House-Wife*, 1824) called the magazan "the smallest and most delicate of the Windsor beans."

In *American Cookery* (1796), Amelia Simmons mentioned two varieties of green bean, the Windsor and the Horse Bean. The more refined Windsor bean was popular in the kitchen gardens of the upper class and is mentioned in several early Southern cookery books. The Horse Bean was a much less refined but heartier bean variety that was found in the gardens of the working class or farms in the Southern backcountry.

For culinary purposes, beans can be divided into bush varieties, pole beans, half runners and dry beans. Green bush beans, such as the popular Blue Lake, are non-climbing plants fifteen to twenty inches tall. All the pods on many of this type of bean come to maturity at the same time, making them easy to harvest with mechanized pickers and cheaper to produce. This is a major reason that the Blue Lake is so widely available in grocery stores.

Pole beans send out "runners" that require a trellis to climb. As a rule, they are broader and flatter than bush types. The most popular pole bean is a variety called Kentucky Wonder, although Scarlet Runner is also found frequently at farmer's markets. Half runners are also pole beans, but they are bushier, with shorter runners. Dry beans, such as red kidney beans, great northern beans, pintos and white kidney beans, are allowed to grow to maturity, and then the beans are removed from the pods and dried for later use.

Cooking techniques for green beans vary widely depending on the type of bean. Using the same low, slow boil that will make a pot of pole beans tender and flavorful will turn French haricots into "flavorless mush."

Early nineteenth-century cooks such as Mary Randolph and Lettice Bryan published recipes calling for different cooking times for different types of beans, but by the 1870s, it was nearly universal for Southern cookbooks to call for simmering beans for a long period of time with salt pork.

Southern-Style Green Beans

Yield: 6 to 8 servings

2 pounds fresh pole beans, trimmed and snapped into 1-inch pieces
1 smoked ham hock
1⅓ cups water
Soul Food Seasoning (see page 43) to taste
½ teaspoon sugar

In a 4-quart saucepan over medium heat, combine beans, ham hock, water, seasoning and sugar. Bring to a rolling boil. Reduce heat to low, cover and simmer until tender, about 45 minutes to 1 hour.

Lima or Butter Beans

Originally called "bushel beans" or "sugar beans," butter beans are a smaller and more heat-resistant variety of lima beans, although in the South, the term is used rather universally to refer to any variety of lima beans.

Lima beans are one of the oldest documented New World vegetables, going back to at least 5,000 BCE in Peru. It is believed that the Spanish introduced lima beans to the Indians of Florida in the 1500s.

Lima beans that date from the very early eighteenth century have been found in the Richneck slave quarters archaeological site at Colonial Williamsburg, and John Lawson reported in *The History of Carolina* (1714) that they were grown by Native Americans and colonists alike.

Yield: 6 servings

1 pound butter beans, fresh or frozen, drained, thawed	⅛ teaspoon salt
1 tablespoon bacon drippings	pinch of garlic powder
⅛ teaspoon black pepper	4 tablespoons butter, melted

In a 3-quart saucepan, bring beans, drippings, seasonings and enough water to cover to a rolling boil. Reduce heat and simmer until beans are tender, about 10 to 15 minutes. Drain and pour melted butter on top before serving.

Succotash

Succotash, a mixture of corn and lima beans (and sometimes tomatoes), was eaten by various groups of Native Americans prior to the arrival of European settlers.

The earliest settlers in Virginia reported the natives made a corn and bean dish called *pausarowmena* from a type of pole bean and a variety of bush bean mixed with sweet corn that had been roasted and slightly caramelized in the husk and then stored dry and reconstituted with water.

Helen Bullock (*Williamsburg Art of Cookery*, 1937) cites what is quite possibly the earliest recipe as being for "Lima Beans and Sweet Corn" in a receipt book circa 1837 in the collection of Elizabeth Labbe Cole of Williamsburg, Virginia.

Yield: 6 to 8 servings

2½ pounds fresh lima beans, shelled
12 ears of corn
⅔ cup cream

2 tablespoons butter
salt and pepper to taste

In a 4-quart saucepan over medium heat, place lima beans in just enough salted water to cover. Bring to a rolling boil, then reduce heat, cover and simmer until almost tender, about 25 minutes, checking frequently and adding more water as needed.
Using a sharp knife, carefully cut corn from cob and place it in a small bowl, using the back of the knife to scrape the bare cob to remove any juice and add to the corn kernels.
Add corn with liquid and cream to the beans; simmer for 5 minutes. Add butter, salt and pepper to taste. Heat succotash thoroughly.

Pinto Beans

Pinto beans are another food gift to the South from our South American neighbors by way of our Spanish and Portuguese delivery service. The Spaniards named these beans "pinto," their word for paint, because of their tan skin that is covered with splotches of different colors.

    Pinto beans were (and still are) especially loved by folks in the Appalachians, where pintos are slowly simmered with a ham hock until they are so tender they are bursting out of their skins. Pintos prepared this way are called "soup beans" in the Southern highlands and are a rite of seasonal passage when the warm sunshine of summer gives way to the chill winds of autumn.

Yield: 6 servings

one 1-pound package dried pintos
1 smoked ham hock
1 large sweet onion

Place dried beans in a 6- to 8-quart Dutch oven and cover with cold water to a depth of 4 inches. Let beans soak for at least 6 hours, preferably overnight. Drain beans in a colander and return to Dutch oven. Add the ham hock and cover with fresh water to a depth of 3½ to 4 inches. Bring to a rolling boil and reduce heat to a simmer.
Cover pot and allow to simmer until beans are very tender, about two hours. Add the onion during the last 30 minutes of cooking time.
Remove the bones of the ham hock from the pot and discard. Take about ½ cup of the beans, put them in a shallow bowl and mash them with a fork until they form a smooth paste. Stir this back into the pot to thicken the beans. Serve hot with turnip or collard greens, corn bread and chow chow.

Black-Eyed Peas

Black-eyed peas originated in the Niger River Basin of West Africa and were being cultivated by Egyptians as early as 2,500 B.C. They made their way to the Southern colonies via the slave trade. Their need for a long, warm growing season meant black-eyed peas grew best in the Southern colonies, making them an early part of Southern foodways.

Also called cowpeas and field peas (and referred to as Indian peas and Virginia peas in eighteenth-century diaries), black-eyed peas have been a staple of the Southern diet for more than three hundred years.

Black-eyed peas were an early export crop of the Virginia colony and were even used to settle debts between planters. Thomas Jefferson planted a French variety of black-eyed pea alongside his corn crop in 1774, and black-eyed peas were also a staple in the diet of soldiers during the American Revolution.

Black-eyed peas were a cheap and easily produced part of the diet of African American slaves, usually grown in small garden plots the slaves tended at night after their regular workday was over. They were also a staple among poor white Southerners, who called them "crowder peas" after the Scottish word *crowdy*, which refers to porridge.

Yield: 4 to 6 servings

1 pound dried black-eyed peas
1 ham hock, piece of salt pork or several slices of bacon
2 quarts water
salt and pepper to taste

Wash peas and soak in cold water for at least 6 hours, preferably overnight. Drain.
In a 6- to 8-quart Dutch oven over medium heat, place peas and ham hock in water to cover. Add salt and pepper and bring to a rolling boil. Reduce heat and simmer until peas are tender, about 2 hours.

Squash

Squash is the third and final member of the "Three Sisters." The plants' broad leaves provided shade for the base of the corn and beans it was planted with and prevented the growth of weeds.

Squash is native to the western hemisphere and was grown in Mexico as early as 5,500 BC. The word comes from the Algonquian Indian term *askoot asquash*, meaning "eaten green." It was well known to the Jamestown settlers and was one of the first crops cultivated by Europeans in the New World.

Squash is usually divided into summer and winter varieties. Summer squash have thin skins and mature in the early months after spring planting; the winter varieties mature later and have a thick, inedible skin. The most common varieties of summer squash used in Southern cooking are the yellow crookneck and the patty pan. Winter squashes grown in the South include acorn squash and pumpkins.

Summer Squash Casserole

Yield: 8 to 10 servings

6 summer squash
¼ pound butter
1¼ cup cheddar cheese, shredded
1 cup sour cream
½ cup onion, chopped
⅓ cup grated Parmesan cheese
1½ tablespoons white wine
breadcrumbs

Using a sharp knife, slice squash cross-wise into ¼-inch-thick pieces. Place the squash into a 4-quart saucepan with enough water to cover to a depth of 2 inches and bring to a rolling boil over medium-high heat. Reduce heat and simmer until squash is tender, about 10 minutes.
Preheat oven to 350 degrees F. Drain squash and add butter, cheddar cheese, sour cream, onion, Parmesan cheese and wine. Mix well and pour into casserole dish; top with breadcrumbs. Bake until breadcrumbs are golden brown, about 30 minutes.

Tomatoes and Okra

Tomatoes are native to South and Central America and were cultivated by the Aztecs and Incas as early as AD 700. Spanish explorers returning from Mexico introduced them to Europe, where tomatoes were first mentioned in 1556.

In sixteenth-century England, the tomato was suspect because of its relationship to the nightshade, a wild plant with toxic berries. Because of this, tomatoes were called "mad apples" or "rage apples" and were mostly used as an ornamental plant. The French, however, called tomatoes *pomme d'amour* or "apple of love," as they considered them powerful aphrodisiacs.

Southerners took to tomatoes early on. They were grown in Carolina in the 1680s, and there are various recipes from colonial times for tomato catsup, tomato soup and assorted cooked tomato dishes. Southern humorist Lewis Grizzard probably best summed up the South's love affair with tomatoes, especially in the summer when they're picked fresh from the vine: "It's difficult to think anything but pleasant thoughts while eating a homegrown tomato."

There are more than four thousand varieties of tomato, ranging from the thumbnail-sized Sugar Babies to the Ponderosa, which can weigh as much as three pounds.

Fried Green Tomatoes

Recipes for this uniquely Southern dish date back at least to the turn of the twentieth century; Minerva Fox published her recipe in *The Blue Grass Cook Book* in 1904, the same year Martha Pritchard Stanford published a similar recipe in her *Old and New Cookbook*. This recipe is similar to both.

Yield: 4 to 6 servings

¼ cup vegetable oil
1 egg
1 cup milk
3 or 4 green tomatoes, washed, cored and sliced (do not peel)
1 cup cornmeal, seasoned to taste with salt and pepper

In a 12-inch cast-iron skillet over medium heat, heat the oil until it begins to shimmer but does not smoke, about 360 degrees F on an instant-read thermometer.
Whisk together egg and milk; dip each tomato slice into the milk/egg mixture and then roll in the cornmeal to coat.
Carefully place battered tomato slices in the preheated skillet. Brown on both sides. Remove to a paper towel to drain; season immediately with salt and pepper to taste.
Serve plain or with remoulade sauce (page 191).

Tomato Sandwiches

There are few things more dear to the hearts of Southerners than the first homegrown tomato of summer; more often than not, the first tomato of summer becomes the first tomato sandwich of summer. The identity of the first person to put tomato, bread and mayonnaise together has been lost to antiquity; the earliest recipe for a tomato sandwich I have found dates only to the 1920s, but surely this Southern summer staple predates that.

The traditional Southern tomato sandwich is made on thick, white bread with lots of mayonnaise, salt and freshly ground black pepper, ideally accompanied by an ear of fresh corn on the cob and a glass of iced tea.

Stewed Tomatoes

Mary Ann Bryan Mason gave excellent advice on how to make stewed tomatoes in *The Young Housewife's Counsellor* [*sic*] *and Friend*. (1875). This recipe works as well today as it did more than a century ago: "Scald and skin the tomatoes (unless canned), and place them in a stewpan without water. Simmer for half an hour. Add pepper, salt, a large piece of butter, a spoonful of white sugar and very little bread finely grated. Boil up once and serve hot."

Okra

Okra came to the South from Africa, probably via the slave trade, and was cultivated in Egypt by the twelfth century BC.

Okra, or "ochra," as it was often spelled in early days, probably arrived in the South by the mid- to late 1700s. Thomas Jefferson reported that okra was being grown in Virginia by 1781, and he was growing it at Monticello by 1809.

While most Southerners are fond of okra, probably none was fonder—or waxed more poetically on the subject—than Mrs. T.P. O'Connor in *My Beloved South* (1914): "Okra is a poetic and historic plant, as it grew in luxuriance along the banks of the Nile in 50 B.C. Caesar, Mark Antony, and Cleopatra ate of it, and it is not only a succulent vegetable, with its tender green pod, but it is worthy of being grown in the handsomest flower garden, for its lovely bell-shaped blossom of thick canary-coloured petals, ending where they join the stem in a deep rich shade of garnet."

Okra and Tomatoes

One of the earliest published recipes for okra as a side dish was Mary Randolph's "Ochra and Tomatoes," from 1824.

Yield: 4 to 6 servings

1 tablespoon bacon grease
1 medium Vidalia onion, chopped
1 pound okra, cut into ½-inch slices
3 fresh tomatoes, preferably Big Boy
1 teaspoon sugar
salt and pepper to taste

In a 10-inch, non-reactive (not cast iron or aluminum) skillet, heat bacon grease over medium high heat. Sauté onion until translucent, about 3 to 4 minutes. Add okra and cook until it begins to brown, about another 5 to 6 minutes. Stir in tomatoes, sugar, salt and pepper to taste. Cover skillet and simmer over low heat until thickened, about 20 to 30 minutes.

Fried Okra

Yield: 6 servings

1½ cups sliced fresh okra
1 cup cornmeal
½ cup all-purpose flour
pepper to taste (optional)
vegetable oil for frying
½ teaspoon salt

Salt okra and let sit for a few minutes.
In a 1-quart mixing bowl, combine cornmeal, flour and pepper. Gently toss okra in cornmeal, coating each piece. Place okra pieces on a wire rack and allow to rest for 1 hour.
In a 12-inch cast-iron skillet, heat ½ inch oil until it shimmers but does not smoke.
Carefully add okra pieces in a single layer. Allow to cook, turning gently with a fork until browned on all sides. Drain on paper towels and season immediately with salt and pepper.

Sweet Potatoes

Sweet potatoes are native to South America and made their way to the South long before the Jamestown colonists. In 1705, Robert Beverly listed the sweet potato as one of the plants "our Natives had originally amongst them."

Enslaved African cooks in the New World took to the sweet potato immediately, as it was very close to the yams they were used to eating back home. Although a staple of the Southern diet from colonial days, the research and recipes put out by Dr. George Washington Carver at Tuskegee Institute in the late nineteenth and early twentieth centuries helped make the noble sweet potato one of the truly iconic foods of the South.

Baked Sweet Potatoes

Sweet potatoes are much more nutritious if they are cooked in their skins. To prepare them for baking, wash them in cold water and then pat them dry and pierce the skin several times with a sharp knife. They can be roasted in a 350-degree F oven for one hour or wrapped in aluminum foil and buried in hot coals in a fireplace or campfire. Serve with butter, brown sugar and cinnamon.

Candied Sweet Potatoes

"Candied" sweet potatoes are sweet potatoes that have been baked with a glaze over them.

Yield: 4 to 6 servings

2 large sweet potatoes
¼ cup butter
½ teaspoon cinnamon
½ cup packed brown sugar

¼ cup orange juice
¼ cup raisins
¼ cup chopped pecans

Peel sweet potatoes and, using a chef's knife, carefully cut them into bite-sized pieces.
In a 6- to 8-quart Dutch oven over high heat, bring sweet potatoes and enough water to cover to a depth of 2 inches to a rolling boil. Reduce heat and simmer until the potatoes are fork tender, about 10 to 12 minutes.
In a 2-quart saucepan over medium heat, melt butter, cinnamon and brown sugar together. Add orange juice and stir until smooth. Add the sweet potatoes and cook slowly, turning occasionally until the sweet potatoes are caramelized, about 20 minutes. If syrup is too thin, add more brown sugar. Garnish with the raisins and nuts.

Irish Potatoes

White, or Irish, potatoes were native to South America. They were brought to Spain by the early explorers and show up in the accounts of Spanish voyages to the New World as early as 1553. There is a regular donnybrook among historians as to how the potatoes got from Spain to Ireland. Some credit Sir Francis Drake, some Sir John Hawkins, some Sir Walter Raleigh and others the shipwreck of the Spanish Armada. Regardless of how they got there, the potato was a prefect crop for the Irish, who didn't have much in the way of land; two acres of potatoes could sustain nine people for a full year. This led to a population boom in the Emerald Isle but also set up a dependence on the crop that eventually led to the Potato Famine in the 1840s.

The potato probably reached the Southern colonies at least by the middle of the eighteenth century. One early recipe is for the "Irish Method for Boiling Potatoes" in a manuscript receipt book by the Cameron family of Orange County, North Carolina, dated 1816.

Stewed Irish Potatoes

Yield: 4 to 6 servings

4 large baking potatoes
2 tablespoons half and half
salt and freshly ground black pepper to taste

Peel and cube potatoes.
In a 4-quart saucepan over medium-high heat, bring potatoes and enough water to just cover to a rolling boil. Reduce heat and simmer until potatoes are extremely tender and water has become a thick gravy. Add half and half, salt and pepper. Serve warm.

Southern Potato Salad

There is no doubt in my mind that on countless occasions, two dear old Southern ladies have engaged in at least a cuss fight (if not outright fisticuffs) over the *only* right way to make potato salad. Some Southern cooks will maintain that potato salad *must* contain (mustard, onions, sweet pickles…) while others will tell you that potato salad containing (mustard, onions, sweet pickles…) isn't fit for the hogs. The basic recipe, along with any or all of the embellishments, is typical for "True" Southern potato salad.

Yield: 8 to 10 servings

5 pounds Irish potatoes
5 tablespoons (more or less) Southern
  mayonnaise (see page 41)
salt and pepper to taste

Optional (or Essential) Embellishments,
  Amounts Adjusted to Suit Your Tastes:
2 tablespoons sweet pickle cubes
2 tablespoons yellow or Creole mustard
8 hard cooked eggs, chopped
¼ cup sweet onions, diced
¼ cup celery, diced
¼ cup green or red bell pepper, chopped

Peel and cube potatoes. In a 6- to 8-quart Dutch oven over medium-high heat, bring potatoes and enough water to cover to a depth of 2 inches to a rolling boil. Reduce heat and simmer until potatoes are just fork tender, about 8 minutes. Do not overcook. Drain into a colander and allow to cool.

Place potatoes and other ingredients into a large mixing bowl. Using a rubber spatula, combine ingredients and mix well. Note that the amount of mayonnaise is subjective and should be just enough to hold all the ingredients together; the more of the embellishments you add, the more mayonnaise you'll need to use. Chill before serving.

Greens

If there was an "official" Southern vegetable, greens would be it. You'll find them everywhere from the finest restaurants in Richmond to the lowliest barbecue joint in a backwater town in Alabama. They transcend all social, racial and economic barriers throughout the region.

Greens are defined as any type of cabbage in which the leaves do not form a head but, instead, branch up to form a stalk. In the South, plants used for greens include collards, turnips and mustard greens.

Collards are thought to have been native to Asia Minor and were spread to all parts of the world by the ancient Romans. They were eaten in England and were among the plants brought to Virginia by the earliest colonists. Collards are a winter crop and were ideally suited for the mild winters in the South.

Although early recipes for greens are scarce, they were part of the diet of middle- to lower-class Southerners since colonial days. When Pleasant Henderson was appointed steward at the University of North Carolina in 1797, he was charged with providing each student "a Dish or Cover of Bacon and Greens" for supper each night.

The traditional way to cook greens is to simmer them slowly for a couple hours with a piece of salt pork or ham hock. Some modern Southern chefs sauté greens in olive oil with a little onion and garlic powder, which retains more of the natural vitamins and minerals that otherwise are lost to the cooking liquid, which is referred to as "pot liquor" or "pot likker."

In 1931, Huey P. Long (U.S. senator-elect of Louisiana) and the editors of the *Atlanta Constitution* got into a print debate over the proper way to eat pot likker and corn bread. Long favored dunking the corn bread in the pot likker, while the *Constitution* advocated crumbling. The debate raged for more than three weeks in February and March of that year, with both sides claiming a moral victory.

Greens also play a role in the folk traditions of the region. A fresh leaf of collard greens placed on the forehead was said to cure headaches, and hanging a fresh leaf over the door is supposed to ward off evil spirits. Greens served alongside black-eyed peas and hog jowl on New Year's Day are said to ensure a year of good luck and plenty of money.

Collard Greens

Mary Ann Bryan Mason gave some good advice on cooking collards in *The Young Housewife's Counsellor* [*sic*] *and Friend* (1875): "Greens must be boiled with ham or pork. They are insipid and flat without. Butter does not seem to be congenial. Let them boil half an hour just before you take up your dinner. Tender sprouts from the cabbage-stalks, in the spring, mustard, or turnip tops, are an acceptable adjunct to ham or pork, when other vegetables are scarce. Let them boil soft and tender, drain them, and serve them very hot."

Yield: 4 to 6 servings

4–6 bunches of collards
5 slices of salt pork or bacon
1 large onion, chopped
1 ham hock

Soul Food Seasoning (page 43) to taste
salt and black pepper to taste
water to cover

Place collards in kitchen sink. Fill sink with water, pushing leaves under running water as sink fills. Allow to soak for five minutes, then drain, rinse collards under running water and fill sink again. Repeat until no dirt is present on leaves, about 5 or 6 times.
Remove collards from sink and allow to drain. Pull leaves from stems; discard stems.
Lay collard leaves on top of each other, roll lengthwise and, using a sharp knife, cut into pieces.
In a 6- to 8-quart Dutch oven over medium heat, cook salt pork or bacon until crisp; drain on paper towel and set aside. Remove all but 1 tablespoon of the grease from the Dutch oven; add the collard greens, salt pork or bacon, onion, ham hock, soul food seasoning, salt and pepper to taste.

Cover with water and bring to a rolling boil over medium-high heat. Reduce heat and simmer slowly, covered, until greens are tender, about one to two hours. Serve with corn bread and hot sauce or pepper vinegar.

DRESSED SALADS

As tempting as it may be to equate salads with the twentieth century, Southerners were eating lettuce and other greens with boiled salad dressings in the eighteenth century and before. Lettuce was one of the first crops to be harvested in the spring, and after a winter of sauerkraut, it was very welcome. Thomas Jefferson was particularly fond of dressed salads, and they were frequently served at Monticello.

CABBAGE AND SLAW

Cabbage originated on the sea coasts of southern and western Europe and was an important food in the European diet from the Middle Ages into the seventeenth century. Cabbage was another of the vegetables that arrived with the earliest colonists and was mentioned by Alexander Whitaker in *Good Newes from Virginia* (1612) as growing well in the New World. Cabbage was an important crop in the colonial South, and there are more varieties of cabbage and its relatives listed by Virginia sources than any other garden vegetable.

Recipes for cabbage are found in the earliest Southern cookbooks, and it was eaten boiled, pickled, cooked in sauce and as a salad green.

Fried Cabbage

This dish is popular in the southern Appalachians. The recipe is adapted from one found in *Mountain Cooking* by John Parris (1978).

Yield: 4 to 6 servings

3 slices bacon, chopped
¼ cup chopped onion
6 cups cabbage, cut into thin wedges
2 tablespoons water

1 pinch white sugar
salt and pepper to taste
1 tablespoon cider vinegar

In a 12-inch cast-iron skillet over medium heat, cook bacon until tender, drain on paper towel and set aside. Add onion and cook in the bacon grease until tender. Add cabbage and stir in water, sugar, salt and pepper. Cook until cabbage wilts, about 15 minutes. Remove to serving dish. Add vinegar and stir to coat; crumble reserved bacon over top and serve hot.

Coleslaw for Fried Chicken or Fish

Coleslaw came to the South by way of the Dutch and Germans; the name "coleslaw" is a corruption of the Dutch word *koolsla*, which means "cabbage salad," and was used in print in the United States by 1785.

Cookbooks from the nineteenth century commonly refer to coleslaw as "cold slaw" to differentiate it from several slaws made with boiled dressings poured over the cabbage. Lettice Bryan gave recipes for warm and cold "slaugh" in *The Kentucky Housewife* (1839).

Coleslaw is served throughout the region as an accompaniment to fried fish and seafood, fried chicken and barbecue, as well as a general side dish.

This recipe is based on several typical of the late nineteenth century but uses premade mayonnaise for convenience.

Yield: 4 to 6 servings

4 cups grated cabbage
½ to 1 cup mayonnaise, to taste
1 tablespoon sugar, or to taste
1 teaspoon salt
½ teaspoon black pepper

Using a grater or food processor, grate cabbage.
Place cabbage in a 4-quart mixing bowl. Add mayonnaise until slaw is desired consistency (amount will depend on the moisture in the cabbage and personal taste). Add sugar, salt and pepper; chill before serving.

North Carolina Red Barbecue Slaw

In the Piedmont and mountains of North Carolina, pork barbecue is served accompanied by a spicy, mildly hot and definitely red slaw on the side or on top of a barbecue sandwich. These slaws have been around since at least the 1940s, and the recipes are carefully guarded family secrets, passed down by the owners of each barbecue joint. This recipe is an amalgamation of several different ones from the Piedmont.

Yield: 2 cups

2 cups finely chopped cabbage
¼ cup Western North Carolina–style barbecue sauce (page 98)
¼ cup ketchup
1 tablespoon sugar
1 tablespoon salt
¼ cup apple cider vinegar
1 teaspoon hot sauce or to taste

In a 4-quart mixing bowl, combine cabbage, barbecue sauce, ketchup, sugar, salt, vinegar and hot sauce; mix well. Chill for at least 3 hours (preferably overnight) for flavors to combine.

Courtesy of Lewis P. Watson Photographic Collection, Olivia Raney Local History Library, Raleigh, NC.

Chapter 11

Glory in a Jar

Pickles, Relishes, Jams and Preserves

On a hot day in Virginia, I know nothing more comforting than a fine spiced pickle, brought up trout-like from the sparkling depths of the aromatic jar below the stairs of Aunt Sally's cellar.
—Thomas Jefferson

Food Preservation in the Old South

Pickling and preserving the bounty of the garden is a time-honored tradition in the South. Even in the twenty-first century, there are still a goodly number of folks who spend their summer Saturdays "putting up" fruits and vegetables for the winter.

Before in-home refrigeration became commonplace, food preservation was literally a matter of life and death. The struggle to grow food and preserve enough of it to last through the period from the last harvest of the fall to the first harvest of the spring was a vital concern to families throughout the South.

Vegetables and fruits were preserved by several methods that included salting, pickling, drying and "putting up" in root cellars. Although effective for preventing spoilage, each method changed the taste and texture of the food.

Canning, a method of preserving food by sealing it in sterilized glass jars or metal cans, was the answer to preventing food from spoiling while also preserving much of its taste, texture and nutritional value.

The basic canning process was invented in France in 1795, but it wasn't until the invention of the metal can in 1810 that the commercial canning industry came into being (ironically, the can opener wasn't invented for another forty-eight years). In 1858, John Mason invented the glass jar that still bears his name, and home canning became feasible.

The process for home canning has remained essentially the same since it was invented more than two hundred years ago. Food is cooked thoroughly to kill bacteria and placed into sterilized glass jars. The jars are sealed and then placed in a boiling water bath that raises the interior temperature of the food to about 250 degrees, pressure sealing the jar. The length of time each food needs to be processed varies based on the food and its acidity. Some foods, such as green beans, which have low acidity, must be processed in a steam canner.

Although the basic technique of canning has changed little since our great-grandmothers' day, the bacteria that canning tries to kill have changed quite a bit, evolving into potentially lethal organisms. Because of this, it is important to keep up on the latest information on canning safety. One of the best sources for this information is the consumer sciences service at your state university or your state department of agriculture. They have lots of free reference material and advice.

Pickles

Although cucumbers are the most common, any vegetable or fruit preserved in an acidic liquid is a pickle. The earliest record of pickles dates back to 2030 BC in Mesopotamia, where they pickled cucumbers brought to the region from India. Pickles are mentioned in the books of Numbers and Isaiah in the Bible and are common to nearly every culture on Earth.

The word pickle comes from the Middle English *pikel*, which came into use around AD 1400. Pickles were extremely popular in Elizabethan England, with the Queen herself reported as a serious connoisseur.

Pickles came to the South with the Jamestown colonists and were being produced in Virginia by 1608.

Bread and Butter Pickles

Bread and butter pickles are truly one of the most delightful Southern foods. Sweet, slightly hot and a little sour, they are enjoyed throughout the region. This recipe is based on several from the late 1950s.

Yield: about 8 pints

4 quarts pickling cucumbers, peeled and thinly
   sliced
8 medium sweet onions, peeled and thinly
   sliced
½ cup pickling salt

5 cups sugar
1½ teaspoons turmeric
1 teaspoon celery seed
2 tablespoons mustard seed
5 cups apple cider vinegar

In a 4-quart mixing bowl, combine cucumbers, onions and salt. Cover with crushed ice and allow to stand, tightly covered, for 3 hours. Drain completely.

Sterilize eight 1-pint jars with lids and bands, ladle and canning funnel; leave in hot water until ready to use.

Place cucumber mixture in an 8- to 10-quart stockpot. Add the sugar, spices and vinegar and bring to a simmer, stirring constantly with a wooden spoon.

Using the sterilized ladle and funnel, pack the pickles into hot, sterilized jars, leaving ½ inch of head space in each jar; process in a boiling water bath as directed by manufacturer of the canner.

Watermelon Rind Pickles

Watermelons hail from Africa and were brought to the South by Spanish and Portuguese explorers. Native Americans took to the new plant, and they were being cultivated in Florida prior to 1654 and along the banks of the Mississippi by the time Father Marquette passed through in 1673. One of the oldest named varieties is the Carolina watermelon, listed by Bernard McMahon, Thomas Jefferson's seed supplier, in his 1802 catalogue.

Mark Twain, an avowed watermelon aficionado, wrote: "The true Southern watermelon is a boon apart, and not to be mentioned with commoner things. It is chief of this world's luxuries, king by the grace of God over all the fruits of the earth. When one has tasted it, he knows what the angels eat. It was not a Southern watermelon that Eve took; we know it because she repented."

Pickles made from the white rind of watermelons have been around since the early 1800s. Lettice Bryan published a recipe for them in *The Kentucky Housewife* (1839), which is the earliest printed recipe I'm aware of.

Although there are variations in the recipes, the pickles are almost universally sweet and flavored with stick or ground cinnamon. Some contain additional spices such as nutmeg, mace or ginger. This recipe is typical of several from the late nineteenth century.

Yield: 10 pints

7 pounds watermelon rind	1 quart white vinegar
1 tablespoon slaked lime (calcium carbonate)	1 tablespoon whole allspice
1 gallon water	10 teaspoons cloves
3¾ pounds granulated sugar	10 (2-inch-long) sticks cinnamon

Using a sharp knife, remove pink and green from watermelon. Cut remaining white rind into 1- to 1½-inch cubes.

In a nonreactive pot or bowl, combine lime and water and stir until dissolved. Place cubed rind in limewater and soak overnight.

Remove rind from limewater; wash in several changes of water.

In a large canning kettle, cover rind with water and bring to a rolling boil. Reduce heat and simmer until rind is tender, about 2 hours. A broom straw should easily pierce rind.

Drain fruit. In a 4-quart saucepan over medium heat, dissolve sugar into vinegar, stirring constantly. Add allspice and bring to a boil.

Divide rind evenly between 10 sterilized, 1-pint canning jars; add 1 teaspoon cloves and 1 cinnamon stick to each jar. Carefully pour boiling sugar and vinegar solution into each jar, leaving ½ inch headspace. Seal jars with sterilized lids and process in boiling water bath according to manufacturer's directions.

Chow Chow

Chow chow (also called pickalilly or picadilli) is a spicy, sweet, hot relish popular in all parts of the South. It originated in India or China, depending on which story you believe, and made its way to the West by way of British seamen. One of the earliest printed recipes for chow chow was published in 1867 by Annabella P. Hill in *Mrs. Hill's New Cook Book*.

There are many variations on the recipe. Cabbage is usually universal; it can also contain any and all combinations of okra, zucchini, corn, various peppers, tomatoes, onion and carrots.

Chow chow is served as a condiment or garnish, especially with pinto beans; this recipe is typical of several from the early twentieth century.

Yield 5½ pints

5 red bell peppers, diced	3 cups sugar
2 large green tomatoes, diced	2 cups white vinegar
2 large sweet onions, diced	1 cup water
1 small head cabbage, diced	1 tablespoon mustard seeds
¼ cup pickling salt	1½ teaspoons celery seeds

Place vegetables in a 6- to 8-quart Dutch oven. Sprinkle salt evenly over vegetables, cover and refrigerate overnight.

Place vegetables in colander; rinse and drain; return mixture to Dutch oven and add remaining ingredients.

Bring to a boil over medium-high heat; reduce heat and simmer for 3 to 5 minutes.

Using a sterilized ladle and canning funnel, pack hot chow chow into hot, sterilized half-pint jars, filling to ½ inch from top. Remove air bubbles and wipe jar rims with clean, dry, lint-free cloth. Cover immediately with metal lids and screw on bands.

Process for 15 minutes in a boiling water bath.

Glory in a Jar

Preserving Fruit

Preserved fruits were highly sought after by early Southerners to add nutrients and flavor to their rather bland winter diets. There were several methods for preserving fruits: drying, pickling in vinegar, using brandy or other alcohol and either packing in sugar or using sugar to make jams, jellies or preserves. In colonial times, when sugar was scarce and expensive, pickled, brandied and dried fruits were far more common; as sugar became easier to obtain and more affordable, nineteenth-century cookbooks exploded with recipes for jams, jellies and conserves.

Pickled Blackberries

Pickled blackberries are an addictive combination of tart and sweet and are traditionally served over ice cream or pound cake. This recipe is based on several recipes from the late 1800s and early 1900s.

Yield: 16 half-pint jars

4 quarts blackberries
1 pint apple cider vinegar
1 teaspoon ground cinnamon
1 teaspoon allspice

1 teaspoon cloves
1 teaspoon nutmeg
1 pound sugar

Wash and pick over blackberries.
In a 2 quart nonreactive saucepan, mix together vinegar, cinnamon, allspice, cloves and nutmeg. Bring to a boil over medium-high heat, then reduce heat, stir in sugar and simmer for 5 minutes. Place blackberries in hot, sterilized half-pint jars. Pour hot vinegar mixture over berries. Seal and process in boiling water bath for 5 minutes.

Brandied Peaches

As the name implies, brandied peaches use brandy as the acid to preserve the fruit (when vinegar is used, the fruit is called "pickled"). The practice of preserving fruits in brandy goes back to colonial times. In *The Virginia House-Wife* (1824), Mary Randolph gave instructions for preserving peaches, cherries and plums in brandy.

161

Yield: 6 quarts

8 pounds firm fully ripe freestone peaches
2 cups lemonade (see page 196)
6 pounds sugar, divided
2 teaspoons salt
2 quarts boiling water
2 pints peach brandy

In a 6- to 8-quart Dutch oven, place a few of the peaches in the bottom of the pot and fill with enough water to cover the peaches to a depth of 2 or 3 inches. Remove peaches and bring water to a rolling boil. Using a slotted spoon, carefully place peaches two or three at a time into boiling water for one minute to loosen the skins; immediately plunge into a bowl of ice water.

Drain the peaches and cut in half. Remove stone and peel.

Place lemonade into a 1-quart mixing bowl; drop the peach halves into the lemonade to prevent discoloration.

In the Dutch oven, bring 2 quarts of water to a rolling boil. Dissolve 3 pounds of sugar (about 6¾ cups) and 2 teaspoons of salt in the boiling water.

Using a slotted spoon, transfer peaches from the lemonade to the syrup mixture; boil for 6 minutes. Remove peaches from the syrup and put into a large deep bowl, reserving the syrup. Return syrup to a boil and cook for another 5 minutes; pour over the peaches, cover the bowl and let it stand overnight.

Drain the syrup off the peaches into the Dutch oven and add the remaining sugar; boil another five minutes and pour back over the peaches, cover and allow to stand overnight again.

Return peaches and syrup mixture to Dutch oven and simmer over medium heat until fruit is heated through.

Using a slotted spoon, carefully pack the peach halves cavity side down in hot, sterilized glass jars, overlapping the layers. Leave ½ inch head space in each jar.

Add 4 tablespoons of peach brandy to each jar.

Bring the syrup to a boil and, using a hot, sterilized ladle and canning funnel, pour the syrup over the peaches, leaving ¼ inch headspace in each jar.

Seal jars and process for 5 minutes in a boiling water bath. Remove from bath and allow to cool on a wire rack. Remove bands and store in a cool, dry place.

Jams, Jellies, Preserves, Conserves and Compotes

Jelly, jam, preserves, conserves, marmalades and fruit butters are very similar to one another and all have roots that reach back to the earliest days of Southern settlement. All are made from fruit, preserved by infusing it with sugar and thickened either by boiling down or, after the dawn of the twentieth century, by a thickening agent such as pectin.

Jelly is a mixture of fruit juice and sugar that is clear and firm enough to hold its shape, while jam is made from crushed or chopped fruit. Jam holds its shape but is less firm than jelly. When jams were made from a mixture of fruits, they were usually called conserves, especially when the recipes contained citrus fruits, nuts, raisins or coconut.

Preserves are made of small, whole fruits or pieces of fruits in a clear, thick, slightly gelled syrup; marmalades are soft, transparent fruit jellies that contain small pieces of fruit or citrus peel.

Fruit butters, such as apple or peach butter, are made from fruit pulp cooked with sugar until thickened.

In *The Virginia House-Wife* (1824), Mary Randolph gave recipes for marmalade made from peaches and pears, jelly from currants, quince and cherries and jams from strawberries, gooseberries and raspberries.

Strawberry Jam

Modern jam recipes usually call for adding pectin, an enzyme that helps the jam to thicken. This recipe, based on several from the late 1800s, uses the pectin naturally released by the strawberries when they are crushed to thicken the jam.

Yield: 5 pints

8 cups strawberries, hulled
2 tablespoons lemon juice
5 cups sugar

Wash a canning funnel, six 1-pint jars, bands and new flat lids in hot soapy water and rinse well. Put jars in a 6- to 8-quart saucepan with enough water to cover; bring to a boil. Put funnel, bands and lids in a separate container and pour boiling water to cover.
In a 6- to 8-quart Dutch oven, combine strawberries, lemon juice and sugar. Using a potato masher or the back of a metal spoon, crush berries. Heat to a rolling boil over high heat, stirring frequently.

Allow mixture to boil uncovered, stirring frequently until jam is translucent and thick, about 25 minutes. Skim off foam and immediately pour jam into hot sterilized jars, leaving ¼ inch headspace. Wipe rim of jars using a clean, lint-free cloth. Seal jars and process in a boiling water bath as directed by manufacturer.

Mrs. S.W. Wengrow's Spiced Tomato Jam

Mrs. Wengrow is a delightful young lady (101 on her most recent birthday) from South Carolina who has made tomato jam for many years as presents for friends and family.

Tomato jam dates back at least to the early nineteenth century; Lettice Bryan gave directions for making a similar jam in *The Kentucky Housewife* (1839). Mrs. Wengrow adapted this recipe from one published many years ago on the Sure-Jell Pectin package.

Yield: 5 pints

about 2½ pounds tomatoes, to make 3 cups
  prepared tomatoes
1½ teaspoon grated lemon rind
¼ cup lemon juice
½ teaspoon allspice

½ teaspoon cinnamon
¼ teaspoon ground cloves
1 box Sure-Jell or other powdered pectin
4½ cups sugar

Scald tomatoes in boiling water for 30 seconds, then plunge into ice water. The skins should peel off easily.

Core and seed tomatoes and cut into small pieces, discarding any pieces of skin and white pith. Simmer tomatoes in a 6- to 8-quart saucepan for 10 minutes.

Meanwhile, wash a canning funnel, six 1-pint jars, bands and new flat lids in hot soapy water and rinse well. Put jars in a 6- to 8-quart saucepan with enough water to cover; bring to a boil. Put funnel, bands and lids in a separate container and pour boiling water to cover.

As tomatoes are simmering and jars are sterilizing, grate the rind of one lemon, making sure to get only the yellow skin. (Chilling the lemon makes grating easier.) Squeeze lemon juice and, if necessary, top up with bottled lemon juice to make ¼ cup. Measure spices, lemon rind and sugar. Measure 3 cups of simmered tomatoes and return to saucepan. Add lemon rind, lemon juice, spices and pectin. Cook and stir over high heat until mixture comes to a hard boil. Add sugar all at once and bring to a full rolling boil on high heat. Continue to stir, until the boil cannot be stirred down. The mixture will become foamy. Boil hard, stirring constantly, for 1 minute. Remove from heat and skim off foam with a metal spoon.

Using canning tongs, take one jar at a time out of the boiling water, drain well and, using the canning funnel, ladle in tomato mixture, leaving ¼ inch space at the top. Wipe jar rim and threads well with damp cloth, place a flat lid on and screw on bands until tight. Repeat until you have filled 5 jars. (Any excess can be put in the extra jar and kept in the refrigerator; it will be ready to eat in about two hours.)

Process the filled jars in a boiling water bath for 10 minutes. You will hear a little "ping" as the jars seal. After they cool completely, press middle of lid lightly with your fingertip. It should feel depressed. If lid pops back, it is not sealed and jar should be refrigerated. Store sealed jars in a cool place away from sunlight.

Hot Pepper Jelly

This sweet and spicy Southern classic is often served with country ham or green beans. Recipes date back to the last quarter of the nineteenth century.

Yield: about 5 pints

½ cup hot red chilies, seeded and coarsely chopped
½ cup hot green chilies, seeded and coarsely chopped
1 cup onion, chopped
1½ cup vinegar
5 cups sugar
2 pouches liquid pectin

In a food processor fitted with a metal blade, process the hot chilies, onion and vinegar until minced very fine.

In a 4-quart, nonreactive saucepan over medium-high heat, combine sugar, vinegar and chili mixture and bring to a boil. Cook for 1 minute. Remove from heat and stir in the pectin. Let sit 5 minutes and then remove the foam with a slotted spoon.

Ladle into sterilized jars and seal according to manufacturer's directions. Turn the jars upside down occasionally to keep the chilies mixed until the jelly is cool and has set.

Blackberry Preserves

Blackberries ripen in late June or early July and have been a staple for making jams, jellies and preserves for generations. This recipe is adapted from one by Annabella P. Hill, published in 1872 in *Mrs. Hill's Southern Practical Cookery and Receipt Book*.

Yield: about 6 pints

1 pound blackberries
1 pound sugar
2 tablespoons lemon juice

In a 6- to 8-quart Dutch oven with lid, combine blackberries, sugar and lemon juice. Let sit, covered, for one hour.

Place Dutch oven on stove and bring mixture to a boil over medium heat. Reduce heat and simmer until the mixture thickens enough for the liquid to coat the back of a spoon. If desired, strain through a large strainer to remove seeds.

Using a sterilized ladle and canning funnel, place blackberry mixture into sterilized one-pint jars, leaving ½ inch head room in each jar. Follow manufacturer's directions for processing.

Apple Butter

Apples are a favorite food in the mountain South, especially in the Blue Ridge and Great Smoky Mountains. Families scattered by time and distance often return to the family homeplace in the fall when the apple harvest is ready for picking to make apple butter from treasured family recipes. This one is based on several from the early twentieth century.

Yield: 6 pints

12 pounds apples
2 cups apple cider
5 cups sugar

4 teaspoons cinnamon
2 teaspoons allspice
1 teaspoon cloves

Place apples in a large kettle, cover with water and bring to a boil. Reduce heat and simmer until apples are tender, about 1½ hours. Drain.

Using a food mill or food processor, puree apples, discarding seeds and skins.

Place apple pulp into a 6- to 8-quart Dutch oven. Add remaining ingredients and bring to a simmer over medium heat; reduce heat and cook over low heat, stirring occasionally, until thickened. (This takes about 1½ hours.) Pour into hot, sterilized pint canning jars to within ¼ inch of top. Seal and process in a boiling water bath canner for 10 minutes.

Dried Apples

Apples have been a part of the English diet since at least the late 1470s and came to the South with the earliest settlers. Native Americans took a shine to the new fruit, and they also cultivated apple trees. The early trees bore only a small amount of fruit because native bees didn't favor the trees and there was little pollination. It took the arrival of the European honey bee in the early 1700s before apple trees became plentiful in the South.

Apples kept well in root cellars, and Southerners developed varieties such as the Arkansas Black that matured late in the season (generally in October) and would keep for several months in cool, dry places.

Drying was another popular method of storing apples for winter use. The apples were cored and cut into thin wedges or rings and dried in the sun for twenty-four to forty-eight hours until all the moisture had evaporated. In the colonial South, small batches of apples were sometimes dried whole by stringing them together and hanging them from the rafters of backcountry cabins.

Dried apples were eaten out of hand and also reconstituted with water to use for cooking.

1 dozen ripe, firm apples
¼ cup lemon juice
1 quart water

Wash, core and peel apples.
Using a sharp paring knife, cut into wedges and slice into slices about ¼ inch thick.
Dip apple slices into lemon juice and water mixture to prevent apples from turning brown while drying.
Lay treated apple slices on trays and cover with cheesecloth. Place in a well-ventilated area in full sunlight, turning slices every few hours. Drying takes two to three days; take trays inside at night.

Robert Lahser photo.

CHAPTER 12

Corn Bread, Biscuits and Other Breads

The idea that one can consume too much cornbread is a myth perpetrated by corn-haters and small-minded bureaucrats. I myself eat more cornbread than some small nations, and I'm an epitome of health, vigor, vim, charm, and good posture. I also control the weather.
—Jeremy Jackson, The Cornbread Book

The idea that bread is the staff of life took firm hold in the South. Southerners, if left unsupervised, will have biscuits and gravy with breakfast, corn bread or white bread with the noontime meal and biscuits, corn bread, spoon bread or rolls (if not a combination thereof) with supper.

Although the buttermilk biscuit is the hallmark of Southern bread making, breads made from corn were staples for settlers on the Southern frontier and have always been an important part of the region's foodways.

ASH CAKES, HOECAKES AND PONE

When the first European settlers arrived in the New World, they found Native Americans making several different types of breads from maize (corn) and beans.

Colonists called maize "Indian corn" or simply "Indian." The earliest recipes use the term (as in Indian bread, Indian cakes, Indian pudding) to differentiate these corn breads from breads made from wheat flour. To the gentry, who were used to fluffy, finely ground wheat flour baked into loaves in the baker's oven, eating these coarse native breads made from cracked corn was probably about as appealing as chewing on a pine cone. But for the vast majority of European settlers, the corn pone of the Indians wasn't any worse than the rye bread or oatcakes they were used to eating back home, and they adapted quite well to the new grain.

As the colonists worked with the new corn flour, they soon learned an interesting quirk: yeast doesn't have much effect on cornmeal, so these early corn breads were flat as a flitter.

By whatever name, these early breads were all made of coarse cornmeal mixed with water and a little salt. As the name implies, ash cakes were cooked on rocks placed in the ashes of the fire; hoecakes were cooked on a clean (relatively speaking) hoe propped over the fire; and pone was simmered in a pot or skillet.

Hoecakes or Johnny Cakes

Some sources suggest the name "Johnny cake" came from "journey cake," a name given to the flat breads because they were well adapted for eating on the move. Others believe it was derived from the Native American term *joniken*, a type of flat, fried cornmeal bread.

The earliest recipe for Johnny cakes or hoecakes is found in *American Cookery* by Amelia Simmons, published in 1796. For contemporary gardeners pondering how they got enough batter on the hoe, it should be noted that eighteenth-century hoes were considerably larger than the ones found in today's tool shed. The same recipe will work for ash cakes by making the dough thicker and baking at 400 degrees F until lightly browned.

Yield: 6 to 8 servings

2 cups sifted cornmeal
½ teaspoon salt
cold water to mix
1 tablespoon lard or vegetable shortening

In a medium bowl, mix meal with salt. Add enough water to make a thick batter.
Heat lard or shortening in a 10-inch cast-iron skillet over medium-high heat. Pour batter into skillet to make cakes with a diameter of about 6 inches, smoothing out with spatula if necessary. Cook until bottom is golden brown, then turn and cook other side. Serve hot with butter and honey or cane syrup.

Corn Pone

The name for this early bread comes from the Algonquian Indian word *apan*, meaning, "baked." The Virginia colonists learned how to make apan from the Native Americans around Jamestown in the early seventeenth century, making this one of the earliest Southern breads.

Yield: 6 to 8 servings

3 tablespoons lard
3 cups cornmeal
2½ cups boiling water
3 teaspoons salt

Place lard in 10-inch cast-iron skillet and place in oven. Preheat oven to 350 degrees F. When oven is ready, remove skillet, carefully swirl to coat with melted lard and pour remaining lard into other ingredients. Mix well and pour batter into hot skillet. Bake until golden brown, about 45 to 50 minutes.

Cornmeal Mush

This simple breakfast cereal goes far back into the history of the early South. In the Carolina backcountry of the eighteenth century, cornmeal mush was oftentimes the only thing served for both breakfast and supper, with the noontime meal being the only one of the day to feature meat and vegetables. It was simple to prepare and was always available when other food was scarce.

For all its simplicity, it still has an appealing taste today, served as it was in colonial times with butter and sweetened with sorghum molasses or honey and cinnamon.

Yield: 2 to 4 servings

2¾ cups water
½ cup cornmeal
¾ teaspoon salt

In a heavy 2-quart saucepan over high heat, bring water to a rolling boil. Sprinkle cornmeal into boiling water, stirring constantly. Add salt, reduce heat to medium low and cook until mixture has consistency of hot cereal, about 30 minutes.

CORN BREAD

After the colonists set up gristmills and were able to grind corn to a consistency closer to wheat flour, recipes using cornmeal began showing up in early Southern cookbooks. The earliest corn bread recipes were essentially just corn pone baked in a skillet. As the recipes evolved, fat was added to improve flavor (on the Southern frontier, this was usually deer fat or bear grease), and milk and eggs were added to help with leavening.

Grandma Hill's Corn Bread

This is the quintessential Southern corn bread, made from white cornmeal with buttermilk added for extra flavor and lift. It has a light texture inside and a crunchy brown crust.

Yield: 6 to 8 servings

¼ cup shortening
1 egg
1⅓ cups whole buttermilk
1 cup all-purpose flour

1 cup cornmeal
1 tablespoon double-acting baking powder
1 teaspoon baking soda
½ teaspoon salt

Place the shortening into a 10-inch cast-iron skillet and place in the oven; preheat oven to 425 degrees F.
In a medium bowl, beat together egg and buttermilk; sift together flour, cornmeal, baking powder, baking soda and salt. Add to the buttermilk and egg mixture and mix until just blended.
When oven is ready, carefully remove hot skillet, pour melted shortening into batter and mix well. Pour batter into hot skillet and return to oven.
Bake until top is golden brown, about 25 minutes.

Cracklin' Corn Bread or Cracklin' Bread

Cracklins are the crispy goodies that float to the top when pork fat is rendered into lard. They were then added to the corn bread before baking. This bread was traditionally made in the late fall and early winter at "hog-killin' time."

Corn Dodgers or Corn Sticks

Corn dodgers and corn sticks are made from essentially the same recipe as other corn breads, but the cooking method is different. Corn dodgers are either fried in hot grease in a skillet or are dropped into simmering liquid, such as the pot liquor from a simmering pot of collard greens. Corn sticks are made in a special cast-iron pan with indentations shaped like little ears of corn.

Hush Puppies

These simple bits of fried cornmeal dough, often found next to a mess of catfish or a pile of steaming pulled pork barbecue, are among the most beloved of Southern breads.

Although their origin is lost to antiquity, they date back at least to the time of the First World War. The story goes that folks frying fish on creek banks would drop bits of cornmeal into the hot oil and throw them to the hound dogs to keep them quiet and away from the kettle of fish.

Yield: about 5 dozen

oil for frying
2 cups self-rising cornmeal
2 cups self-rising flour
½ teaspoon salt
½ teaspoon pepper

1½ teaspoons sugar
1 large onion, finely grated
2 cups buttermilk
1 large egg

In a large Dutch oven, pour enough oil to cover the bottom to a depth of 4 to 6 inches. Using a deep-fat thermometer, heat the oil to 375 degrees F.
In a large mixing bowl, mix together cornmeal, flour, salt, pepper, sugar and onion.
In a separate bowl, whisk together buttermilk and egg and slowly add to dry ingredients, whisking just enough to blend.
Drop batter by level tablespoonfuls into hot oil, being careful not to crowd.
Fry 5 to 7 minutes or until golden. Drain on paper towels.

SPOON BREAD

This dish represents the fusion of three cultures—Native American corn combined with the French soufflé technique by African American cooks—to create a uniquely Southern dish.

While spoon bread traces its ancestry back to Native American *apan*, this refined, light and fluffy cornmeal soufflé is about as far removed from corn pone as sleeping on a creek bank is from a night at one of Charleston's historic inns.

Spoon bread by other names first appeared in early eighteenth-century cookbooks; the name spoon bread first appeared in print in 1904.

Spoon bread, as the name implies, is soft and light and is spooned onto supper plates as an accompaniment to meat and vegetables, usually in place of rice or potatoes.

Awendaw

Awendaw was a Native American village north of Charleston where their cooking traditions mingled with African American and European influences.

Sarah Rutledge published the recipe for "Owendaw Cornbread" in *The Carolina Housewife* in 1847; although this is the first printed recipe for what we consider spoon bread, the dish is almost certainly older than that.

Yield: 8 servings

2 tablespoons unsalted butter, melted
4 large eggs, slightly beaten
2 cups milk

2 cups cooked hominy (grits—see page 59)
1 cup cornmeal
½ teaspoon salt

Preheat oven to 375 degrees F.
In a medium bowl, stir butter, eggs and milk into hot grits.
Stir in cornmeal and salt and mix until a very thin batter forms.
Pour batter into a greased 2-quart baking dish and bake until set, about 30 minutes.

Virginia Spoon Bread

Early recipes relied on just eggs for leavening, but this modern version gets extra help from baking powder and baking soda. This recipe is adapted from one by Laura Thornton Knowles in *Southern Recipes Tested By Myself*, published in 1913.

Yield: 6 servings

1 cup boiling water	1 tablespoon baking powder
1½ cup cornmeal	1 tablespoon lard or shortening
1½ cup milk	3 eggs, separated
½ teaspoon salt	1 tablespoon butter

Preheat oven to 375 degrees F.
In a 2-quart mixing bowl, pour boiling water over cornmeal and stir until smooth; beat in milk, salt, baking powder, lard or shortening and egg yolks.
In a small metal bowl, beat egg whites until stiff peaks form; fold into mixture.
Turn into a lightly buttered 1½-quart casserole dish. Bake until set, about 25 to 30 minutes.

THE RISE OF THE SOUTHERN BISCUIT

Biscuits have always been the hallmark of a true Southern cook. Light, hot and fluffy, they grace breakfast plates and supper tables throughout the region, alone or filled with all manner of goodies from country ham to blackberry preserves.

Before biscuits could take their place at the Southern table, several hurdles had to be overcome by a combination of economics, chemistry and technology.

Beaten Biscuits

These were probably the first biscuits to grace the Southern table; a recipe for a similar type of bread is found in Mary Randolph's *The Virginia House-Wife* (1824) with the Indian-sounding name "*Apoquiniminc Cakes.*"

In the 1700s, before the invention of baking soda, baking powder or commercially available yeast, a substance called pearl ash (calcium carbonate for the chemically curious) started to gain popularity in home baking as a means of rising bread dough without having to wait for yeast to act. Pearl ash did a fine job of leavening, but it had a slight drawback.

Pearl ash was made by pouring water over wood ashes and collecting the solid that remained. The problem was that this is the same process used to make lye; add a little animal fat to lye and you have lye soap. When the pearl ash was used to leaven biscuits, there was enough residual lye in it to react with the lard or butter in the dough and give the biscuits a slightly bitter, soapy taste.

Searching for a quicker way to leaven biscuits, cooks found that when unleavened dough was folded over and pounded with a mallet or an axe handle and the process repeated enough times, tiny air pockets formed in the dough. When the dough was baked, the air pockets expanded and caused the biscuits to rise, although the result was somewhere between a cracker and a biscuit rather than the light, fluffy biscuits we know today. Nevertheless, beaten biscuits were a staple in the early South.

Mary Stuart Smith wrote in her *Virginia Cookery-Book* (1885), "In the Virginia of the olden time no breakfast or tea-table was thought to be properly furnished without a plate of these indispensable biscuits."

Yield: about 24 small biscuits

4 cups flour
1 teaspoon salt
¼ cup lard or vegetable shortening
1 cup cold milk

Preheat oven to 400 degrees F.
In a large bowl, mix flour and salt. Add lard or shortening and work into flour with your fingers until mixture is crumbly. Add milk and mix well with dough whisk or spatula.
Turn out onto lightly floured surface and knead 3 or 4 times; pat out dough about 1 inch thick.
Using a wooden mallet, gently beat dough over entire surface. Fold dough in half and repeat. Continue to beat and fold until dough contains many small blisters (about 20 to 30 minutes).
Roll out dough ½ inch thick and cut into rounds with a floured 2-inch biscuit cutter; re-roll and cut scraps. Using a fork, prick the top of each biscuit several times. Place biscuits on greased baking sheet; bake until golden brown, about 20 to 25 minutes.

The Modern Biscuit

After the invention of baking soda in the mid-1840s and baking powder in 1856, the biscuit as we know it became part of Southern foodways. The widespread availability of inexpensive, mass-produced wheat flour in the last two decades of the nineteenth century put biscuits on the tables of all but the poorest Southerners. Since the baking powder and baking soda leavened without having to spend all that time beating dough, making biscuits became a matter of minutes instead of hours, and their popularity greatly increased.

Buttermilk Biscuits

Also called "soda biscuits" in early cookbooks, the combination of baking soda and buttermilk makes for culinary magic.

Buttermilk was widely used in early Southern biscuit recipes. Buttermilk is the "clabber," or liquid that was left over after milk was churned into butter. Historically, buttermilk was used in cooking because in the days before refrigeration, whole milk (or "sweet" milk, as it was mostly called) was not always readily available.

In addition to providing extra flavor, buttermilk is acidic; it combines with the baking soda (which is a base, chemically speaking) to produce carbon dioxide, which makes the biscuits rise.

Yield: 8 biscuits

2 cups flour
½ teaspoon baking soda
1 tablespoon sugar
¼ teaspoon salt

½ cup shortening (or ¼ cup plus ¼ cup lard), chilled
¾ cup buttermilk

Preheat oven to 450 degrees F.

In a large mixing bowl, sift together flour, soda, sugar and salt. Using a pastry blender or your fingers, cut in shortening until mixture resembles coarse crumbs. Make a well in the center; add buttermilk. Stir just until dough comes together.

Place dough on lightly floured work surface. Using your hands, gently push dough together and pat it out to ½ inch thickness; repeat 3 or 4 more times. Cut with biscuit cutter dipped in flour between each cut.

Transfer biscuits to a baking sheet and bake until golden brown, about 10 to 12 minutes. Serve warm.

Sweet Milk (Baking Powder) Biscuits

After baking soda came along in the mid-1840s, chemists and cooks began to experiment with ways to make it better. In 1855, Eben Norton Horsford and George F. Wilson founded what was to become Rumford Chemical Company, makers of the country's most successful baking powder. They combined baking soda with cream of tartar, which is an acid, and a drying agent to keep the two from reacting until liquid was added. This made biscuits rise better, and

Rumford Baking Powder became one of the South's favorite brands for generations. Double-acting baking powder, which caused dough to rise once while it was being mixed and then again when the dough was baked, came along in 1899.

Since baking powder already contained an acid, buttermilk was no longer needed to act with the soda, so recipes for "Sweet Milk Biscuits" started appearing in Southern cookbooks in the last quarter of the nineteenth century.

This recipe is adapted from one by Mary A. Wilson, published in *Rumford Southern Recipes*, put out by the Rumford Chemical Works in 1930.

Yield: 8 to 12 biscuits

2½ cups flour
4 teaspoons baking powder
1 tablespoon sugar
1 teaspoon salt

½ cup shortening (or ¼ cup plus ¼ cup lard), chilled
⅔ cup whole milk

Preheat oven to 450 degrees F.
In a large mixing bowl, sift together flour, baking powder, sugar and salt. Using a pastry blender or your fingers, cut in shortening until mixture resembles coarse crumbs. Make a well in the center; add milk. Stir just until dough comes together.
Place dough on lightly floured work surface. Using your hands, gently push dough together and pat it out to ½ inch thickness; repeat 3 or 4 more times. Cut with biscuit cutter dipped in flour between each cut.
Transfer biscuits to a baking sheet and bake until golden brown, about 10 to 12 minutes. Serve hot.

Fried Biscuits

These sinful delights that folks in Maryland call "chicken biscuits" are a guilty pleasure enjoyed in several parts of the region.

Fried biscuits are cooked in the fat left over after chicken is fried and in Maryland are served (along with the fried chicken) smothered in cream gravy.

Fried biscuits can be made with any of the biscuit recipes on the previous pages, with a slight variation in technique: knead the dough a little more vigorously and roll it thinner so the biscuits will absorb less fat.

The frying fat should be hot, about 360 degrees F, and come a little less than halfway up the sides of the biscuit. Be sure not to crowd the biscuits; fry them until browned on one side (about 4 minutes) then turn and brown on the other side.

Sweet Potato Biscuits

Sweet potato biscuits are another gift to Southern cooking from African Americans. They trace their roots back to the African tradition of using mashed starchy tubers to make bread rather than milled flour.

In the New World, the biscuits go back to colonial times; Thomas Jefferson was reported to be a fan of biscuits made with sweet potatoes.

During the food shortages that plagued the South during the Civil War and the five years following its end, they became familiar to all Southerners as a way to stretch out flour, which was a scarce and expensive commodity.

Yield: about one dozen

1⅔ cups flour
1 tablespoon brown sugar
2½ teaspoons baking powder
1½ teaspoons salt

6 tablespoons unsalted butter, cut into small
  pieces
¾ cup cooked and pureed sweet potato
¼ cup half and half
vegetable oil cooking spray

Preheat oven to 425 degrees F.
In a large mixing bowl, combine flour, sugar, baking powder and salt.
Using a pastry blender or your fingers, cut butter into flour mixture until mix resembles coarse crumbs.
Add sweet potato and half and half; using a wooden spoon or dough whisk, mix until dough comes together.
Turn dough out onto lightly floured work surface and knead gently until dough holds together, about five or six times.
Roll out dough to a thickness of ½ inch. Using a biscuit cutter dipped in flour between each cut, cut out biscuits and place on a sheet pan sprayed with vegetable oil cooking spray.
Bake until golden brown, about 10 to 12 minutes.

YEAST BREADS

Although yeast was used in brewing by ancient Egyptians, reliable, predictable and commercially available yeast didn't come along until 1872. Beginning at the turn of the twentieth century, Southern cookbooks started to feature more recipes for yeast breads, and they took their place at the Southern table with increasing regularity.

Angel Biscuits

Angel biscuits are a curious culinary hybrid; they are extremely light, bread-like biscuits that use both yeast and chemical leavening.

It's highly likely that this unusual combination of leavening agents may have come about as a culinary insurance policy (another name for angel biscuits is "bride's biscuits"), with the double dose of leavening intended to help ensure success for beginning cooks. Note that the dough for this recipe must rise in the refrigerator overnight.

Yield: about one dozen biscuits

2½ teaspoons yeast
½ cup warm water (not over 110 degrees F)
5 cups flour
1 teaspoon baking soda
1 teaspoon salt
3 teaspoons baking powder

3 tablespoons sugar
¾ cup vegetable shortening
2 cups warm buttermilk (not over 110 degrees F)
cooking spray

In a small bowl, dissolve yeast in warm water.

In a large mixing bowl, sift together flour, baking soda, salt, baking powder and sugar.

Using a pastry blender or your fingers, cut in shortening until mixture resembles coarse meal. Stir in buttermilk and yeast mixture, gently stirring until dough forms a loose ball.

Spray the inside of a 1-gallon zipper-lock food storage bag with cooking spray and place dough inside; refrigerate overnight.

Preheat oven to 400 degrees F.

On a floured work surface, roll dough out to a thickness of ½ inch. Cut out biscuits and place 2 inches apart on an ungreased baking sheet. Bake until golden brown, about 10 to 12 minutes.

Sixty-Minute Rolls

This is an old tried and true recipe that is easy to make even for beginners. As the name implies, you can make these rolls from start to finish in one hour.

Yield: 24 rolls

1 cup whole milk	3 tablespoons sugar
½ cup water	2 (¼-ounce) packages active dry yeast
¼ cup butter	3½ cups flour

Preheat oven to 450 degrees F.

In a 1-quart saucepan over low heat, combine milk, water and butter; heat until barely warm, no more than 110 degrees F.

Dissolve sugar and yeast in the milk mixture. Pour mixture into a large mixing bowl.

Add the flour a little at a time, gently stirring until dough forms.

Knead dough for 2 to 3 minutes; place in oiled, covered container and let rise in a warm place for 15 minutes.

Punch dough down and shape into 24 small rolls; place in a shallow greased baking pan with the sides of the rolls just touching.

Let the rolls rise 15 minutes. Bake until golden brown, about 12 to 14 minutes.

Sally Lunn

This high-rising, buttery yeast loaf has been called the aristocrat of Southern breads. Although long identified with the South, this bread is more than likely English, and the recipe probably came to America with the early colonists.

There is quite a dispute as to where this bread got its name. One story goes that Sally Lunn was a teahouse proprietress in Bath, England, during the 1700s and gave us the bread that bears her name. Great story, but several generations of culinary historians and researchers have yet to find any evidence of a resident of Bath named Sally Lunn.

Another story is that the bread's golden top and pale bottom look like the sun and moon; therefore "Sally Lunn" must be a corruption of the French *soliel et lune* (sun and moon). There are even some who maintain that Sally Lunn was George Washington's cook!

One thing we can be sure of is that recipes for breads very similar to Sally Lunn appear in early American cookbooks dating back to about 1770, and it is well loved in the South, particularly in Virginia.

Some modern versions have sweetened this elegant bread beyond all hope of repair; this recipe is closer to the originals.

Yield: 1 loaf

¾ cup milk
6 tablespoons unsalted butter
¼ cup warm water (not over 110 F)
one ¼-ounce package active dry yeast
4 tablespoons sugar, divided

3¼ cups bread flour
1¼ teaspoons salt
3 eggs
Thoroughly butter a 10-inch kugelhopf pan or Turk's head mold; set aside.

Grease bottom and sides of a large bowl; set aside.

In a small saucepan, combine milk and butter; heat until liquid just simmers and allow to cool until barely warm to the tough (no more than 110 degrees F).

In a glass measuring cup, mix warm water, yeast and 1 tablespoon of the sugar. Allow yeast to dissolve until mixture is foamy on top.

In a large mixing bowl, combine flour, remaining sugar, salt and eggs. Using a large wooden spoon, blend ingredients together. Add yeast mixture and milk mixture; stir until dough comes together. Dough will be very wet, like a thick batter.

Pour dough into greased bowl and cover bowl with plastic wrap. Let rise in a warm place until dough has doubled in volume (about 1½ hours).

After rising, stir dough with a wooden spoon and turn out into buttered kugelhopf pan or Turk's head mold. Cover pan loosely with a floured towel and let dough rise again until it again doubles in volume (about 1 hour).

Preheat oven to 350F.

Remove towel; bake loaf until it sounds hollow when tapped, 45 to 50 minutes. Turn loaf out onto a wire rack and cool completely before slicing.

BREAKFAST BREADS

Southerners do not consider breakfast complete without some form of bread. Biscuits fill the bill for savory fare, but sometimes we need a little something sweet.

Pumpkin Gingerbread Bread

Gingerbread came over with the earliest English colonists; this recipe adds Native American pumpkin to the English original.

    The recipe is a scaled-down adaptation of the one used by my friends John and Julie Stehling at their famous Early Girl Eatery in Asheville, North Carolina.

Yield: 3 loaves
vegetable oil cooking spray

graham cracker crumbs
4 cups flour
1½ teaspoons salt
2 teaspoons baking soda
1 teaspoon baking powder
4 teaspoons ground ginger
1 teaspoon ground nutmeg
1 teaspoon ground cinnamon
½ teaspoon ground cloves

½ teaspoon dry mustard
3 cups sugar
½ pound unsalted butter at room temperature
4 large eggs
⅔ cup strong black coffee
one 15-ounce can pumpkin puree
1 cup pecan halves

Preheat oven to 350 degrees F.

Spray 3 loaf pans with vegetable oil cooking spray and coat with crumbs.
In a large mixing bowl, sift together flour, salt, baking soda, baking powder, ginger, nutmeg, cinnamon, cloves, mustard and sugar.
Add butter, eggs, coffee and pumpkin. Mix well. Fold pecans into batter and spoon batter evenly into prepared loaf pans.
Bake until cake tester inserted in center of loaf comes out clean, about 1½ hours.

Moravian Sugar Cake

The Moravians were a German-speaking Protestant sect (from what is now the Czech Republic) who settled the Wachovia Tract in the Piedmont of North Carolina. They founded the village of Salem in 1766, which is now part of present-day Winston-Salem, North Carolina. According to the Historic Foodways staff at Old Salem, the earliest mention of sugar cake, which is traditionally eaten as a breakfast bread, is in a diary left by Maria Rosina Unger dated 1789. Sugar cakes are still given as Christmas gifts in North Carolina to this day.

Yield: 4 cakes, each 7½ by 9 inches

one ¼-ounce package active dry yeast
½ cup warm water (not over 110 degrees F)
1 cup warm, unseasoned mashed potatoes
1 cup sugar
½ cup shortening
¼ cup butter, softened
1 teaspoon salt
2 eggs, beaten
5–6 cups sifted flour
brown sugar
butter
Saigon cinnamon

Dissolve yeast in warm water and set aside.
In a large mixing bowl, mix mashed potatoes, sugar, shortening, butter and salt.
Add yeast mixture and stir until blended. Cover mixing bowl and put bowl in a warm place to rise (about 30 to 45 minutes).
When mixture has started to ferment, stir in eggs and enough sifted flour to make a soft dough. Shape dough into a ball and place in a bowl coated with vegetable oil, turning dough in bowl to evenly coat with oil. Cover bowl with a moist towel and allow dough to rise until it doubles in size, about 2 hours.
Turn dough onto a lightly floured surface and knead 5 minutes or until dough is smooth and elastic.
Divide dough in half and spread out into two greased 13- by 9-inch baking pans. Set aside to rise again.
Preheat oven to 375 degrees F.

After the dough has again doubled in volume, use the handle of a wooden spoon to make a series of holes 1½ to 2 inches apart over the surface of the dough. Fill holes with brown sugar and pieces of butter about the size of a peanut. Sprinkle cinnamon liberally over entire top of bread. Bake until golden brown, about 20 minutes. Allow cakes to cool completely, then cut each cake in half crosswise.

Chapter 13

Gravies, Sops, Sauces and Condiments

On a large dish she gently placed the festive possum done to a turn. Then she carefully arranged some baked sweet potatoes around it. Over all she poured some gravy that had been simmering in a saucepan by the fire. She placed this dish in front of the plate on the table, and flanked it on one side by a dish of rice as white as milk, and on the other by some delicious cornbread. She surveyed the table a moment then announced, "Supper ready."
—*Sam Aleckson,* Before the War and After the Union

Southerners have an endearing and enduring relationship with sauces and gravy. From the elegance of béchamel and Hollandaise sauces in the French Quarter of New Orleans to the more plebeian sawmill gravy of the nineteenth-century Blue Ridge Mountain timber camps, gravies and sauces have played their part in the foodways of the American South.

In the days before there was a chain grocery store every two blocks, Southern cookbooks and handwritten family receipt books were filled with recipes for all kinds of gravy, sauces, sops and condiments, all made at home by the mistress of the house.

The ultimate guide to Southern sauces is probably *The Piccayune's Creole Cookbook* (1901), which weighs in with sixty-seven sauce recipes.

Gravy is a pan sauce made from cooked meat or poultry drippings, usually thickened with flour browned in the hot pan juices. Simple pan gravy in the English style came to the South with the earliest colonists. According to *The Oxford English Dictionary*, the word is believed to have come from the Old French word *grane* and dates to about 1390.

One of gravy's most enduring charms is that it is an extremely versatile sauce. It can be made with the simplest of ingredients or dressed up with rich cream and butter. It can also take on many different tastes, depending on how simple or complex the seasonings.

Hoover Sop

This is the most elemental form of gravy, a simple dish that sustained Southerners through the hardest times of the twentieth century.

Herbert Hoover was president of the United States when the stock market crashed in 1929, sending the nation into the worst economic disaster in the history of the world. Although Hoover didn't directly cause the Great Depression, his lack of leadership caused many people, especially in the largely Democratic South, to vilify the Republican president.

Meat suddenly became a luxury on many tables, and as jobs and food became scarcer, gravy made with leftover salt pork grease or lard and water instead of milk became a staple food for many Southerners.

Yield: 4 to 6 servings

2 tablespoons flour or cornmeal
2 tablespoons bacon drippings
2 cups water
salt and pepper to taste

In a 10-inch cast-iron skillet over medium heat, whisk flour into hot bacon drippings. When flour turns golden brown, stir in water and allow to simmer until it reaches the desired thickness. Season to taste with salt and pepper.

Traditional Milk Gravy

Although any liquid from water to stock to heavy cream can be used to make gravy, milk is the traditional liquid used to make Southern gravies.

Gravy made using milk is variously called milk gravy, white gravy, chicken gravy and (erroneously) sawmill gravy.

Yield: 4 to 6 servings

2 tablespoons flour or cornmeal
2 tablespoons bacon drippings
2 cups milk
salt and pepper to taste

In a 10-inch cast-iron skillet over medium heat, whisk flour into hot bacon drippings. When flour turns golden brown, stir in milk and allow to simmer until it reaches the desired thickness. Season to taste with salt and pepper.

Cream Gravy for Fried Chicken

This gravy (or a slight variation thereof) is the traditional accompaniment to fried chicken throughout the region. In Maryland, the gravy is served poured over the chicken; elsewhere, it is served on the side, usually over rice. To make it, substitute cream for the milk in the milk gravy recipe.

Sausage Gravy

Sausage gravy is made from the pan drippings left over from frying sausage. The sausage is crumbled into the gravy and served over hot biscuits.

Yield: 6 to 8 servings

1 pound hot sausage
½ cup flour
½ teaspoon salt
½ teaspoon black pepper
1¼ cups milk

In a 10-inch cast-iron skillet over medium heat, cook crumbled sausage until done, about 8 minutes. Remove from heat and drain on paper towels, reserving 8 tablespoons of drippings.
Put drippings back into skillet, increase heat to high and whisk in flour, salt and pepper. Stir until flour is golden brown, then add milk, stirring until gravy is desired thickness. Stir in drained sausage, stirring until heated through. Serve hot with biscuits.

Sawmill Gravy

According to Joe Dabney, author of *Smokehouse Ham, Spoon Bread and Scuppernong Wine* (1998), this classic Southern gravy dates back to the Treemont Logging Camp in the Blue Ridge Mountains at the dawn of the twentieth century.

The story goes that after making enough biscuits to feed the loggers, the cook didn't have enough flour left to make gravy. The cook substituted coarsely ground cornmeal. When the men asked what kind of gravy it was, he replied, "It's made from sawdust," and the loggers started calling it "sawmill gravy."

Yield: 6 to 8 servings

3 heaping tablespoons white cornmeal   ½ teaspoon black pepper
1 tablespoon bacon drippings   dash of salt
2¼ cups milk

In a 10-inch frying pan, combine cornmeal and bacon drippings; stir until brown. Add milk and simmer until gravy thickens, stirring constantly. Add pepper and salt to taste.

Red Eye Gravy

This simple sauce is the traditional accompaniment to country ham.

One story goes that Mark Twain, on being served this yet-to-be-named delicacy by a hotel cook who was more than a little hungover at the time, quipped, "That fellow's gravy is as red as his eyes."

Another version of the tale says it was Andrew Jackson who gave the tasty treat its name. More than likely, the name comes from the natural red color of the ham juice, without benefit of comment from Messieurs Twain or Jackson.

Yield: 1 cup

several slices of country ham
1 cup water (or black coffee)

In a 10-inch cast-iron skillet over medium heat, fry ham until done. Remove from pan. Add water or coffee to ham drippings and stir, scraping brown bits off the bottom of skillet. Serve with country ham, biscuits and honey.

Remoulade Sauce

Shrimp remoulade is one of the classic dishes of New Orleans: boiled shrimp served cold over salad greens with a spicy mayonnaise dressing. The sauce is also used on po' boy sandwiches and as a topping for cold beef, pork and chicken. This recipe is based on several from the 1880s to the 1960s.

Royce W. Smith photo.

Yield: 1 pint

1 pint mayonnaise
2 tablespoons Creole mustard
2 tablespoons grated onion
3 tablespoons prepared horseradish
¼ teaspoon salt
1 tablespoon lemon juice
1 tablespoon white wine Worcestershire sauce
¼ teaspoon pepper
¼ teaspoon cayenne
¼ teaspoon hot sauce

Mix ingredients well. Serve over cold shrimp or roast beef.

Robert Lahser photo.

CHAPTER 14

Iced Tea (and a Few Stronger Beverages)

Iced tea is too pure and natural a creation not to have been invented as soon as tea, ice, and hot weather crossed paths.
—John Egerton, Side Orders

The South is dry and will vote dry. That is, everybody sober enough to stagger to the polls will."
Will Rogers

How Iced Tea Became Southern

Ask any Southerner to picture in their mind a lazy summer day, and chances are that vision will include a porch, a rocking chair and a glass of iced tea.

So how did a drink made from a plant that grows on the other side the world become, as many have called it, the house wine of the South?

Iced tea begins life as the leaves of a bushy evergreen shrub indigenous to Tibet and western China. There's some controversy as to exactly when the Chinese started drinking tea, but it was so popular by the sixth century that merchants commissioned a book extolling the pleasures of drinking it.

Tea drinking spread to Europe in the sixteenth century, when the English began trading with China. The English began importing tea and then switched to growing it themselves in their Asian colonies.

Despite attempts in the early 1800s to grow tea in South Carolina, the British continued to dominate the tea market after the American Revolution.

In 1859, the Great Atlantic & Pacific Tea Company began selling tea at one-third the price of British tea and later grew into a chain of supermarkets under the name A&P.

One of the most enduring myths associated with iced tea is that it was "invented" at the 1904 World's Fair. While this *might* have been the earliest commercial sale of iced tea, and definitely served to popularize black tea (instead of the green tea popular since colonial days), Southerners had been enjoying this cool and refreshing drink for at least a generation prior to the dawn of the twentieth century.

Although there were recipes such as Regent's punch (essentially a spiked version of iced tea) dating back to colonial times, iced tea became an essential part of Southern life sometime around the mid-nineteenth century.

It's been theorized that the birth of iced tea probably occurred in New Orleans sometime after the first commercial ice production began in 1868, but there are recipes for other iced drinks that predate commercially produced ice by at least three decades.

The earliest mention of iced tea in print is a passage from *Sea-Gift*, a novel written by North Carolinian Edwin Wiley Fuller in 1873. Mary Ann Bryan Mason, another North Carolinian, gave this advice about iced tea in 1875: "Three things it would be well to avoid in tea—tea of inferior quality, weak tea, and cold tea, unless persons desire iced tea—then it should be well iced. Tepid tea is nauseous, especially if weak."

The earliest printed recipe for iced tea is found in Marion Cabell Tyree's *Housekeeping in Old Virginia* (1877), so by at least the early 1870s, iced tea was a well-established part of Southern cuisine.

How to Make Southern Iced Tea

Start with a 4- to 6-quart nonreactive pot and fill it with three quarts of cold water. Put four to six regular (or three or four family-size) tea bags into the cold water, cover and bring to a boil, then immediately remove from the heat. After three or four minutes (depending on how strong you like your tea), remove the tea bags (don't squeeze them) and pour the hot tea into a gallon pitcher. Add a small pinch of baking soda to counter any bitterness, and add sugar to taste—1 to 2 cups, depending on whether you like your tea sweet, seriously sweet or stand up and bark sweet. Add enough cold water to fill the pitcher, stir well and let the tea cool to room temperature before pouring; otherwise the hot tea will melt the ice in the glasses and the tea will be watery. Do not refrigerate until the tea is completely cool or it will become cloudy.

To serve, fill a tall glass three-quarters full of ice. Quarter a lemon and squeeze it over the ice, then drop in the lemon and pour the tea over the ice.

Iced Tea (and a Few Stronger Beverages)

Robert Lahser photo.

Other Southern Beverages

Lemonade

Lemonade, while not unique to the South, has been a favorite drink on verandas and side porches since before Mary Randolph mentioned ice cream made from lemonade in *The Virginia House-Wife* in 1824. The Spanish brought lemons to Florida, and they were also regularly imported from Europe.

Yield: 4 to 6 servings

1 cup water
1 cup sugar
juice of 4 to 6 lemons

In a 1-quart saucepan over medium heat, add sugar to the water and cook, stirring occasionally, until sugar dissolves and mixture thickens slightly.
Using a juicer, extract one cup of juice from the lemons.
In a 2-quart pitcher, stir together sugar syrup, lemon juice and enough water to fill the pitcher. Refrigerate at least 45 minutes before serving.

Soft Drinks

Southerners can lay firm claim to soft drinks as their own. Although ginger ale was invented in Ireland in 1851 and commercial root beer was around by the time Americans were celebrating their centennial in 1876, the soft drink brands we are familiar with today began to spring up in the South beginning in 1885 when pharmacist Charles Alderton invented Dr. Pepper in Waco, Texas.

In 1886, an Atlanta pharmacist named John S. "Doc" Pemberton invented a tonic he hoped would help his chronic headaches. It contained caffeine and small amounts of cocaine in addition to sugar, cocoa and carbonated water. Pemberton's bookkeeper coined the name Coca-Cola and wrote out the name in his flowing handwriting, which became the logo that appears on every bottle of Coca-Cola today.

In New Bern, North Carolina, another pharmacist was at work on what would become Coca-Cola's biggest rival. "Brad's Drink," the creation of Caleb Bradham, was invented in the summer of 1893. In 1889, Bradham renamed his soda Pepsi Cola after the pepsin and cola nuts that made up part of the formula.

In 1905, newly graduated pharmacist Claude Hatcher started the Union Bottling Company (later Royal Crown Company) in Columbus, Georgia, and RC Cola was born. The company also invented the Nehi fruit flavor sodas in the 1920s. It wasn't until a Chattanooga, Tennessee bakery salesman named Earl Mitchell invented the Moon Pie in the early 1920s that the combination of the five-cent Moon Pie and the five-cent RC Cola came together to become a paragon of Southern culinary culture.

Cheerwine, the cherry-flavored soda beloved by Carolinians, made its debut in 1917 from the basement of a wholesale grocery store owned by L.D. Peeler in Salisbury, North Carolina.

Sun-Drop, a yellow, citrus-flavored soda was invented in St. Louis in 1928 by Charles Lazier and quickly became a Southern staple, marketed under the names "Sun-Drop Golden Cola," "Golden Girl Cola" and "Golden Sun-Drop Cola."

Whiskey

Despite the best efforts of the Ladies Christian Temperance League and other groups, whiskey (both legal and illegal) has always been the favored alcoholic libation in most parts of the South.

Astute observers will notice that the letter "e" disappears from the word whiskey on occasion. This is because of the different way our Scottish and Canadian friends spell. If you are referring to Scottish or Canadian spirits, it's whisky; American hooch is whiskey with an "e." When Scottish settlers began pouring into the South in the eighteenth century, they brought with them a long tradition of making Scotch whisky.

Although wheat, barley and rye were planted in the Southern colonies (George Washington made nearly eleven thousand gallons of whiskey from wheat and rye in 1799), Southerners soon discovered that an acre of corn produced far more usable grain. The Scots who flocked to Kentucky soon turned any corn not used for grits or cornmeal into corn liquor.

By the end of the eighteenth century, Kentuckians were shipping the fruits of their labor down the Mississippi to New Orleans. The finest of the corn liquor came from Bourbon County and was shipped in barrels marked with the county's name. It wasn't long before people started asking for this premium whiskey by name, and bourbon became synonymous with high-quality corn liquor. Although bourbon can be made anywhere, almost all of it comes from Kentucky.

By federal law, bourbon must contain at least 51 percent corn; most bourbon contains at least 65 to 75 percent. It must also be aged for at least two years in new, charred oak barrels and have nothing that adds sweetness, flavor or color added to it at bottling.

Tennessee whiskey is similar to bourbon in that it starts out as a mash that is between 51 and 80 percent corn and is also aged in new, charred oak barrels for at least two years. At the end of the two-year aging, Tennessee whiskey is filtered through a layer of sugar maple charcoal about ten feet thick. This gives Tennessee whiskey a uniquely mild, smoky flavor.

Moonshine

On March 3, 1791, the newly minted United States government imposed a federal excise tax on stills and distilled spirits. This didn't set well with the Scotsmen who settled the rugged coves and hollows of the Appalachian Mountains, as it reminded them a little too much of the tax the British had made them pay back home. Since they had dodged the British tax collectors for years, they pretty much ignored the tax and started making liquor on the sly.

For some Southerners, it was the amount of tax levied by the government that kept their whiskey making on the other side of the law. As one mountaineer explained to Horace Kephart, author of *Our Southern Highlanders* (1913): "Nobody refuses to pay his taxes for taxes is fair and squar'. Taxes costs mebbe three cents on the dollar; and that's all right. But revenue costs a dollar and ten cents on twenty cents' worth o' liquor; and that's robbin' the people with a gun to their faces. Now, yan's my field o' corn. I gather the corn, and shuck hit, and grind hit my own self, and the woman she bakes us a pone o' bread to eat—and I don't pay no tax, do I? Then why can't I make some o' my corn into pure whiskey to drink, without payin' tax?"

Although moonshining occurred in many areas of the South, it was mostly concentrated in the Blue Ridge Mountains of western North Carolina, eastern Tennessee and northeast Georgia.

Courtesy of North Carolina State Archives.

Corn liquor was a valuable trading commodity in a region where cash money was scarce. Someone who had corn liquor could trade for powder and shot, flour, gingham and calico for the lady of the house, chewing tobacco or whatever else they needed or wanted to make life in the wilderness more pleasant.

Oftentimes would-be moonshiners went in with family or friends to pool resources to purchase a used still or to procure the parts to assemble a new one. The basic still consisted of a sealed copper kettle or pot in which to cook the mash and a copper condensing coil called a worm.

The distillation process for moonshine required a fire to "cook" off the alcohol. Since this produced large amounts of smoke and steam, the process was carried out at night far back in the woods, where the fire was indistinguishable from any normal campfire. Since the operation was carried out by the light of the moon, the word moonshine entered the American vernacular as both noun and verb.

From 1910 until national Prohibition began in 1920, states such as Georgia, Tennessee and West Virginia passed laws prohibiting the manufacture, sale and transportation of alcohol. This meant that moonshiners, who had taken to the new technology of the automobile to transport their goods to customers as far away as New York, now had to contend with state and local law officers chasing them in their own cars. This led to a war of automotive technology, as the moonshine runners put larger engines and stiffer suspensions in their cars so they could outrun the law. Impromptu races between these "shine haulers" led to loosely organized races, and in 1948 the National Association for Stock Car Auto Racing (NASCAR) was founded. One of the sport's earliest heroes was Junior Johnson of Wilkes County, North Carolina, who had been running 'shine since he was fourteen years old.

COCKTAILS

The mixed drink was born in New Orleans, where the idea for cocktails, and even the name, originated.

In the late 1700s, an apothecary in the French Quarter named Antoine Amedée Peychaud invented a digestive aid and general cure-all he called bitters. To help ease the bitter taste, Peychaud mixed his concoction with brandy and served the drink in small, egg-shaped cups the French called *coquetiers*. Soon, other New Orleans watering holes were serving Peychaud's drink. The local pronunciation (especially after downing a few) was corrupted to "cocktail," and the little egg-shaped cups evolved into the jigger.

Mint Julep

There is no alcoholic drink more readily identified with the moonlight-and-magnolias image of the Old South than the mint julep. The julep has its roots in the English practice of infusing alcohol with fruit, fruit juices, cucumbers or other cooling ingredients in the summertime.

Although there are many recipes for this drink, in its purest (and earliest) form, it consists of sugar, bourbon, mint leaves and ice. This passage from William Alexander Percy's *Lanterns on the Levee: Recollections of a Planter's Son* (1941) is the only recipe needed to make a good mint julep:

> *Certainly her juleps had nothing in common with those hybrid concoctions one buys in bars the world over under that name. It would have been sacrilege to add lemon, or a slice of orange or of pineapple, or one of those wretched maraschino cherries.*
>
> *First, you needed excellent bourbon whiskey; rye or scotch would not do at all. Then you put half an inch of sugar in the bottom of the glass and merely dampened it with water.*
>
> *Next, very quickly—and here was the trick in the procedure—you crushed your ice, actually powdered it, preferably in a towel with a wooden mallet, so quickly that it remained dry, and, slipping two sprigs of fresh mint against the inside of the glass, you crammed the ice in right to the brim, packing it with your hand.*
>
> *Last you filled the glass, which apparently had no room left for anything else, with bourbon, the older the better, and grated a bit of nutmeg on the top. The glass immediately frosted and you settled back in your chair for half an hour of sedate cumulative bliss. Although you stirred the sugar at the bottom, it never all melted, therefore at the end of the half hour there was left a delicious mess of ice and mint and whiskey which a small boy was allowed to consume with calm rapture.*

Corinthian Julep

"Mrs. Harris says, 'Give her a Corinthian julep if she wants one and by the time I get in the house she won't know whether I'm wearing a sunbonnet or a crown.'"

Thus wrote ten-year-old Virginia Cary Hudson in *O Ye Jigs & Juleps* (1900) about this potent Southern libation. The drink draws its name from Saint Paul's letter to the provincial churches in First Corinthians, chapter 13.

The drink is made in the same manner as a regular mint julep but with three jiggers of bourbon, one each for Faith, Hope and Love.

Sazerac

The Sazerac is one of the oldest and most famous of New Orleans cocktails. This blend of bitters, bourbon and sugar, born in an Exchange Street bar in the mid-1800s, is still being served today.

Yield: 1 cocktail

crushed ice
1 dash Herbsaint or Pernod
1 cube of sugar
2 dashes Peychaud bitters

2 dashes Angostura bitters
1½ ounces bourbon
1 lemon peel twist

Chill an old-fashioned glass by filling with crushed ice. When the glass is chilled, discard the ice and pour in the Herbsaint or Pernod, tilting and rotating the glass carefully to completely coat it. Discard the excess if you wish.

Place the sugar cube in the bottom of the glass and pour the bitters over it. Using the back of a spoon, crush the sugar cube. Fill the glass two-thirds full with ice; add the bourbon and sugar mixture and lemon twist. Swirl (don't stir) to chill and serve.

Rum

After bourbon, rum is probably the second most "Southern" of spirits. Rum came into the Southern liquor cabinet early in the colonial period by way of the English settlements in the West Indies and Barbados.

In colonial times, most of the rum consumed in the South was made from molasses brought by ship from the British sugar plantations in the Caribbean to New London, Connecticut, where it was distilled into rum and sent south.

In 1764, the British imposed the Sugar Act, forbidding the import of rum and sugar from "foreign ports," making the lucrative American rum distilling industry illegal. During the Revolution, American ports were blockaded, preventing rum from being imported. Since whiskey was made from American grain and produced in America (and thus was cheaper than rum), whiskey became the choice of patriotic Americans.

Rum was not considered a proper drink for a lady, nor would a gentleman ever consider drinking it straight; then and now rum is mixed with fruit juices to make some of the South's favorite summer cocktails.

Planter's Punch

There are numerous recipes for this drink dating back to the early part of the nineteenth century. The common ingredients found in all variations are rum, sugar and lemon or lime juice.

Yield: 6 servings

1½ cup dark rum
1½ cup orange juice
1½ cup pineapple juice
1½ cup guava nectar
3 tablespoons fresh lime juice
2 tablespoons light brown sugar
1 teaspoon Angostura bitters

6 fresh pineapple
  rings
6 orange slices
6 cinnamon sticks
6 Maraschino
  cherries

Robert Lahser photo.

In a 1-gallon pitcher, mix rum, fruit juices, brown sugar and bitters.
Pour into six tall glasses filled with ice. Garnish each drink with pineapple ring, orange slice, cinnamon stick and cherry.

Hurricane Punch

Hurricane Punch is probably the cocktail most often identified with New Orleans. The drink is most often identified with Pat O'Brien's, one of the French Quarter's best-loved bars. The drink is served in a tall, distinctive glass shaped like a hurricane lamp, but any large glass or cup will do in a storm.

Yield: 1 cocktail

1 ounce white rum
1 ounce Jamaican rum
1 ounce Bacardi 151 proof rum
3 ounces orange juice, with pulp
3 ounces unsweetened pineapple juice

½ ounce
  Grenadine
crushed ice

Robert Lahser photo.

Combine all ingredients and mix well by shaking or stirring. Pour over crushed ice in hurricane or other tall glass. Garnish with orange or pineapple ring and drink through a small straw for maximum-strength winds.

Chatham Artillery Punch

The Chatham Artillery is the oldest military organization in the state of Georgia, founded just after the American Revolution.

Regimental functions were always a hit when this rather stout punch was served. If you make this recipe, be advised that it must be made a few days in advance, and that I will not be responsible for anything you do or say after consuming it.

Yield: 20 servings

2 cups sweet red wine
2 cups strong tea
⅔ cup rum
½ cup packed brown sugar
½ cup rye whiskey

½ cup orange juice
⅓ cup gin
⅓ cup brandy
⅓ cup lemon juice
1 bottle dry champagne

Mix all ingredients except champagne. Cover and refrigerate for several days. Stir in champagne just before serving.

Charleston Light Dragoon Punch

Not to be outdone, Charleston has its own potent punch named for a military organization. This is a modernized version of a recipe that appeared in *The Sewanee Cook Book* by Queenie Woods Washington in 1926.

Yield: 20 to 30 servings

1 pint bourbon
1 pint light rum
1¼ cups granulated sugar
1 pint strong iced tea (see page 194)
2 quarts Apollinaris or other sparkling water

1 fresh pineapple, sliced
1½ (2-liter) bottles ginger ale
12 lemons, sliced ¼ inch
one 16-ounce jar Maraschino cherries, drained
bagged or block ice

Mix all liquid ingredients well; float lemon slices, cherries and ice in punchbowl.

Beer

Beer was consumed with gusto from the earliest days of the Southern colonies. The English believed that beer was healthier than water; given the sanitation practices of the day, this was true.

Nearly every household brewed "small" beer (beer with a low alcohol content) for their own use. Records at Monticello show that Thomas Jefferson's wife, Martha, brewed fifteen-gallon batches nearly every two weeks.

George Washington's Beer Recipe

To Make Small Beer:
Take a large sifter full of bran hops to your taste—boil these 3 hours. Then strain our 30 gallons into a cooler put in 3 gallons molasses while the beer is scalding hot or rather draw the molasses into the cooler.

Strain the beer on it while boiling hot, let this stand till it is little more than blood warm. Then put in a quart of ye[a]st if the weather is very cold cover it over with a blanket let it work in the cask—Leave the bung open till it is almost done working—Bottle it that day week it was brewed.

Wine

"Grapes grow wild there in an incredible plenty and variety, some of which are very sweet and pleasant to the taste." Thus wrote Robert Beverley in 1705 of the abundance of grapes in colonial Virginia.

Winemaking was one of the tasks the Jamestown Company in London set forth for the early English settlers. Winemaking in England had come to a screeching halt during the Middle Ages due to climate changes, making France the main wine producer in Europe. Since England and France weren't on the best of terms, wine was expensive and reserved for the wealthy.

European grapes didn't grow well in Virginia. The native wild grapes, known as scuppernongs or muscadines, had a strong flavor, and while the wine produced from them was drinkable, it was too astringent to pair with food and never found favor at the tables of the wealthy planters.

Jefferson and other Southern gentry imported Madeira, port, sherry and clarets from France or Spain rather than suffer wine made from the rough American grapes. For the average Southerner of the colonial and antebellum periods, wine or cordials made from muscadines, blackberries, cherries, dandelions or any other substance would do just fine.

Mrs. Sinkler's Blackberry Wine

When Emily Wharton Sinkler started her handwritten receipt book in August 1855, she included three different recipes for blackberry wine, including this one from her grandmother: "Measure the berries and bruise. To every gallon ad a quart of boiling water, Let stand 24 hours stirring occasionally. Strain into a cask, adding to [each] gallon 2 lbs [pounds] sugar. Cork tight and let remain til October."

Royce W. Smith photo.

Chapter 15

Just a Little Something Sweet

Southern Desserts

The table held only the kickshaws—cakes, candy, nuts, syllabub and custard. Wide handsome plates piled high with tempting sliced cake sat up and down the length of it, with glass dishes of gay candies in between.
—*Martha McCulloch-Williams,* Dishes & Beverages of the Old South, *1913*

The Southern Sweet Tooth

As a region, the South has a legendary collective sweet tooth; from sweet breads and coffee cakes in the morning to slices of pie from the diner at noontime to the slice of pound cake after supper, we must satisfy our urge for sweets of all types.

While the French had a large influence on the rest of Southern cooking, our desserts are decidedly English; from the earliest days, English desserts such as trifles, puddings and sweetmeats dominated the dessert section of Southern cookery books.

The development of desserts in the culinary history of the American South has several stages, all of them tied to certain social and economic events.

In the colonial South, sugar was the provenance of the wealthy; even then, it was imported and expensive, so its use wasn't as lavish as it was destined to become. Colonial-era cookery books relied heavily on puddings and trifles to satisfy the sweet tooth; in an era when baking was done in brick ovens that turned an already hot kitchen into something resembling the inner rings of Hell, cakes and baked goods were reserved for company and special occasions. In the nineteenth century, as sugar refining began in earnest in Louisiana, sugar prices dropped, and the dessert sections of period cookbooks began to expand.

By the last quarter of the nineteenth century, advances in stove design and the general prosperity of those years led to an incredible wealth of recipes for every type of sweet imaginable, from ambrosia to macaroons and meringues to a bevy of cakes named for Confederate heroes. The period between 1875 and 1910 produced some of the region's most noteworthy desserts.

Ambrosia

Ambrosia is the simplest of all the Southern desserts, an heirloom made with fresh fruit, sugar and grated coconut. Recipes for ambrosia by that name first began appearing in Southern cookbooks in the last quarter of the nineteenth century.

There are many variations on the theme, but coconut is always present. Oranges are also found in the vast majority of recipes, and miniature marshmallows are a late twentieth-century abomination. Marietta Powell Gibson gave a recipe in *Mrs. Charles H. Gibson's Maryland and Virginia Cook Book* (1894) that captured the simple elegance of the dish: "Slice oranges or pineapples in a glass bowl, sweeten well. Put a layer of fruit and a layer of coconut, grated, and so on till the bowl is full. Cover with grated coconut."

Puddings and Trifles

Trifles and puddings came over with the earliest English settlers. They were elegant yet easy to prepare; as an added bonus, they took very little sugar, so they were economical.

Real Banana Pudding

This rich combination of cookies, custard and bananas has been a staple in the dessert section of Southern community cookbooks for many generations.

Bananas have been imported into the South since colonial times. In 1787, Eliza Lucas Pinckney wrote to her daughter Harriott Pinckney Horry that "the oranges and bananas are not good enough to send" when Mrs. Pinckney sent food gifts from her plantation to Hopewell, Harriott's home near Georgetown, South Carolina.

Mary Harris Frazer gets the nod for the earliest recipe in a Southern cookbook for the one in her *Kentucky Receipt Book*, published in Louisville in 1903.

Yield: 6 servings

For the Custard:
4 whole eggs, separated
⅔ cup sugar
⅛ teaspoon salt
3 cups milk
2 tablespoons cornstarch
1 teaspoon vanilla extract
vanilla wafer cookies
2 or 3 ripe bananas, sliced

For the Meringue:
5 tablespoons sugar
½ teaspoon vanilla extract

Preheat oven to 300 degrees F.

In a 2-quart saucepan over medium high heat, whisk together egg yolks, sugar, salt, milk and cornstarch and cook, stirring constantly, until the mixture thickens enough to coat the back of a spoon. Remove from heat and add vanilla extract.

In an 8-inch square baking dish, place a layer of vanilla wafers, standing some of the vanilla wafers up around sides of baking dish. Add banana slices and pour cooled custard over vanilla wafers and bananas.

In a 2-quart mixing bowl using an electric hand mixer, make meringue by beating egg whites until frothy and adding sugar. Beat until stiff peaks form, then add vanilla extract. Spread on top of pudding and bake until meringue is golden brown on tips, about 20 minutes.

Tipsy Parson (Tipsy Hedgehog)

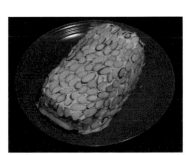

Royce W. Smith photo.

Tipsy Parson (also referred to as Tipsy Squire, Tipsy Cake or Tipsy Pudding) is another dessert with English roots, a cousin of the trifle. It dates back to colonial times and, like the rest of the English-inspired pudding and cake desserts, was wildly popular in the last quarter of the nineteenth century.

Tipsy Parson (and its other aliases) is a multilayered dessert made up of sponge cake soaked in sherry, brandy or wine and boiled custard.

One interesting variation on the Tipsy Parson is the Tipsy Hedgehog. This dessert, developed sometime in the late nineteenth century, is a pound cake baked in a loaf pan and then soaked in brandy, sherry or sweet wine. After it is placed on the serving dish, the cake is covered with custard, and then toasted almond slices are stuck into the cake to resemble the spines of a hedgehog. This recipe is based on one from *The Queen of Appalachia Cook Book*, published about 1910 by Loula Roberts Platt; she called it Tipsy Squirrel.

Yield: 2 loaf cakes

one recipe Old-Fashioned Pound Cake (see page 217)
½ cup brandy or sherry
4 egg yolks
⅔ cup sugar

⅛ teaspoon salt
3 cups milk
2 tablespoons cornstarch
1 teaspoon vanilla extract
sliced almonds

Make cake according to recipe, baking in loaf pans. After allowing to cool, pour brandy or sherry over cake, a little at a time, until cake is well soaked. Allow to sit overnight before covering with the custard.

In a 2-quart saucepan over medium high heat, whisk together egg yolks, sugar, salt, milk and cornstarch and cook, stirring constantly, until the mixture thickens enough to coat the back of a spoon. Remove from heat and add vanilla extract. Allow to cool and then, using a rubber spatula, spread custard over tops and sides of cakes. Stick almonds into cakes in rows to resemble the quills of a hedgehog.

PIES, COBBLERS AND OTHER FRUIT DESSERTS

When Europeans first settled the South, they marveled at the abundance of wild native fruits. They soon discovered that the region's mild weather and rich soil made for ideal growing conditions for apples, peaches, pears, plums, figs and all manner of other fruits.

The English loved their savory and sweet "pyes," as the early cookery books called them, and soon the fruits of the new land were happily bubbling in pies and cobblers.

Pie Crust

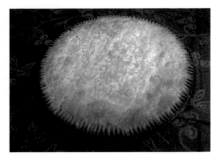

Mary Ann Bryan Mason imparted just about everything you need to know about making pie crusts in *The Young Housewife's Counsellor* [*sic*] *and Friend* (1875): "Pastry should be made up with cold water—in summer, the coldest you can get; and it should be made in a cool place. It should be mixed with a knife-blade, and touched as little as possible with the hands."

Chilling the dough and working it as little as possible will yield a flakier crust; substituting ½ cup vegetable shortening or lard for ½ cup of the butter in this recipe will also make the crust flakier.

Yield: enough dough for two 9-inch piecrusts

1½ cups all-purpose flour
1 teaspoon salt
1 teaspoon sugar
1 cup (2 sticks) cold unsalted butter, cut into small pieces
¼ to ½ cup water

In a 4-quart mixing bowl, combine flour, salt and sugar. Using a pastry blender or your fingers, cut butter into flour until mixture resembles coarse meal.

Using a wooden spoon, stir flour mixture and add water a little at a time until dough just holds together.

Turn dough out onto piece of waxed paper on a flat work surface. Form dough into flat disc, wrap in plastic wrap and refrigerate at least 1 hour.

Remove dough from refrigerator. Remove plastic wrap from one of the dough discs and place disc onto well-floured work surface (or wax paper). Using a rolling pin, use short, even strokes to roll dough out until it overlaps pie plate by one inch all the way around. Fold dough over rolling pin and center over pie plate. Gently slide dough off rolling pin and into pie plate. Using your fingers, gently smooth dough out into bottom and up sides of pie pan. Repeat for other dough disc.

If crust is for a single crust pie, use a dinner fork to press the edges of the dough onto the lip of the pie plate, sealing the dough to the pie plate. If dough is for double crust pie, fill pie shell and top with upper crust before sealing. If pie recipe calls for pre-baking crust, return to refrigerator and chill for at least 30 minutes before pre-baking.

Aunt Ruth's Sweet Potato Pie

Sweet potato pies have been a fixture on Southern tables since at least the early 1800s; Lettice Bryan published an early recipe in *The Kentucky Housewife* (1839).

Traditionally, sweet potato pie is flavored with the same spices as its cousin, pumpkin pie—cinnamon, nutmeg, cloves, ginger and allspice. The surprise in this version is that it eschews the heavy, heady flavor of the "fall spices" for a light, lemony taste that brings to mind warm spring or summer days.

For a more traditional sweet potato pie, eliminate the lemon extract and add 1 teaspoon cinnamon and ¼ teaspoon each of ginger, allspice and nutmeg.

Yield: two 9-inch dish pies

2 or 3 large sweet potatoes (about 2½ pounds total)
1 stick butter
3 eggs, beaten
one 14-ounce can evaporated milk (not sweetened condensed)

2 cups sugar
1 ½ teaspoons cornstarch
1 teaspoon vanilla extract
1 teaspoon lemon extract
dough for 2 single crust pies (see page 211)

In a 6-quart Dutch oven, bring 3 quarts water to a rolling boil.
Peel sweet potatoes, then cut into small pieces. Place potatoes into boiling water; return to a boil and cook until fork tender, about 10 to 15 minutes. Drain and set aside.
Preheat oven to 350 degrees F.
Using a potato masher or electric hand mixer, cream butter into sweet potatoes. Add eggs and milk. Combine sugar with cornstarch; add to potato mixture along with vanilla and lemon flavoring. Pour into pie shells. Bake until center is set and top is golden brown, about 45 to 50 minutes.

Fresh Peach Cobbler

Peaches are one of the main cash crops in South Carolina and Georgia. Brought to the South by way of Spain, this native Chinese fruit has become forever identified with the South.

Cobblers have been enjoyed in the South since before the American Revolution. The name "cobbler" refers to a deep-dish fruit pie with a sweetened biscuit dough crust. The dough is dropped by spoonfuls onto the filling; as it bakes, it looks like the stones in a cobblestone street, hence the name cobbler. This recipe is typical of late nineteenth- and early twentieth-century cobblers.

Yield: 6 to 8 servings

For the Crust:
1 cup self-rising flour
2 tablespoons sugar
2 tablespoons butter
whole milk

For the Filling:
2 cups fresh peaches, peeled and sliced
1¼ cups sugar
1 tablespoon flour
dash of salt

Preheat oven to 350 degrees F.

In a 4-quart mixing bowl, combine flour and sugar. Using a pastry blender or your fingers, cut butter into flour and sugar mixture until mixture resembles coarse crumbs. Add enough milk, stirring after each addition, so that dough comes together into a soft ball. Set aside.

In a 2-quart baking dish, combine peaches, sugar, flour and salt; stir until mixed. Drop dough by spoonfuls over top of cobbler. Bake at 350 degrees for 1 hour.

Jefferson Davis Pie

Jefferson Davis pie, named for the Confederate president, was one of a series of existing desserts (in this case, a version of chess pie) named for the leaders of the Confederacy in the years immediately after the South's defeat in 1865.

Davis was imprisoned without trial and held for two years after the war; he refused to take the oath of allegiance to the U.S. government after the war and died without ever regaining his United States citizenship.

Jefferson Davis pie was a fixture in Southern cookbooks of the late nineteenth century. I have also seen two recipes for a Jefferson Davis cake, but for the most part, the cake has faded into obscurity. The pie lives on, though, as a delicious tribute to "the man without a country." This recipe is based on several from the 1890s.

Yield: one 9-inch pie

½ cup butter (at room temperature)
2 cups light brown sugar, packed
4 egg yolks
2 teaspoons flour
1 teaspoon cinnamon
1 teaspoon nutmeg
½ teaspoon allspice

1 cup light cream
½ cup chopped pecans
½ cup raisins
½ cup dates
dough for a single crust 9-inch pie (see page 211)

Preheat oven to 350 degrees F.

In the bowl of an electric mixer, beat butter until soft. Add sugar and beat until mixture is light and fluffy. Add egg yolks one at a time, beating well after each addition.

Combine flour, cinnamon, nutmeg and allspice and add to creamed butter mixture. Stir in cream until well blended, then stir in pecans, raisins and dates.

Pour into pie crust and bake until center is just set, about 35 to 40 minutes.

Buttermilk Pie

Buttermilk pie is another custard pie in the English tradition, cousin to chess pie and Jefferson Davis pie. One of the earliest mentions of buttermilk pudding (remember that in nineteenth-century terms, puddings and pies were fairly interchangeable) is Annabella P. Hill's recipe in *Mrs. Hill's New Cook Book* (1867). Early recipes often call for a meringue topping, but this recipe doesn't. It's based on one by Mrs. Vivian Hodges of Gillis, Louisiana, in *Favorite Southern Recipes by Southern Ruralist Readers*, published in 1912.

Yield: one 9-inch pie

3 eggs, slightly beaten
1½ cups sugar
½ cup butter, melted
3 teaspoons flour

1 cup buttermilk
1 teaspoon vanilla
dough for a single crust 9-inch pie (see page 211)

Preheat oven to 350 degrees.

In a 4-quart mixing bowl using a wire whisk, beat all ingredients together until smooth. Pour into pie shell and bake until filling is golden, about 45 to 50 minutes.

Pecan Pie

Pecan pie is a rich mixture of eggs, sugar, corn syrup and pecans that traces its ancestry back to the treacle pies of the Middle Ages in Europe. Although there are tales of pecan pies in Louisiana from the early years of the 1800s, there are no written records or recipes to back up the claim. Even late nineteenth-century cookbooks with enormous dessert sections offer up not one recipe for the gooey delight. In 1912, when housewives from all over the South sent in their favorite recipes for *Favorite Southern Recipes by Southern Ruralist Readers*, all the pecan pie's cousins were well represented—molasses pie, sugar pie, syrup pie, caramel pie, vinegar pie and transparent pie—but not a single pecan pie recipe. Given the lack of evidence to the contrary, it's entirely possible that pecan pie is a twentieth-century invention.

Yield: one 9-inch pie

3 eggs
1 cup brown sugar
1 cup white corn syrup
⅓ teaspoon salt
⅓ cup melted butter
1 teaspoon vanilla
2 cups pecans
dough for a single crust 9-inch pie (see page 211)

Preheat oven to 350 F.
In 4-quart mixing bowl using an electric hand mixer on low speed, beat eggs until light. Add sugar, corn syrup, salt, butter and vanilla; beat until blended. Stir in pecans. Place pie dough in pie pan and crimp edges with fork. Pour pecan filling into pie crust.
Bake until knife inserted halfway between center and edge comes out clean, about 55 to 60 minutes. Cool completely on wire rack before cutting.

Southern Fried Pies

Martha McCulloch-Williams wrote about this Southern favorite in *Dishes & Beverages of the Old South* (1913): "To be perfect these must be made of sun-dried peaches, very bright and sweet, but any sort of sound dried fruit will serve at a pinch."

The basic recipe below may be modified to include any dried fruit. Although the pies may be made with fresh fruit, dried fruit is traditional and gives the best flavor. If you do use fresh fruit, increase the amount to 4 cups and simmer in just enough water to cover until tender.

Yield: about 6 to 8 pies

3 cups dried apples
1½ cups water, boiling
½ cup sugar
¼ teaspoon cinnamon (optional)
¼ teaspoon allspice, ground (optional)
one recipe Basic Pie Crust (see page 211)
shortening or lard

Cook fruit in boiling water, covered, for 30 minutes, or until very tender; cool and mash slightly. Stir in ½ cup of sugar and add spices.

Divide chilled pastry in half; roll each half to ¼ inch thickness and cut into circles about 5 inches in diameter.

Place 2 to 3 tablespoons of fruit mixture on half of each pastry circle; moisten edges of dough and fold over filling, making sure the edges line up. Press edges together, using a fork dipped in flour.

In a 12-inch cast-iron skillet over medium-high heat, melt enough lard or shortening to fill the skillet to a depth of ½ inch and heat until it shimmers but does not smoke, about 365 degrees on an instant-read or deep fat thermometer.

Fry pies until browned on both sides. Drain on paper towels. Serve hot, warm or cold.

Cakes and Their Place in Southern Food History

Cakes have always held a special place on the Southern table. They have always had a connection to celebrations and special occasions unmatched by even the fanciest pudding, pie or trifle and are the crowning glory of the holiday table.

One reason for the association of cakes with special occasions is that prior to the early years of the twentieth century, making a cake was a huge amount of trouble and expense.

Like most other Southern desserts, the cake reached its zenith in terms of recipes in the late nineteenth century, when the wood- or coal-burning cookstove made baking more practical.

From about 1870 until 1900, Southern cookbooks featured a dazzling parade of cakes for every occasion imaginable. Among the nearly two hundred cakes Mrs. M.E. Porter listed in *Mrs. Porter's New Southern Cookery Book* (1871) were introduction cake, acquaintanceship cake, flirtation cake, love cake, engagement cake, wedding cake and groom's cake. In other cookbooks of the period, there were cakes named for places (Columbia cake, Norfolk cake), people (Robert E. Lee cake, Nathan Bedford Forrest cake) and events (election cake and commencement cake).

Pound Cake

While not unique to the region, the simple pound cake holds a fond place in the memories of most Southerners.

The first pound cake recipes began to appear in the early years of the eighteenth century in English cookery books. They got their name because the original recipes were simply a pound each of butter, sugar, flour and eggs.

The cakes were usually flavored with lemon juice or zest, rose water or some type of alcohol such as brandy. Currants were also a popular addition to eighteenth- and early nineteenth-century pound cakes.

Old-Fashioned Pound Cake

This cake is typical of an eighteenth-century recipe; it contains one pound each of butter, sugar, flour and eggs.

Yield: 10 to 12 servings

2 cups butter
2 cups sugar
9 medium eggs
4 cups flour

½ teaspoon salt
½ teaspoon mace
2 tablespoons brandy

Do not preheat oven.

Grease and flour a 10-inch tube pan.

In an electric stand mixer, cream butter and sugar together until light and fluffy. Add eggs, one at a time. Sift together flour, salt and mace; add to creamed mixture and beat to blend. Add brandy and beat until well blended; pour batter into prepared pan.

Bake in a 325-degree oven until a cake tester or broom straw inserted in the center of the cake comes out clean, about 1 hour and 20 minutes. Cool on a wire rack for 15 minutes and remove from the pan. Allow to cool for at least half an hour before serving.

Robert Lahser photo.

Grandma Hill's Fresh Coconut Cake

Coconut cakes are the crowning glory of the Christmas feast in many a Southern household. They are found throughout the region, and recipes date back to the early years of the nineteenth century.

Yield: 10 to 12 servings

For the Cake:

flesh of 1 coconut
1 cup coconut milk (see note below)
½ pound butter at room temperature
1 cup vegetable shortening

3 cups sugar
5 large eggs, added one at a time
2 teaspoons orange extract
½ teaspoon baking powder
¼ teaspoon salt
4 cups cake flour

Do not preheat oven.

Hold the coconut firmly between your knees and use a hammer and a large, clean nail to pierce the coconut through two of the "eyes" on its top. Carefully pour the coconut milk into a large glass or bowl and set aside. Hit the coconut with the hammer to crack it open, and carefully remove the white flesh with a small paring knife and set aside.

Grease and flour a 10-inch tube pan. Cream butter, shortening and sugar together until light and fluffy. Add eggs, one at a time, beating well after each addition. Pour orange extract into coconut milk. Sift dry ingredients together into separate bowl. Measure the coconut milk, adding whole milk (if necessary) to make 1 cup. Add 1/3 of the dry ingredients to creamed mixture, then follow with ½ of the coconut milk. Beat at slowest speed until flour is just mixed. Add second third of dry ingredients and the rest of the coconut milk and beat until the flour is just blended. Scrape the bowl and add the rest of the dry ingredients. Mix until just blended and pour into pan.

Bake in a 350-degree oven for 1 hour and 20 minutes, or until a cake tester or broom straw comes out clean. Don't open the door for the first hour or the cake will fall. Cool on a wire rack for 15 minutes and remove from the pan. Let cool for ½ hour before slicing.

Cut the cake into four layers by sticking toothpicks into the side of the cake as a guide and then looping strong thread or dental floss around the cake and pulling it tight until it slices the cake. Alternately, a large serrated knife and a steady hand may be used. Carefully lift off layers and set aside.

For the Frosting:
1½ cups sugar
½ teaspoon cream of tartar
⅛ teaspoon salt

½ cup water
4 egg whites (at room temperature)
½ teaspoon coconut extract
fresh coconut, grated

In a 2-quart saucepan, combine sugar, cream of tartar, salt and water. Cook over medium heat, stirring constantly, until mixture is clear. Cook until mixture reaches 240 F on a candy thermometer (soft ball stage).

Beat egg whites until soft peaks form. Let mixer continue to run and slowly pour the sugar mixture in a thin stream down the side of the mixing bowl (don't let the sugar mixture come into contact with the beaters). Add the coconut extract. Continue beating until stiff peaks form and frosting thickens to desired consistency. Using a rubber spatula, fold in coconut.

Spread frosting between layers, then frost top and sides of cake. Refrigerate overnight before serving, and keep refrigerated.

Eudora's Double Caramel Cake

Caramel cake is a Southern favorite, one of those cakes that if you notice one on a church buffet table, you might have to strong-arm your way past the preacher and head deacon to get a piece before it gets gone.

The cake dates at least to the last quarter of the nineteenth century; the earliest published recipe I have found is in *The Dixie Cook-Book* by Estelle Woods Wilcox, published in Atlanta in 1883.

This recipe is typical; it comes from *Eudora Garrison's Favorite Carolina Recipes*. Mrs. Garrison was a longtime food editor of the *Charlotte Observer*.

Yield: 10 to 12 servings

For the Cake:

⅓ cup plus 1¼ cups granulated sugar, divided

¼ cup boiling water

¾ cup butter or margarine

3 eggs

3 cups sifted cake flour

3½ teaspoons baking powder

1 teaspoon salt

1 cup milk

1 teaspoon vanilla extract

Melt the 1/3 cup sugar in a heavy skillet, stirring constantly until deep brown syrup is formed—a process called caramelizing. Remove from heat and slowly stir in boiling water, being careful that steam does not burn your hand. Set syrup aside to cool.

Preheat oven to 375 degrees. Grease two 9-inch cake pans, place parchment paper in the bottoms and then grease and flour the bottoms and sides.

Cream butter in bowl of electric mixer. Add sugar and continue to beat until light and fluffy. Add eggs one at a time, beating until each is well incorporated. Stir in 4 tablespoons of the reserved syrup.

Sift together the cake flour, baking powder and salt. Combine milk and vanilla. Add flour mixture to the batter alternately with the milk mixture, beginning and ending with the flour mixture. Beat until smooth. Divide batter evenly between the two prepared pans and bake 25 minutes, or until wooden toothpick inserted in the center comes out clean.

Remove pans from oven and let stand about 10 minutes, then turn out cakes onto wire rack, peel off paper and cool completely.

For the Frosting:

3 cups (light) brown sugar, firmly packed

1 cup plus 2 tablespoons half and half

½ stick (4 tablespoons) butter

1 teaspoon vanilla extract

Mix sugar and half and half in a heavy saucepan and cook, stirring over low heat until syrup reaches the soft ball stage, 235 degrees on a candy thermometer. If lacking a thermometer, check doneness by dropping a tiny bit of syrup into a cup of cold water. When the syrup can be gathered up in fingers and will almost hold its shape, it has reached the soft ball stage.

Remove pan from heat. Stir in butter, then let syrup cool. Add vanilla and beat until frosting reaches spreading consistency. A little cream (or half and half) may be added if mixture is too thick.

Lane Cake (Mrs. Lane's Prize Cake)

The Lane cake joined the pantheon of Southern sweets courtesy of Mrs. Emma Rylander Lane of Clayton, Alabama, who printed the recipe for her "Prize Cake" in her 1898 cookbook, *Some Good Things to Eat*.

This cake is challenging to make, and most bakers agree that the Lane cake is best if made a day or so in advance of serving to allow those flavors to blend.

Coconut, dried fruit such as figs and cherries and nuts are frequent additions to modern recipes, but they are not included in the original. If desired, 1 cup chopped pecans and 1 cup flaked coconut may be added to the filling for the "modern" version; this recipe is true to Mrs. Lane's 1898 original.

Yield: 10 to 12 servings

For the Cake:

1 cup softened butter
2 cups sugar
3¼ cup flour
1 tablespoon baking powder
¾ teaspoon salt
1 cup milk
1 teaspoon vanilla extract
8 egg whites

Grease and flour four 8-inch cake pans: preheat oven to 325 degrees F.

In a 4-quart mixing bowl or the bowl of an electric stand mixer, cream butter and sugar, beating until light and fluffy. Sift together flour, baking powder and salt and add to creamed mixture alternately with milk, mixing well after each addition. Stir in vanilla.

Using a rubber spatula, gently fold in egg whites and pour batter into prepared pans. Bake until a toothpick inserted in the center comes out clean, about 25 to 30 minutes. Remove from oven and place on a wire rack; after 10 minutes, remove cake layers from pans and place on wire rack to cool completely before filling and frosting.

For the Filling:

8 egg yolks
1½ cups sugar
½ cup butter
1 cup raisins, finely chopped
½ cup bourbon or brandy

In a 2-quart saucepan over medium heat, combine egg yolks, sugar and butter; cook, stirring constantly, until thickened, about 18 to 22 minutes.

Remove from heat and stir in raisins and bourbon or brandy. Allow mixture to cool completely, then spread between cake layers and on top of cake.

For the Frosting:

¾ cup sugar

2 tablespoons plus 2 teaspoons water

1 egg white

½ tablespoon light corn syrup

dash of salt

½ teaspoon vanilla

In a 1-quart stainless steel mixing bowl, combine sugar, water, egg white, corn syrup and salt. Using a hand-held electric mixer, beat on low speed until ingredients are just blended, about 30 seconds. Place bowl into the top of a saucepan containing boiling water; beat constantly on high speed until stiff peaks form, about 7 minutes. Remove from heat. Add vanilla and beat until the mixture is thick enough to spread, about 1 minute. Spread on sides of cake.

Lady Baltimore Cake

This beloved Southern confection traces its roots to Charleston sometime around the turn of the twentieth century.

Owen Wister, a popular novelist, described the cake in his 1906 work, *Lady Baltimore*; it is a matter of debate if the cake inspired the novel or the novel inspired the cake.

Lady Baltimore Cake is a three-layer white cake made with egg whites, filled with dried fruits and nuts and covered with a fluffy white boiled frosting. It became wildly popular after Wister's novel appeared and is still a popular Christmas treat all across the South, but particularly in Charleston. This recipe is based on an early one by Mrs. Starkey Willis of Graysport, Mississippi, published in *Favorite Southern Recipes by Southern Ruralist Readers*, published in Atlanta in 1912.

Yield: 10 to 12 servings

For the Cake:

1 cup butter

2 cups sugar

3½ cups flour

2 teaspoons baking powder

1 teaspoon vanilla

1 cup whole milk

6 egg whites

Preheat oven to 350 degrees F; butter and flour three 9-inch cake pans.

In a 4-quart mixing bowl using an electric hand mixer, beat butter until light, then add sugar a little at a time, beating until light and fluffy. Sift together flour and baking powder; pour vanilla into milk and stir. Add the flour mixture to the creamed mixture alternately with the milk, beating just until all the flour is incorporated.

In a 2-quart mixing bowl using an electric hand mixer or wire whisk, beat egg whites until they form stiff peaks. Using a rubber spatula, fold beaten whites into cake batter. Pour batter into prepared pans; bake until a cake tester inserted in the middle of the pan comes out clean, about 30 to 35 minutes. Remove pans to a wire rack and allow to cool for ten minutes, then turn cake layers out onto wire rack. Allow to cool completely. Put filling between layers and on top of cake.

For the Filling and Frosting:

3 cups sugar

1 cup water

3 egg whites

1 cup seedless raisins, chopped

1 cup pecans, chopped

5 figs, chopped

In a 2-quart saucepan over medium-high heat, stir together sugar and water until sugar dissolves. Bring to a boil, stirring frequently. Reduce heat and cook, stirring constantly, until sugar mixture forms a thread when poured from the spoon.

In a 2-quart mixing bowl using an electric hand mixer or wire whisk, beat egg whites until they just begin to hold soft peaks. Slowly drizzle the sugar syrup over the egg whites, beating continuously, until mixture is a spreadable consistency. Make the filling by placing one half of the frosting into another bowl; using a rubber spatula, fold in raisins, pecans and figs. Spread this mixture evenly between cake layers; use the plain frosting to ice the top and sides of the cake.

Stonewall Jackson Cake

This interesting cake is one of the "Southern Hero" desserts that sprang up in the years following the Civil War. These were everyday recipes for cakes, pies and cookies that were renamed in honor of the heroes of the "Lost Cause." Stonewall Jackson cake is one of four cakes I have found named for Confederate generals; the others were Generals John B. Gordon, Nathan Bedford Forrest and Robert E. Lee.

Thomas Jonathan Jackson was an eccentric professor of mathematics and artillery at the Virginia Military Institute when the Civil War broke out. Devoutly religious and antislavery, Jackson became one of the South's fiercest and most victorious generals before his untimely death at the Battle of Chancellorsville in 1862.

Stonewall Jackson cake is a rarity; I have only found three published recipes for it in thirty years of studying old cookbooks. This recipe is adapted from one found in *Key to the Pantry*, published by the ladies of the Church of the Epiphany in Danville, Virginia, in 1898.

Yield: 10 to 12 servings

For the Cake:
1½ cups butter
2 cups sugar
9 medium eggs, separated
4 cups flour
½ teaspoon salt
½ teaspoon baking powder
¼ cup brandy

Do not preheat oven. Grease and flour a 10-inch tube pan.
In a 4-quart mixing bowl using an electric hand mixer, cream butter and sugar together until light and fluffy. Add egg yolks, one at a time, beating well after each addition.
Sift dry ingredients together into separate bowl, then add to creamed mixture, alternating with the brandy, beating just enough to blend.
In a 2-quart mixing bowl, beat egg whites until soft peaks form. Using a rubber spatula, fold egg whites into batter, then pour into prepared tube pan.
Bake in a 350-degree oven until a cake tester inserted in the middle comes out clean, about 60 to 70 minutes.

For the Frosting:
1½ cups sugar
½ teaspoon cream of tartar
⅛ teaspoon salt
½ cup water
4 egg whites (at room temperature)
½ teaspoon vanilla extract
1 square semi-sweet chocolate, melted
½ pound English walnut halves
½ pound pecans

Combine sugar, cream of tartar, salt and water in heavy saucepan. Cook over medium heat, stirring constantly, until mixture is clear. Cook until mixture reaches 240 degrees F on a candy thermometer (soft ball stage).
Beat egg whites until soft peaks form. Let mixer continue to run and slowly pour the sugar mixture in a thin stream down the side of the mixing bowl (don't let the sugar mixture come into contact with the beaters). Add the vanilla extract and the chocolate. Continue beating until frosting thickens to desired consistency.
Spread frosting over tops and sides of cake, then stick walnuts and pecans into frosting so that cake resembles a stone wall.

Dixie Hummingbird Cake

This cake became an instant favorite when it arrived on the scene in the late 1970s. The first recipe for this cake has long been attributed to Mrs. L.H. Wiggins of Greensboro, North Carolina, who submitted it to the February 1978 issue of *Southern Living* magazine. But Helen Moore, a former food editor at the *Charlotte Observer*, says that hummingbird cake actually hails from Jamaica, where it is called Doctor Bird cake. .

Royce W. Smith photo.

There are two major schools of thought as to where the name came from. The first is that the cake is so sweet it could attract hummingbirds; the second is that the cake is so good, people spontaneously begin to hum while eating it. No matter which story is true, this is one of the most delicious of all Southern cakes. The recipe is adapted from Mrs. Wiggins's original.

Yield: 10 to 12 servings

For the Cake:
3 cups all-purpose flour
2 cups sugar
1 tcaspoon salt
2 teaspoon baking soda
1½ teaspoon ground cinnamon
3 eggs, beaten

1¼ cups vegetable oil
1½ teaspoons vanilla extract
one 8-ounce can crushed pineapple, drained
   (reserve ¼ cup juice)
2 cups chopped pecans, divided
2 cups mashed bananas

Grease and flour three 9-inch cake pans; preheat oven to 350 degrees F.

Sift together flour, sugar, salt, soda and cinnamon; place into a 4-quart mixing bowl. Add eggs and vegetable oil, stirring with a rubber spatula until dry ingredients are moistened (do not use an electric mixer). Stir in vanilla, pineapple, pineapple juice, 1 cup of the pecans and bananas; spoon batter into pans.

Bake until cake is golden brown and a cake tester inserted in the middle comes out clean, about 25 to 30 minutes. Allow to cool in pans for ten minutes, then turn out onto a wire rack to cool completely.

For the Frosting:
two 8-ounce packages cream cheese, softened
1 cup unsalted butter, softened

two 16-ounce boxes powdered sugar
2 teaspoons vanilla extract

In a 2-quart mixing bowl, combine cream cheese and butter; using an electric hand mixer, cream until smooth. Add powdered sugar, beating until light and fluffy; stir in vanilla. Spread frosting between layers and on top and sides of cake. Sprinkle with 1 cup chopped pecans.

Robert E. Lee Cake

It is fitting that a book devoted to the history of Southern food should close with a dessert named after the South's most revered figure.

Robert E. Lee cake (also referred to in old cookbooks as Lee cake, General Lee cake, R.E. Lee cake and General Robert E. Lee cake) existed by other names long before Robert E. Lee became the South's most beloved icon. The cake began appearing by its new name in the 1870s; there are two recipes in Marion Cabell Tyree's *Housekeeping in Old Virginia*, published in 1879.

Most recipes from the late nineteenth century use the citrus filling to top the final layer, leaving the sides unglazed; but in the twentieth century, variations calling for a boiled or seven-minute frosting for the top and sides began to appear. Coconut is sometimes called for and seems to have joined the original ingredients for the filling by the 1890s; the earliest recipe I've found that uses coconut is in *A Collection of Virginia Recipes*, published by Mrs. William S. Donnan in 1891.

The cake is labor-intensive but well worth the effort. This recipe is based on several written between 1877 and 1891. If you would like a more "modern" version with boiled frosting, use the frosting recipe from the Lane cake on page 222.

Yield: 10 to 12 servings

9 eggs, separated
1½ cups sugar
2 cups sifted all-purpose flour
½ teaspoon salt
1 tablespoon lemon juice
½ cup lemon juice, divided

zest of 5 oranges
zest of 3 lemons
2 cups orange juice
1½ cups sugar
1½ cups unsweetened shredded coconut, divided

Preheat oven 350 degrees; grease and flour three 8-inch round cake pans.
In a 4-quart mixing bowl, beat egg whites until they just form stiff peaks. In a separate large bowl, beat egg yolks until pale yellow and light. Slowly beat in sugar. Sift together flour and salt in a 1-quart mixing bowl and set aside.
Using a rubber spatula, fold in egg whites, then flour mixture and 1 tablespoon of the lemon juice, mixing only enough to blend in flour.
Divide batter equally among the three cake pans. Bake until cake tester inserted in the middle comes out clean, about 35 to 45 minutes. Set pans on a wire rack to cool; after 10 minutes, remove cake layers from pans and place on wire rack to cool completely.
In a 2-quart mixing bowl, combine orange and lemon zest and the leftover lemon juices, 1½ cups sugar and one cup of the coconut, stirring to dissolve sugar.
Spoon citrus mixture over tops of cake layers. Stack layers and allow to stand several hours before serving to allow cake to absorb liquid. To serve, sprinkle with remaining ½ cup coconut.

References Consulted

Aleckson, Sam. *Before the War and After the Union*. Boston: Gold Mind Publishing Co., 1929.

Arthur, Stanley Clisby. *Famous New Orleans Drinks & How to Mix 'Em*. New Orleans, LA: Rogers Printing Company, 1937.

Avirett, James Battle. *The Old Plantation: How We Lived in Great House and Cabin Before the War*. New York: F. Tennyson Neely Co., 1901.

Barbour, Philip L., ed. *The Complete Works of Captain John Smith, (1580–1631)*. Chapel Hill: University of North Carolina Press, 1986.

Bashinsky, Elizabeth Burford. *Tried and True Recipes*. Troy: Alabama Division, United Daughters of the Confederacy, 1922. Third Ed. Montgomery, AL: Paragon Press, 1937.

Betts, Edwin M., ed. *Thomas Jefferson's Garden Book, 1767–1824* Philadelphia: American Philosophical Society, 1981.

Beverley, Robert. *The History and Present State of Virginia*. London: 1705. Reprint. Louis B. Wright, ed. Chapel Hill: University of North Carolina Press, 1947.

Booth, Sally Smith. *Hung, Strung & Potted: A History of Eating in Colonial America*. New York: C.N. Potter; distributed by Crown Publishers, 1971.

Bowers, Lessie. *Plantation Recipes*. New York: R. Speller, 1959.

Brown, John Hull. *Early American Beverages*. Rutland, VT: C.E. Tuttle Co., 1966.

Bruner, Peter. *A Slave's Adventures Toward Freedom*. Oxford, OH: self-published, late 1800s?

Bryan, Lettice. *The Kentucky Housewife*. Cincinnati, OH: Shepherd and Stearns, 1839.

Bullock, Helen Claire Duprey. *The Williamsburg Art of Cookery*. Richmond: A. Dietz and his son, 1938.

Burge, Dolly Lunt. *A Woman's Wartime Journal: An Account of the Passage over Georgia's Plantation of Sherman's Army on the March to the Sea*. New York: Century Co., 1918.

Burnaby, Andrew. *Travels Through the Middle Settlements in North America, 1759–60*. New York: A. Wessels Company, 1904.

Burton, Annie L. "Memories of Childhood's Slavery Days." In *Six Women's Slave Narratives*, edited by Henry Gates Jr. New York: Oxford University Press, 1988.

Carlton, Helen T. *The Practical and Fancy Cook Book for Every Household*. Louisville: Courier-Journal Printing Company, n.d. [prob. late 1800s–early 1900s].

Chesnut, Mary Boykin Miller. *A Diary from Dixie*. New York: D. Appleton and Company, 1905.

Church of the Epiphany. *Key to the Pantry: Choice, Tried Recipes*. Danville, VA: Boatwright Bros., 1898.

Colquitt, Harriet Ross, ed. *The Savannah Cook Book*. New York: Farrar & Rinehart, 1933.

"A Confederate Lady." *Confederate Receipt Book*. Richmond, VA: West & Johnston, 1863.

Dabney, Joeseph Earl. *Moonshine Spirits: A Chronicle of Corn Whiskey from King James' Ulster Plantation to America's Appalachians and the Moonshine Life*. Asheville, NC: Bright Mountain Books, 1974.

———. *Smokehouse Ham, Spoon Bread and Scuppernong Wine*. New York: Cumberland House Publishing, 1998.

Deetz, James. *Flowerdew Hundred: The Archaeology of a Virginia Plantation, 1619–1864*. Charlottesville: University Press of Virginia, 1993.

Devereux, Margaret. *Plantation Sketches*. Cambridge: privately printed at Riverside Press, 1906.

Donnan, William S., Mrs. *A Collection of Virginia Recipes*. Richmond, VA: Whittet & Shepperson, 1891.

Douglass, Frederick. *Narrative of the Life of Frederick Douglass*. Boston: Anti-slavery Office, 1845. Reprint. New York: Dover Publications, 1995.

Dull, Henrietta Stanley (Mrs. S.R.). *Southern Cooking*. Atlanta: Ruralist Press, 1928.

Egerton, John. *Side Orders: Small Helpings of Southern Cookery & Culture*. Atlanta: Peachtree Publishers, 1990.

———. *Southern Food: At Home, on the Road, in History*. New York: Knopf, 1987.

Estes, Rufus. *Good Things to Eat, as Suggested by Rufus*. Chicago: self-published, 1911.

Eustis, Célestine. *Cooking in Old Créole Days*. New York: R.H. Russell, 1904.

Felton, Rebeca Latimer. *Country Life in Georgia in the Days of My Youth*. Atlanta: Index Printing Company, 1919.

Fisher, Abby. *What Mrs. Fisher Knows About Old Southern Cooking*. San Francisco: Women's Co-operative Printing Office, 1881.

Fitchett, Laura Simkins (L.S.F.). *Beverages and Sauces of Colonial Virginia, 1607–1907*. New York: Neale Pub. Co., 1906. Reprint. Richmond, VA: William Byrd Press, 1938.

Fowler, Damon Lee. *Classical Southern Cooking*. New York: Crown Publishing Group, 1995.

———. *Dining at Monticello*. New York: Thomas Jefferson Memorial Foundation, Inc., 2005.

Fox, Minnie C. *The Blue Grass Cook Book*, comp. by Minerva Carr Fox, with an introduction by John Fox Jr. New York: Fox, Duffie & Co., 1904.

Frazer, Mary Harris. *Kentucky Receipt Book*. Louisville, KY: Press of the Bradley & Gilbert Co., 1903.

Fries, Adelaide L., et al. *Records of the Moravians in North Carolina*. Raleigh, NC: Edwards & Broughton Print. Co., 1922.

Fuller, Edwin Wiley. *Sea-Gift: A Novel*. New York: E.J. Hale & Son, 1873.

Garrison, Eudora. *Eudora Garrison's Southern Cook Book*. Charlotte, NC: Charlotte Observer, n.d. [1950s?].

———. *Eudora's Cook Book*. Charlotte, NC: Charlotte Observer, n.d. [1950s?].

Gawalt, Gerald W. "Jefferson's Slaves: Crop Accounts at Monticello, 1805–1808." *Journal of the AfroAmerican Historical and Genealogical Society* (Spring/Fall 1994): 19–20.

Gibbs, Patricia A. "Daily Schedule for a Cook in a Gentry Household." *Fresh Advices: A Research Supplement to the Colonial Williamsburg Interpreter* 7, no. 3 (1986).

———. "Little Spots allow'd them: Slave Garden Plots and Poultry Yards." *Colonial Williamsburg Interpreter* 20, no. 4 (1999).

Gibson, Marietta (Mrs. Charles H.). *Mrs. Charles H. Gibson's Maryland and Virginia Cook Book*. Baltimore, MD: J. Murphy, 1894.

Ginter Park Woman's Club (Richmond). *Famous Recipes from Old Virginia*. Richmond, VA: Clyde W. Saunders and Sons, Printers and Publishers. Second Revised Edition, 1941.

Glasse, Hannah. *The Art of Cookery Made Plain and Easy*. London: W. Strahan, 1774.

Gray & Dudley Hardware Co. (Nashville, Tenn.). *Southern Cook Book of Famous Southern Dishes*. Nashville, TN: Gray & Dudley, 1900s.

Harriot, Thomas. *A Briefe and True Report of the New Found Land of Virginia*. New York: J. Sabin & Sons, 1871.

Harrison, Molly. *The Kitchen in History*. New York: Charles Scribner's Sons, 1972.

Hearn, Lafcadio. *La Cuisine Creole*. New Orleans: F.F. Hansell & Bro., Ltd., 1885.

Henson, Josiah. *The Life of Josiah Henson*. Boston: Arthur D. Phelps, 1849.

Hess, Karen, ed. *The Carolina Rice Kitchen: The African Connection*. Columbia: University of South Carolina Press, 1992.

———. *Martha Washington's Booke of Cookery*. New York: Columbia University Press, 1981.

Hill, A.P. *Mrs. Hill's Southern Practical Cookery and Receipt Book* by Annabella P. Hill; with a biographical sketch of the author and historical notes and glossary on the cookery by Damon L. Fowler. [Mrs. Hill's new cookbook, 1872] Columbia: University of South Carolina Press, 1995.

Hilliard, Sam Bowers. *Hog Meat and Hoecake: Food Supply in the Old South, 1840–1860*. Carbondale: Southern Illinois University Press, 1972.

Hooker, Richard J. *The Carolina Backcountry on the Eve of the Revolution; The Journal and Other Writings of Charles Woodmason, Anglican Itinerant*. Chapel Hill: University of North Carolina Press, 1953.

———. *A Colonial Plantation Cookbook: The Receipt Book of Harriott Pinckney Horry, 1770*. Columbia: University of South Carolina Press, 1984.

Jefferson, Thomas. *Garden Book* [manuscript], 1766–1824. Thomas Jefferson Papers: An Electronic Archive. 1998. Manuscript Collection, Massachusetts Historical Society, Boston.

Kephart, Horace. *Our Southern Highlanders*. New York: Outing Publishing Company, 1913. Reprint. Knoxville: University of Tennessee Press, 1976.

Knowles, Laura Thornton. *Southern Recipes Tested by Myself*. New York: George H. Doran, 1913.

Ladies of the Raleigh Presbyterian Church. *Capital City Recipes*. Raleigh, NC: Capital Printing Company, 1900.

Lawson, John. *A New Voyage to Carolina*. London: 1709.

LeClercq, Anne Sinkler Whaley. *An Antebellum Plantation Household: Including the South Carolina Low Country Receipts and Remedies of Emily Wharton Sinkler*. Columbia: University of South Carolina Press, 1996.

LeConte, Emma Florence. *Diary, 1864–1865*. Transcript prepared by the Historical Records Survey of the Works Progress Administration, May 1938.

Leigh, Frances Butler. *Ten Years on a Georgia Plantation Since the War*. London: Richard Bentley & Son, 1883.

Marrs, Elijah P. *Life and History of the Rev. Elijah P. Marrs*. Louisville: Bradley & Gilbert Company, 1885.

Mason, Mary Ann Bryan. *The Young Housewife's Counsellor and Friend*. New York: E.J. Hale & Son, 1875.

Master's Workers of First Presbyterian Church. *Old Time Tennessee Receipts*. Nashville, TN: privately published, 1943.

McCulloch-Williams, Martha. *Dishes & Beverages of the Old South*. New York: McBride, Nast & Company, 1913.

McGuire, Judith. *Diary of a Southern Refugee During the War by a Lady of Virginia*. Lincoln: University of Nebraska Press, 1995.

McPhail, Clement Carrington, Mrs. *F.F.V. Receipt Book*. Richmond, VA: West, Johnston & Co., 1894.

M'Mahon, Bernard. *American Gardener's Calendar*. Philadelphia: B. Graves, 1806. Reprint, Ninth Edition. Philadelphia: E.G. Dorsey, 1839.

Moss, Kay. *A Backcountry Herbal of Plants Both Wild and Cultivated Likely to Be Found in Dooryards and Kitchen Gardens in Frontier Communities of the 18th Century*. Gastonia, NC: Schiele Museum, 1993.

Moss, Kay, and Kathryn Hoffman. *The Backcountry Housewife*. Gastonia, NC: Schiele Museum of Natural History, 1985.

Neal, Bill. *Bill Neal's Southern Cooking*. Revised Edition. Chapel Hill: University of North Carolina Press, 1989.

———. *Biscuits, Spoonbread, and Sweet Potato Pie*. New York: Knopf, 1990.

Olmsted, Frederick Law. *A Journey in the Seaboard Slave States, with Remarks on their Economy*. New York: Mason Brothers, 1861.

Page, Thomas Nelson. *Social Life in Old Virginia Before the War*. New York: Charles Scribner's Sons, 1897.

Phipps, Frances. *Colonial Kitchens, Their Furnishings, and Their Gardens*. New York: Hawthorn Books, 1972.

Picayune. *The Picayune's Creole Cook Book*. New Orleans, LA: Picayune, 1900. Reprint. New York: Dover Publications, Inc., 2002.

Pinckney, Eliza Lucas. *Recipe Book*, 1756. Charleston, SC: Committee on Historic Activities of the South Carolina Society of the Colonial Dames of America, 1930.

Pineopolis, SC Civic League. *Old Receipts from Old St. John's*. Charleston, SC: n.d., photocopy of printed cookbook from early 1900s, Hinson Collection, Charleston Library Society.

Platt, Loula Roberts. *Queen of Appalachia Cook Book*. Asheville, NC: privately published, n.d. [early 1900s].

Porter, Mrs. M.E. *Mrs. Porter's New Southern Cookery Book*. Philadelphia: J.E. Potter and Company, 1871.

Pretlow, Mary Denson, comp. *Old Southern Receipts*. New York: R.M. McBride & Co., 1930.

Randolph, Mary. *The Virginia House-Wife*. Washington, D.C.: printed by Davis and Force, 1824.

Rawlings, Marjorie Kinnan. *Cross Creek Cookery*. New York: C. Scribner's Sons, 1942.

Rhett, Blanche S. *Two Hundred Years of Charleston Cooking*. New York: Random House, 1930. Reprint. New York: University of South Carolina Press, 1976.

Simmons, Amelia. *American Cookery*. Hartford, CT: Hudson & Goodwin, 1796.

Smith, Jacqueline Harrison, and Sue Mason Maury Halsey. *Famous Old Receipts*. Philadelphia: J.C. Winston Co., 1906.

Smith, Mary Stuart. *Virginia Cookery-Book*. New York: Harper & Brothers, 1885.

Social Workers, M.E. Church. *Spartanburg Cook Book*. Spartanburg, SC: Band and White Printers, 1917.

Southern Presbyterian Curch (Paris, KY). *Housekeeping in the Blue Grass*. Cincinnati, OH: G.E. Stevens & Co., 1875.

Southern Ruralist. *Favorite Southern Recipes*. Atlanta: Southern Ruralist, 1912.

Stanford, Martha Pritchard. *The Old and New Cook Book*. New Orleans, LA: T. Searcy & Pfaff, Ltd., Printers, 1904.

Stanton, Lucia C. "From Plantation Fare to French Cuisine." *Monticello* 4, no. 2 (Fall 1993).

Stieff, Frederick Philip, comp. *Eat, Drink & Be Merry in Maryland*. New York: G.P. Putnam's Sons, 1932.

Stoney, Louise C.S. *Carolina Rice Cook Book*. Charleston, SC: Carolina Rice Kitchen Association, 1901.

Taylor, Joe Gray. *Eating, Drinking, and Visiting in the South*. Baton Rouge: Louisiana State University Press, 1982.

Thornton, Phineas T. *The Southern Gardener and Receipt Book*. Columbia, SC: privately published, 1840. Reprint. Birmingham, AL: Oxmoor House, 1984.

Tyree, Marion Cabell, ed. *Housekeeping in Old Virginia*. New York: G.W. Carleton & Co., 1877.

Vaughn, Kate Brew. *Culinary Echoes from Dixie*. Cincinnati, OH: McDonald Press, 1917.

Virginia Federation of Home Demonstration Clubs. *Recipes from Old Virginia*. Richmond, VA: Dietz Press, 1946. Revised edition, 1958.

Virginia League of Women Voters. *Virginia Cookery Book: Traditional Recipes*. Richmond: Virginia League of Women Voters, 1921.

Walter, Eugene. *American Cooking: Southern Style*. New York: Time-Life, Inc., 1971.

Washington, Queenie Woods, ed. *The Sewanee Cook Book*. Nashville, TN: Baird-Ward, 1926. Revised edition. Chattanooga, TN: Chattanooga Printing & Engraving Co., 1958.

Whitaker, Alexander. *Good News from Virginia, sent to the Counsell and Company of Virginia, Resident in England*. London: Imprinted by Felix Kyngston for William Welby, 1613.

Wilcox, Estelle Woods. *The Dixie Cook-Book, Carefully Compiled from the Treasured Family Collections of Many Generations of Noted Housekeepers*. Revised edition. Atlanta: L.A. Clarkson & Co., 1883.

Wilson, Mary Elizabeth Lyles. *Mrs. H.W. Wilson's New Cook Book*. Nashville, TN: Foster & Parkes Co., 1914. Third edition, 1916.

Winston-Salem, North Carolina Manuscript Collection, Moravian Museum of the Historic Bethlehem Partnership. Maria Rosina Unger, Journal Kept At Bethlehem Boarding School, entry dated 25 December, 1789.

Wise, John S. *The End of an Era*. Boston: Houghton, Mifflin and Company, Riverside Press, 1899.

Women's Auxiliary of the First Presbyterian Church. *Capital City Cook Book* (Revised). Raleigh, NC: Edwards and Broughton Company, 1927.

Wright, Louis B. *The Cultural Life of the American Colonies, 1607–1763*. New York: Harper & Brothers, 1957.

Young Ladies' Aid Society, Freemason Street Baptist Church (Norfolk, VA). *The Jamestown Cook Book*. Norfolk, VA: Burke and Gregory, 1907.

Zanger, Mark. *The American History Cookbook*. Westport, CT: Greenwood Press, 2003.

Zimmer, Anne Carter. *The Robert E. Lee Family Cooking & Housekeeping Book*. Chapel Hill: University of North Carolina Press, 1997.

Index

About the Author

Polly McDaniel photo.

Rick McDaniel has been a working journalist for thirty years and a full-time food writer for more than a decade. McDaniel learned his love of Southern food from three generations of "small women who were giants in the kitchen." Coconut cakes, vegetables fresh from the garden and abundant Sunday dinners flavored his upbringing in a small North Carolina town in the 1960s.

A member of the Southern Foodways Alliance, he is dedicated to preserving Southern culinary heritage by collecting and publishing historical recipes. The *New York Times*, MSNBC and newspapers and magazines throughout the South have interviewed McDaniel about Southern food history and traditional recipes. He has been a consultant to the producers of *Diners, Drive-ins and Dives* on the Food Network and *Anthony Bourdain's No Reservations* on the Travel Channel, as well as a Southern Regional panelist for the James Beard Foundation's chef and restaurant awards.

His website, chefrick.com, has been featured in the *New York Times* and was selected as one of the best Internet resources on American cookery by the University of Oregon and the Carnegie Library of Pittsburgh.

Visit us at
www.historypress.net